7 PERSONALITY TYPES

Hay House Titles of Related Interest

YOU CAN HEAL YOUR LIFE, the movie,
starring Louise L. Hay & Friends
(available as a 1-DVD program and an expanded 2-DVD set)
Watch the trailer at: **www.LouiseHayMovie.com**

THE SHIFT, the movie,
starring Dr. Wayne W. Dyer
(available as a 1-DVD program and an expanded 2-DVD set)
Watch the trailer at: **www.DyerMovie.com**

◆◆◆◆◆

By Caroline Myss:

Archetype Cards (an 80-card deck and instruction booklet)

Sacred Contracts: An Interactive Experience for Guidance
(with Peter Occhiogrosso)

By Carol Ritberger, Ph.D.:

Managing People . . . What's Personality Got to Do with It?

What Color Is Your Personality?

Your Personality, Your Health

◆◆◆◆◆

All of the above are available at your local bookstore, or may be ordered
by visiting: Hay House USA: **www.hayhouse.com®**; Hay House
Australia: **www.hayhouse.com.au**; Hay House UK: **www.hayhouse.
co.uk**; Hay House South Africa: **www.hayhouse.co.za**; Hay House
India: **www.hayhouse.co.in**

7 PERSONALITY TYPES

Discover Your True Role in Achieving Success and Happiness

ELIZABETH PUTTICK, PH.D.

HAY HOUSE, INC.
Carlsbad, California • New York City
London • Sydney • Johannesburg
Vancouver • Hong Kong • New Delhi

Library of Congress Control Number: 2009922680

ISBN: 978-1-4019-2456-0

12 11 10 09 4 3 2 1
1st edition, August 2009

Printed in the United States of America

For Robin, with all my love

From the Editor: To our North American readers, please note that for the most part, we have maintained the British style of spelling, grammar, punctuation, and syntax of the original text in order to preserve the editorial intent of the author, who hails from the United Kingdom.

Contents

Foreword

BY JOSÉ LUIS STEVENS, LCSW, PHD

For over 30 years I have worked as a clinical social worker and a psychologist as well as a trainer and educator of management in the corporate world and public sector. I have taught graduate students in counselling programs, including theories of personality. Acquainted with all the main personality typologies, I have never found a map to understanding human behaviour as powerful as the Michael Teaching, a philosophy I have professionally referred to as Personnessence™. In my opinion it is hands-down the most comprehensive and insightful description of human nature and human behaviour that I have ever come across. For this reason I have adopted it as my main approach for understanding and assisting people from all over the world and all walks of life, with exceptionally favourable and often extraordinary results.

I have found through my work with thousands of people that by understanding the personality types (Roles), my clients have been able to shift into more appropriate work situations, understand their own natural inclinations better, take advantage of their talents, and stop judging themselves for not being able to do what others do better. When people stop comparing themselves and concentrate on what they do best, they find greater happiness and satisfaction.

The Roles are part of an incredibly rich, comprehensive and multi-dimensional philosophy of life. Yet they are central to the system, so it makes sense to have an entire book devoted to them. Knowing about the seven Roles can be such a key to understanding your life that this knowledge can by itself unlock the secrets to help you meet your full potential.

Elizabeth Puttick has studied and practised methods of self-development, including this system, for many years and worked successfully in the business and media worlds. She has had the opportunity, as I have, to test and apply it practically in life and work. She successfully gets to the core of this system and so is able to communicate it to a much wider audience. Fortunately, this will allow countless people who have not heard of it before to enjoy the benefits of this powerful body of knowledge. Elizabeth has interviewed many examples of each Role and presents directly from their own experience what it is like to be a Warrior, a Priest, a Server, or an Artisan.

Not only will you find this book fascinating and highly informative, but it will also lead you to a greater understanding of why you do the things you do, what your potential is and why there are certain things you find difficult. In this way you will be led to greater self-acceptance and love for what it is to be a human being, the goal of this wonderful teaching.

Introduction

Is it important or useful to know yourself and understand others? Millions of people get along without self-knowledge, like drivers in a city where there are no maps or street names, finding their way by chance and instinct. Some seem to manage well, but most just get by or get lost. Does it matter if you are on a life path that you chose when you were younger, less wise and less experienced, or that was chosen for you by someone else, a parent or teacher? It is quite likely that these elders gave you an identity as well, which you either accepted and strove to live up to or wasted energy in rejecting and rebelling against. You may now be suspecting or discovering that these early choices do not fulfill your deepest needs, maybe because you don't know who you truly are. If that is the case, then this book can help you.

The secret of success, happiness and wisdom lies in self-knowledge. Only when you know yourself can you know what you really want in life. Out of this understanding arise insight and confidence, leading to effective action: a clear vision of the best way to achieve fulfillment. Even if it is not possible to change your outer circumstances for the foreseeable future, self-knowledge is useful in allowing you to see yourself as others see you and understand others as intimately as yourself. It will save you a lot of time and suffering by helping you make choices that are better suited to your personality and talents. It will lead you not only to self-discovery but eventually to self-mastery.

The modern world is so complex and fast-changing that we can no longer rely on old traditions and structures – outdated class systems, jobs for life, stable families and friendship networks. In the past, these things gave us not only support but also identity. Since the outer world no longer serves this purpose, we need to look to inner realities to ground our sense of self. We need a new map – and this book provides one in the form of a personality system that really works.

There are many personality typologies around, derived from psychology, metaphysics, even marketing. As a sociologist who has worked for many years in publishing, specializing in self-help books, I have studied most of them, finding some very helpful, others less so. The Personality Types is the best system I've come across: the most universally true, useful and transformative. It is based on an ancient philosophy known as the Michael Teaching, which was rediscovered in the 1970s. The version I'm presenting here is adapted from the work of the psychologist Dr José Stevens, founder of Pivotal Resources, who modernized the philosophy into a practical system for use in counselling and management training. (*See the Resources section for a list of consultancy services.*) I've trained with Dr Stevens and tested and validated the system for over 20 years. In this book I've adapted and simplified it for the general reader to use in daily life. It provides an accurate easy-to-learn map of the human personality and a powerful set of tools for self-development.

This personality typology is rapidly emerging as an influential force in the counselling and psychotherapy professions and also in business training, for several reasons. First, it is presented entirely in plain English, without scientific or esoteric jargon, which makes it easy and fun to learn. Another great advantage is that it is intuitive, building on what we already know about people and the world, but putting it into a clear and practical structure. As a result, anyone can understand the ideas; it is meant for everyone and works for everyone. Once you have grasped the basic concepts, it is easy to check and verify them by observing yourself and other people in action – at home, in the workplace, at parties, in intimate relationships or on the political hustings.

How to Use This Book

The first step is to take the questionnaire following this introduction; the two sets of answers that most fit you will give you your primary and secondary Roles.

The second step is to read Chapter 1, which gives an overview of the personality types, explains the system and how it works, and defines the main concepts.

The third step is to read the Role chapters corresponding with your highest scores in order to verify your results.

Each chapter gives a complete overview of the personality type or Role, including pointers to help you recognize yourself and others; information on the Role in the workplace, including best occupations and leadership style; communication style, including how to communicate better with someone who has this Role; relationships with romantic partners, parents and children; archetypes of the Role in myth, fiction and film; how to fulfill your Role; and the influence of your secondary on your primary Role.

To end on a lighter note, I've also given a list of famous people past and present who have the Role in question. These attributions have been compiled from the collective observations of the main teachers of this system and supplemented with my own direct observation and study, including biographies, memoirs, interviews and other primary sources. Each chapter also includes a mini-biography of a famous person who strikingly displays the key characteristics of that Role, to serve as an illustration and inspirational role model.

Reading this book is not the end of the story. The final step is validation. You need to check your results by observing yourself in daily life, as well as your friends and colleagues. This will bring you great insight and illumination, clarifying many puzzles and problems in your family and working life. You may understand, for example, that the manager who seems so bossy is a Warrior geared to getting things done as efficiently as possible. They are not out to get you, simply a bit insensitive. You will no longer dismiss your colleague as a dreamer, recognizing that they are an Artisan whose strength is in generating new ideas rather than carrying out routine administration. Similarly, the mysteries of the eternal male–female divide can be illuminated when you see that the differences are as much about Role as gender. In the bigger picture, knowing our Role can help us not only to know ourselves and each other better but to get along together more harmoniously and productively in families, teams and communities.

Find Your True Role

This questionnaire is based on the one developed by Dr José Stevens at Pivotal Resources, which has been used by thousands of people worldwide and has true cross-cultural relevance. For this book I have expanded it and substituted new questions. I've tested the results on a broad range of people with each Role as well as people new to the system, incorporating their feedback to achieve accurate representations of all the personality types.

Instructions

- Check off all the statements you agree with (not necessarily 100 percent but clearly more 'yes' than 'no').

- Don't take too much time to analyse each statement, but go by your gut feeling as to which *resonate* the most for you.

- At the end, add up your checks and note which groups you have the most checks under. Then see page xxiii.

Group 1

1. Everything that happens to me can become a funny story, and I find humour in almost everything. ☐

2. I enjoy telling stories to an attentive audience. ☑

3. People said that I was naturally funny even when I was a child. ☐

4. My social life is a high priority and I have a large circle of friends. ☐

5. I prefer to avoid confrontation and usually tell a joke to defuse the tension. ☐

6. People sometimes tell me I talk too much. ☑

7. I sometimes feel like a performer in the drama of my own life and wonder where the 'real me' is. ☐

8. I have a talent for using language creatively and coining new words. ☐

9. If asked to make an impromptu speech, I could easily rise to the occasion. ☐

10. I seek and value wisdom as the highest attainment. ☑

11. I never let a fact get in the way of a good story. ☐

12. I enjoy watching chat shows and quizzes on television, sometimes against my better judgement. ☑

13. When I'm on form, I'm the life and soul of a party. ☐

14. I like to wear interesting clothes and bright colours to stand out in the crowd. ☑

15. I would enjoy performing in a play and have considered an acting career. ☐

Group 2

1. I love to help people in any way that makes it possible for them to get along in life.

2. At work, I'm the person who takes care of the bits that others avoid but that are important.

3. I'm willing to clear up other people's messes, as long as they thank me for it.

4. I really dislike losing control of a situation.

5. Generally, I prefer working behind the scenes than being the front runner.

6. If someone drops their change, I don't hesitate to help them pick up their coins.

7. I enjoy making people feel at ease and comfortable in any way I can.

8. My friends say they find me caring and inspiring.

9. I usually put the needs of other people before my own.

10. My local community is very important to me, and I give time and energy to support it.

11. I'm practical, competent and thorough at administration.

12. Sometimes people take my help and support for granted.

13. I enjoy having guests to stay and work hard to make them feel welcome.

14. I prefer working for someone who has a positive vision which I can share and support.

15. If volunteers are needed for a job, I'm the first to put my hand up.

Group 3

✓ 1. I enjoy analysing and developing complex ideas. ✓ ☑

✓ 2. I can usually see both points of view in an argument, so I find it hard to take sides. ✓ ☑

✓ 3. I have an insatiable curiosity about life and love to explore its possibilities. ✓ ☑

✓ 4. People often pick my brain, and I can almost always answer their questions. ☑

✓ 5. I prefer to think things through and do extensive research before making a decision. ✓ ☑

✓ 6. My home is full of books, including a big pile on my bedside table. ✓ ☑

✓ 7. I tend to feel a bit distant from people and don't express my feelings easily. ☑

✓ 8. I believe that analysing my experiences is the best way to understand them. ✓ ☐

✓ 9. I enjoy collecting and can spend many hours adding to and enjoying the results. ☐

✓ 10. Often I'd rather stay at home with a good book than go to a party. ☑

✓ 11. I prefer to blend into a crowd and observe rather than be the centre of attention. ☑

✓ 12. I avoid confrontation where possible and prefer to withdraw from conflict. ✓ ☐

✓ 13. I can happily spend hours surfing the internet and following interesting links. ✓ ☐

✓ 14. I am at ease with solitary intellectual labour and prefer to work alone. ✓ ☑

✓ 15. I am fascinated by the past and would make a good historian. ☑

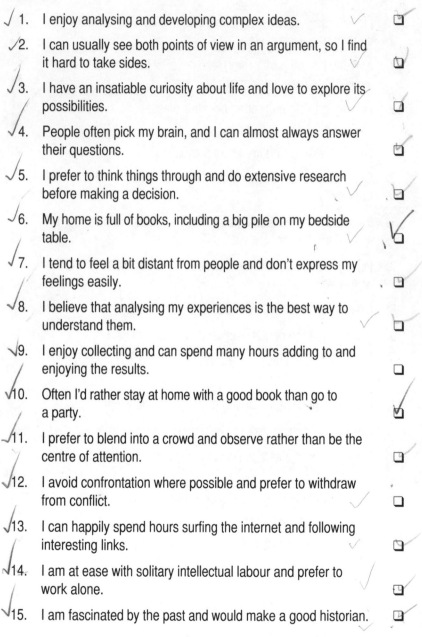

15

Group 4

1. In our family, I'm the one who leads and makes the important decisions. ☐

2. I'm a perfectionist with very high standards. ☑

3. I can often see a way to expand and improve a project far beyond the original concept. ☑

4. I expect people who work with me to share my high standards of capability and integrity. ☑

5. People often put me in a leadership position, even when I'm not looking for it. ☑

6. I strive for mastery in whatever I'm doing and usually achieve it. ☑

7. My dignity is very important to me and anyone who offends it will feel my displeasure. ☑

8. I have a natural authority which most people recognize and respect. ☑

9. Mostly I can't be bothered with small talk and want to get straight down to business. ☐

10. I have often had significant difficulties with intimate and one-to-one relationships. ☐

11. I'm attracted to organizations with problems rather than those that are working well. ☐

12. I'm good at seeing the bigger picture, but like to keep an eye on important details. ☑

13. Sometimes I feel too big or forceful, like a bull in a china shop. ☐

14. When I don't get my way or others fail to perform well, I can fly into a terrible temper. ☐

15. The buck stops with me. ☐

Group 5

1. I enjoy creative work and play and people tell me I'm creative.

2. I pick up on atmospheres and moods as soon as I walk into a room.

3. I enjoy clothes and adapting fashion to my own personal style.

4. When I move, I'd rather take on an old wreck that I can do up the way I want than a place that's decorated to someone else's taste.

5. My personality is fluid, changing with different people and situations.

6. I'm good with my hands and find it easy to make or repair things.

7. People sometimes criticize me for being dreamy or distracted.

8. I have lots of exciting projects in the works, but many of them never get finished.

9. I find it hard to make up my mind and often change it.

10. I love to find old things and reshape them for a new use.

11. I need lots of space for spontaneity and hate being boxed in by routine.

12. I sometimes buzz excitedly with new ideas, almost beyond my capacity to express them all.

13. I love to have my creations or style admired and feel disappointed when they aren't.

14. I strongly dislike explaining myself even if I'm misunderstood.

15. I enjoy making beauty and harmony out of chaos.

Group 6

1. I get great joy from helping people to grow and become more of who they can be. ☐

2. People often unburden their problems to me, treating me like a counsellor or confessor. ☐

3. People tell me they feel better just being with me or talking to me. ☐

4. I am often filled with compassion for humanity and want to take care of everyone. ☐

5. I admire famous figures who have been of great service and inspiration to many. ☐

6. I feel a direct connection with a higher power or being. ☐

7. People sometimes complain that I'm too preachy or probing. ☐

8. To be happy in my work, I need to feel a strong sense of dedication. ☐

9. Other people tell me that I'm charismatic and/or inspirational. ☐

10. Sometimes people seem threatened by me for reasons I don't understand. ☐

11. I often get intuitions or inner guidance. ☐

12. When I meet someone, I tend to move quickly from small talk to soul-to-soul communication. ☐

13. I love ceremonial events and feel at home in spiritual places. ☐

14. I'm a free spirit and don't react well when people try to control me. ☐

15. I have a mission to help make the world a better place. ☐

Group 7

1. I respond positively to challenges and usually feel I can overcome them.

2. I'm very hardworking and will keep going till the job's done.

3. I'm not afraid of confrontation and have a good instinct for when to fight, when to withdraw.

4. I like to have an action plan for a project, but don't want to get bogged down in analysis.

5. I try to fix people's problems and lives, and often rush to defend the underdog.

6. I'm an open and straightforward person – what you see is what you get.

7. I can be very persuasive and get people to do things when required.

8. When the going gets tough, I can keep going better than most people.

9. I'm entrepreneurial and efficient, and would be good at running my own business.

10. Loyalty is among my highest values, and I expect others to share this.

11. I'm sometimes told I see the world too much in black and white.

12. I react strongly to people who criticize me and feel that I must challenge them.

13. If I hear someone say, 'It's time to take action!' my heart leaps a little and I think, 'Yes, that's it!'

14. People sometimes find me bossy when I'm trying to keep things moving.

15. I have a clear sense of 'chains of command' and know where I stand in the pecking order.

Results

Group 1: Sage

Group 2: Server ✓

✓ Group 3: Scholar ✓

✓ Group 4: King

Group 5: Artisan

Group 6: Priest ✓

Group 7: Warrior ✓

How to Interpret your Results

Ideally, you should get high scores for two groups, which are your primary and secondary Roles; which way around they are will become clearer once you've read the chapters. If this is the case, then read the corresponding chapters to confirm your results.

Some people get less clear results. Your results can be skewed by various factors, including:

Family and social conditioning: For example, if you were born into a highly educated or academic family, you will be conditioned into appearing like a Scholar. In an artistic or bohemian family, everyone will have an Artisan or Sage flavour. More generally, in some societies women are expected to behave as Servers or Artisans, men as Warriors or Kings. However, these are social functions which may not necessarily be your own true Role.

Work or profession: If your job corresponds to one of these personality archetypes, it will seem like your Role but may not be. For example, the business world is dominated by Warriors and Kings, while the public sector promotes a Server ethos, and the arts and media express Sage and Artisan values. These influences often override your natural personality.

Your own self-image: Many people have an idealized self-image which can obscure their true selves. It's easy to check or reject statements on this basis, so it's important to be as objective, self-aware and honest as possible in your self-assessment.

If your results are unclear, don't worry. Simply read all the chapters and you will probably recognize yourself in the Role you most identify with.

CHAPTER 1

The Seven Personality Types

This system is built on seven personality types: *Artisan, Sage, Server, Priest, Warrior, King and Scholar*. The personality types represent the core or essence of our being and determine our primary way of being in the world. In this system they are called 'Roles'.

It is important to understand two principles from the beginning:

1. *The Roles do not refer to professions and are not identical with work roles, although there are strong associations, as explained below.*

2. *There is no hierarchy in this system. The Roles are different but equal; each has its advantages and disadvantages.*

Your Role motivates and drives you; it colours how you see the world, affects how you express yourself and relate to other people, and determines what kind of work you are best suited to. It even influences your fashion sense, food preferences and choice of leisure activities. The Roles are universal archetypes regardless of culture, nationality, gender or any other external influences.

The Seven Roles as Archetypes

Once upon a time . . . in the Middle Ages, the world was simpler, with a more ordered and structured society. At the top was the king, who wore a crown so nobody was in any doubt that he was the big boss. The king was supported by a band of loyal warriors, who guarded him with their lives and kept the rest of the population in order. Feudal society was highly religious, and the power of the king in society was balanced by the priesthood, who controlled the spiritual realm. Priests supported the monarchy by anointing and blessing the king and endorsing his divine right to rule, in return for his protection. Priests held the keys to the kingdom of heaven and could save your soul – or condemn you to hell. Medieval society was held together by a large group of serfs (peasants), who worked extremely hard, but were inspired by the promise that the poor were blessed and would be rewarded in the afterlife. Scholarship flourished in the monasteries and the new universities. Medieval scholars, burning the midnight oil, provided a theological framework for the priests' spiritual vision and laid the foundations of science through their experiments. Life was hard and often bleak, but softened and enlivened by art and entertainment, albeit with a religious flavour. Hollywood was just a hill and there was no TV and radio, let alone internet, but every court had its jester to keep people laughing through the long winter nights. Troubadours and travelling players entertained the populace with stories, epic sagas and mystery plays. There were no artists in the sense we now understand of high-status creative individualists, but there was a flourishing class of artisans who built the magnificent cathedrals, decorated them with stunning stained-glass windows and frescoes, illustrated the scholars' manuscripts and composed music to lift the interminable church services. They also decorated the king's palace with tapestries and designed glorious gowns and jewellery for the ladies of the court.

The Middle Ages had their own problems, but medieval society worked well for hundreds of years, enabling Europe to be reborn out of the chaos of the Dark Ages into stability and prosperity. One of the fundamental reasons was its reliance on universal institutions – kingship, priesthood, colleges, the military, arts guilds, et cetera – which have existed in all civilized societies worldwide, including ancient Africa, Egypt, Greece and Rome, India, China and Japan. They have developed into such complex, sophisticated and successful institutions because they were created and run by people with the right qualities and specialised skills: the Roles. It is no accident that the names of these core personality types correspond with these institutions, because without their specialised skills it would not be possible to run them efficiently. Kings and Warriors create systems of government and wage warfare to protect their community. Priests keep evolving religions and other ideologies to inspire people. Scholars are continually adding to human knowledge and organizing it to teach others. Sages keep revitalizing the language to entertain and communicate with people. Artisans are always coming up with new inventions, new media and materials to add beauty and style to the world. Servers are available 24/7 to support all the other Roles and keep the community bonded together. Today of course we live in a much faster changing, more diverse and multi-cultural world, but these archetypes are eternal and still hold true.

In the modern world, Kings are more likely to wear a baseball cap than a crown and drive a Mercedes than a golden coach, but they still rule politically as presidents and prime ministers, supported by Warriors in suits. The balance of power has shifted from governments to business, and many Kings and Warriors prefer to operate in the business world. Religion is a less dominant force in the West, where psychology has taken on much of its authority, so modern Priests are as likely to be counsellors as confessors. Scholars still run the schools and universities, now mainly free from the shackles of religious dogma, and validate the scientific knowledge that underpins our industry and technology. Jesters have transmuted into actors and TV presenters, dominating the entertainment and communication industries. In this system they are given the name of Sage to recognize their wisdom as well as their wit. Artisans are now held in much higher esteem as cultural creatives and are as likely to be found at the cutting edge of multimedia and new technology as in the traditional media of paint and stone. Supporting the whole social structure are the service industries and public sector, maintained by Servers, who, as ever, keep the whole show on the road.

It needs to be clearly understood that this personality typology is much more flexible and humane than feudal society, or the average cut-throat corporation, and is intended to serve people and help them develop rather than put them in their place. It is a truly liberating and democratic system which cuts across the barriers of class, wealth, education, race, religion, age and gender. It is a map but not a trap, describing not prescribing. Despite the associations of their names, all roles are equal and have unlimited potential. A King is as likely to be born into a poor family as a palace, but will still display leadership qualities. It is no better to be a Priest than a Server – who has many advantages, including greater ease in one-to-one relationships. The Roles function more like a team than a hierarchy. They are all important and vital to the greater harmony, like the instruments of an orchestra.

The Structure of the Personality System

The seven Roles are interrelated and organized in a simple but powerful structure:

Axis	Ordinal	Neutral	Cardinal
Expression	Artisan		Sage
Inspiration	Server		Priest
Action	Warrior		King
Integration		Scholar	

The Axes of the Roles:
Expression, Inspiration, Action, Integration

The Roles are divided into four axes: three pairs and one stand-alone Role. These axes are the four primary ways of being in the world. One good starting point to discovering your Role is to ask yourself which axis you most resonate with: Expression, Inspiration, Action or Integration.

Expression is the process of conveying and communicating inner states of feeling and thinking to other people. It can take many forms: speech, facial expressions, gesture and movement, art, performance, to name a few. Without expression there would be no creativity or change and the world would be a dull place. With expression come form, colour, music, style, beauty and fun, along with practical inventions to improve our lives. Expressive people show their emotions and expect others to do the same. Everyone can express themselves, but two Roles in particular have this as their main way of being: Artisans and Sages.

Inspiration literally means 'breathing in', thus connecting body and soul. Inspiration reminds us that there is more to life than bread alone and motivates us to move beyond the immediate practicalities of our existence, rise above the obstacles life throws in our way and achieve our potential. It also takes us beyond our personal concerns to serve the common good of society or a higher cause. Inspiration is particularly important at times of hardship when people are desperate or in fear of their lives, offering comfort and the sense of a deeper meaning and purpose beyond present suffering. Everyone can be inspirational, but the two specialist inspirational Roles are Servers and Priests.

Action is the basis of life. Without it, there would be no progress – nothing would happen at all. Action takes expression and inspiration into the material world and makes them productive. Hospitals and churches need to be built for Servers and Priests to fulfil their missions effectively. Artisans and Sages need art galleries, theatres and people to manage their careers and sell their work. Action is about organizing people and processes to get results; it requires work, collaboration and leadership. Everyone can be active and productive, but there are two specialist action Roles: Warriors and Kings.

Integration is the ability to assimilate information, processing raw data into its higher form: knowledge. There is so much happening in the world all the time that there is a need for people to stand on the sidelines without actively participating so that they can get a better view of the other Roles' activity and pull it all together into a new synthesis. Everyone is capable of integration, but there is one specialist Role for this function: Scholars. They stand alone in a pivotal position at the centre of the pendulum, which enables them to perform an important function in helping a group to cohere and a project to run more smoothly.

The Focus of the Roles: Cardinal, Ordinal and Neutral

The expression, inspiration and action axes are divided into pairs or partners. Each of these three axes comprises one ordinal and one cardinal partner. These partners are complementary in many ways and so get on well together in love, as friends and at work. The integration axis comprises one stand-alone neutral Role, who gets on with all the other Roles and mediates between them.

Ordinal means 'narrow-focused', so ordinal Roles work better at immediate tasks and tend to be more practical and down to earth than other Roles. They are also better at one-to-one relationships and prefer small to large groups. The ordinal expression Role is the Artisan; the ordinal inspiration Role is the Server; the ordinal action Role is the Warrior.

Cardinal means 'wide-focused', so cardinal Roles have a clearer grasp of the bigger picture. In a group they stand out even without trying to draw attention to themselves.

They make good leaders and can manage big projects. They prefer connecting to people in a group than individually and sometimes find personal relationships challenging. The cardinal expression axis Role is the Sage; the cardinal inspiration role is the Priest; the cardinal action Role is the King.

Neutrality is the ability to stand back from a situation or relationship and evaluate it objectively. This makes it easier to perform tests and experiments and come up with the correct answer. It is the midway point between the polarity of cardinal and ordinal, and so it is easy to swing to one or other side like a pendulum. Neutrality brings calmness and balance, though it can become overly detached. The Scholar stands alone as the neutral integration Role.

The Positive and Negative Poles

Each Role has a positive and negative pole or aspect. This is a psychological rather than moral attribute. The positive pole leads you to happiness and wellbeing. If you operate from it, your life will work more smoothly. You will feel more energized and confident and be better able to handle challenges and make good choices. Operating from the negative pole brings dysfunction and unhappiness and is more likely to lead to choices with unfortunate consequences for yourself and others.

Each chapter describes both the positive and negative pole of the Role in question and how these apply to the main areas of life: work, relationship, communication. The goal is to remain in the positive pole as much as possible or move back into it if you slide to the negative pole.

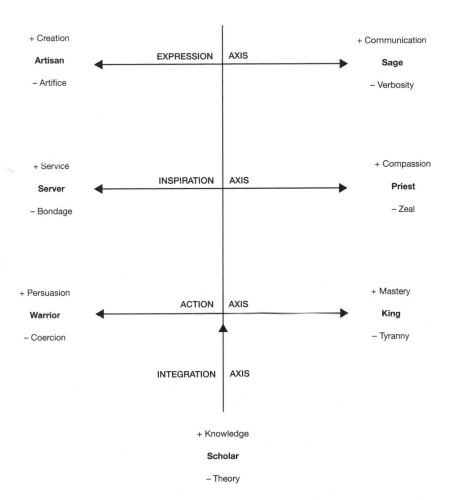

ORDINAL   **NEUTRAL**   **CARDINAL**

+ Creation   + Communication

Artisan   EXPRESSION | AXIS   **Sage**

– Artifice   – Verbosity

+ Service   + Compassion

Server   INSPIRATION | AXIS   **Priest**

– Bondage   – Zeal

+ Persuasion   + Mastery

Warrior   ACTION | AXIS   **King**

– Coercion   – Tyranny

INTEGRATION | AXIS

+ Knowledge

Scholar

– Theory

The Roles in the Population

The Roles are found in different proportions throughout the world population (with some variation in different cultures). This is appropriate, since some functions are most useful in smaller or larger proportions. For example, it's better to have a ratio of one King to 10 or 20 Warriors because it avoids an 'all chiefs and no Indians' scenario. Overall there are more ordinal Roles and fewer cardinal Roles, which is appropriate, as leadership is such a high-impact function.

Servers are the most numerous of the Roles, at 30 percent, reflecting the fundamental importance of service in the world. Artisans come next, at 20 percent, closely followed by Warriors, at 18 percent, reflecting the need for creativity and productivity in a well-functioning society. Scholars comprise 15 percent of the population, Sages 10 percent, Priests 5 percent and Kings 2 percent.

The Perspectives

For added depth and flexibility, I am bringing one more dimension of the system into this book: the Perspective. This is your worldview or outlook on life, including your deepest motivations, values and ethical sense. It is the most important influence on how your Role manifests in your life and how you experience it internally. Like all the elements in this system, it has a positive and a negative pole and the aim is to operate from the positive pole.

The set of five Perspectives is similar (though not identical) to the 'Hierarchy of Needs' theory developed by the psychologist Abraham Maslow:

1. *Survival-oriented Perspective.* This is rare in wealthier countries, though not unknown, and anyone can revert to it if they suddenly lose all their money or get lost in the mountains. For people who have it, life is mainly about their own day-to-day survival. For obvious reasons, if you have this Perspective you are more likely to lead an

obscure than famous life. It can be summed up as 'me against the world'.

In the positive pole, this Perspective ensures the survival of yourself, your family and your community. In the negative pole it produces extreme ruthlessness, as is sometimes found in the desperate situations of disaster, war and prison.

2. *Rule-bound Perspective.* This presumes the absolute authority of rules as the basis for living, for the purpose of feeling secure. These rules are usually believed to be imposed by a divine authority or time-honoured custom and tradition. This Perspective predominates in traditional societies such as those found in the Middle East and East Asia and in pockets in the USA and Europe. All the world religions have rule-bound individuals and sects within them. Rigidly organized professions and work environments often promote these values, particularly the non-commissioned ranks of the military. Though they are in a minority worldwide, such communities can have a great impact when they are vociferous in promoting their ideologies; for example, fundamentalist religious groups who exert pressure on a liberal regime. People at this Perspective only become famous if they represent a large constituency, as did Richard Nixon.

In the positive pole, this Perspective provides structure: a safe 'Pleasantville' kind of environment where everyone knows their place and everything works like clockwork. In the negative pole, it produces extreme inflexibility;

any signs of nonconformity are ruthlessly suppressed. Suburbia expresses the positive and negative values perfectly: safe for child-rearing but stifling to people with different perspectives, particularly teenagers.

3. *Competing Perspective.* This is the dominant outlook in the world today in politics, business and the entertainment industry. It is a powerful, driven outlook, which stresses individual or group success as all-important – winner takes all. Typically, people overcome enormous obstacles such as poverty and illness to scale the heights. As winners they never quit, as losers they pick themselves up and start again. Most corporations have this as their group ethos – they believe that it is essential for their prosperity in the modern market economy. Some are excellent and contribute much to the world, while others, such as certain banking and financial corporations, can be extremely damaging in their pursuit of profits.

The competing motto can be summed up as 'There are only two kinds of people in the world, winners and losers, and I'm going to be a winner!' The predominant belief is that any problem, including those of the world at large, can be solved if you throw enough money at it. Many of the world's movers and shakers share this perspective, from leaders such as Alexander the Great and John F. Kennedy to glitzy entertainers like Frank Sinatra and Fred Astaire. It is the Perspective that leads most easily to fame. The James Bond movies depict its values and aspirations perfectly. People who have it find that relationships are not their strongest suit, and often choose a trophy wife or husband over a deep and meaningful relationship.

In the positive pole, this Perspective creates competence: a well-organized society, thriving economy and spectacular entertainment, including the sporting contests most of us enjoy watching. The negative pole produces extreme selfishness in which ambition and greed overcome all scruples. A few winners enjoy the fruits of success at the expense and suffering of the exploited many.

4. *Relationship-oriented Perspective.* This is becoming increasingly prominent in the world and represents a complete transformation from the outer-directed values of the first three Perspectives to more reflective, empathic, inner-directed values. The motto for this Perspective is: 'You and I are connected, let's try and get along together.' This worldview has produced socialism, public welfare, charities and voluntary services, and most recently a 'soft power' ethos in many companies and enterprises, adding much to the common good.

To work well in these environments, you need empathic skills and a sophisticated, ethical outlook. Success may be important, but people want to achieve it by co-operative rather than competitive means and are sometimes prepared to sacrifice an easy route to fame to be true to their inner vision. A feature of the relationship-oriented Perspective is the high level of intensity and drama experienced in almost all areas of life, especially in personal relationships. Most of the great artists and humanitarians used this Perspective, including Michelangelo, Shakespeare, Mozart, St Francis of Assisi and Martin Luther King.

In the positive pole, this Perspective produces tremendous insight, which can result in great creative innovation, social progress and emotional intelligence. The negative pole produces confusion, which is likely to result in stormy, painful relationships and the collapse of idealistic groups into ideological recrimination.

5. *Philosophically oriented Perspective.* This is currently a minority worldview concerned with understanding the deeper meaning and purpose of life. People with it have little interest in material or worldly success and tend not to join the rat race or compete in the world. Often eccentric (by mainstream standards), they prefer simple living – indeed, simplicity in everything – cultivating their own gardens in a laid-back way. While capable of being enormously productive in their chosen fields, and also outside their own specialisms, they typically lead quiet and secluded lives. Their motto is 'There's you and me, and we're part of something much bigger than we can know.' Some people use their wisdom and talents to do good work for the rest of humanity, which is particularly effective and beneficial from this Perspective and highly recommended. A few, therefore, become famous, such as Carl Gustav Jung, Walt Whitman and Johann Sebastian Bach.

The positive pole of this Perspective can lead to great wisdom, and often takes people in a spiritual direction, though usually outside organized religion. Its negative pole makes people detached from daily life, sometimes arrogant towards others and lazy.

While each Perspective has its value and validity, there is an evolutionary development from the first to the fifth. Each incorporates the insights and understanding of the previous one, but there is a dramatic shift between the third and fourth. The first three Perspectives are outer-directed, concerned with finding your feet and making your mark on the world. At the relationship Perspective the focus changes radically to inner-directed values. Relationships, emotional experience, ethics and spirituality become more important than material success. People put their family before their career, spiritual growth before worldly success, and sometimes sacrifice self-interest for a higher cause. Much of the misunderstanding and conflict between people in personal relationships, business and political life is a result of the clash of values between these two Perspectives. One example is the way the environmental movement is led by relationship- and philosophically oriented people but sometimes hijacked by people operating from the negative pole of the competing Perspective.

Everyone operates predominantly from one Perspective, which usually emerges in adolescence and continues throughout life, although occasionally people switch Perspectives if their life circumstances change dramatically. All Roles can achieve success and happiness at any Perspective. It's pointless and impossible to try and force yourself to the fifth if you're not ready for it. You will feel happiest by discovering and accepting your own natural Perspective.

This book deals mostly with Perspectives 3–5, because these are the most concerned with self-development.

The Roles in Context

The Roles are the core of a highly complex but coherent philosophy and psychology which comprise seven sets of traits. These are summarized in the final chapter for anyone wanting to explore the system in greater depth.

For the sake of clarity and simplicity, I am focusing on the Roles and Perspectives in this book. Since everyone has a secondary as well as a primary Role, this gives you a set of 49 sub-types to choose from. All 49 sub-personalities are described in the book (in the final section of each chapter), so I hope you'll be able to recognize yourself in one of them. If you factor in the Perspective, this gives you nearly 250 variations, which is probably enough to be going on with.

The goal of this system is to become your best self, which will empower you to live a more successful, happy and fulfilled life. The way to do this is to discover your Role, integrate it with your Perspective and live from their positive poles. The process requires sharp and honest self-observation and a certain amount of effort in the early stages, but with practice becomes second nature. I guarantee that it is worth making a commitment to this process of self-discovery and that you will find the results transformative.

CHAPTER 2

The Artisan

'If you can dream it, you can do it. Always remember that this whole thing was started with a dream and a mouse.'
WALT DISNEY

The Artisan Personality

Artisans are the ordinal expression Role, specializing in creativity. They are the great innovators, always seeking or inventing something new, fresh, unique. Fascinated by structure, they can shape and manipulate the material world with impressive dexterity. Their creativity is also applied to their own style and personality, as their individuality is vital to them. They are constantly reinventing themselves in an attempt to stand out from the crowd, to be different or special. Whether or not they achieve fame and fortune, they bring beauty, style and originality into the world – and also useful inventions. Most would agree with the great Artisan architect Frank Lloyd Wright that 'form and function should be one, joined in a spiritual union.'

Since the term 'Artisan' has such strong associations with arts and crafts, it is important to understand that most Artisans are not artists, although art is the ultimate expression of this Role. So don't dismiss this identity for yourself if you are not artistic. It is the broader concept and energy of creativity rather than art in particular that are the essence of the Artisan personality. Conversely, any Role can be an artist, so don't assume all artists are Artisans, although most of the best ones are. Artisans predominate in the arts and media, and these worlds both reflect and shape the Artisan personality. However, Artisans are as likely to work in the skilled trades as the fine arts. They can and do apply their creative talents to any medium, including ideas. Albert Einstein was an Artisan scientist who said of himself: 'I am enough of an artist to draw freely upon my imagination.' Typically, they have several different careers, sometimes simultaneously, and a diverse range of leisure pursuits.

Creativity is the positive pole of the Artisan Role and comes naturally to them. All Artisans are creator gods, refashioning the world out of clay, paint, fabric, music — whatever is their chosen medium. Artisans see the world as a blank canvas, and an empty surface or space is the most appealing thing to them. If nothing else is available, they might cover a wall with graffiti, doodle in a book or decorate their skin with tattoos. Even without any special training, they 'have it in their hands'. Male Artisans often enjoy carpentry and woodworking; they might build and fix computers, set up a furniture refinishing shop in the basement or restore classic cars in their garage. Women often enjoy making and embellishing clothes and soft furnishings, jewellery and other crafts.

Artisans have longer antennae than other people. They receive and process information, impressions and energies from different levels simultaneously. This is the basis of their creativity and makes them highly sensitive, imaginative and good at multi-tasking. However, they can become bombarded with sensory overload and overwhelmed by generating more ideas than they can handle. They instinctively understand form and space and their interrelationship, such as the space between notes in music. They possess a discriminating, multi-dimensional appreciation of beauty and ability to put together materials, colours, sounds and ideas in unexpected combinations which surprise but work.

'My quality of life is marvelously enhanced by an intimate relationship with colour, texture, vibration and the many other scintillating dimensions of experiencing.'
Clementine, bodyworker

Artisans are ahead of the curve, picking up intuitively on the zeitgeist. It's often said that the length of women's hemlines reflects the state of the money markets. The Artisan who designed the season's look probably didn't consult the Dow Jones Index, but was somehow tuned in anyway.

The material world is not solid to an Artisan but fluid and subject to change; this also applies to ideas and rules. They are therefore the role that suffers most from rules and routine. They are highly spontaneous, hate being boxed in or given a blueprint, and prefer to make it up as they go along. As a result they thrive in chaos, as long as it is balanced with stability:

'The transformation of chaos into some sort of order is more exciting than the chaos itself. If I walk into a totally chaotic

space, I cannot stay there very long. I will either need to get out or rearrange and fix it if I have to hang out there. I do make a huge mess (I am told) when I cook, but I like a clean and tidy and organized kitchen and a pleasing presentation of food on a plate. I accept the chaotic process of creation, but my intention is to end up with something beautiful and harmonious and balanced and something more peaceful or healing . . . until perhaps something needs to be shaken and stirred and transformed again as the times change.'

ELIZABETH, CATERER/WRITER

The 'shock of the new' is a positive experience for Artisans, who love change and get bored with routine and repetition. Sometimes they can be *enfants terribles* or iconoclasts who set out to shock, break up the old order and wake people up to a new vision. They are natural anarchists who can be drawn to revolutionary movements, being unafraid of destruction, which they see as the other side of creation. Romanticism was the quintessential Artisan movement, popularizing the idea of the artist as rebellious genius. Rock stars – the new romantics – understand this instinctively. Jim Morrison of the Doors proclaimed: 'I am interested in anything about revolt, disorder, chaos – especially activity that seems to have no meaning. It seems to me to be the road toward freedom.'

Artisans comprise around 20 percent of the population. They feel most at home surrounded by other expressive people and in creative working environments. While they love nature for its healing and inspirational qualities and as a resource, they tend to get bored living in the country and prefer the stimulus and excitement of an urban environment.

Capital cities and towns with a flourishing cultural life like San Francisco, Santa Fe, London, Paris, Berlin and Barcelona suit them well. Sometimes they are fortunate to live in a country where the whole culture has a strong Artisan flavour. While ancient Rome was a Warrior society, Italy from the Renaissance onwards has been an Artisan culture and a thriving centre for art, design, invention and fashion.

The Challenge of the Negative Pole

Artisans can be the most charming and delightful people you will ever meet, and it can be hard to see that they have any flaws. But every Role has a negative pole, and for them it is artifice, which can lead them into self-deception or delusion. Creativity is both an elusive muse and a hard taskmaster, and imitation is easier and often better rewarded. If Artisans have to make a living from their art or craft, it is easier to give the market what it wants – which is more of the same. At the competing Perspective, most Artisans will happily jump on the bandwagon in return for fame and fortune. Authenticity and originality are sacrificed to insincerity, imitation and pastiche. At the relationship Perspective the call of their muse is usually stronger and harder to ignore, despite the pressure of the market. Most will reject anything they see as plastic, derivative or contrived, but they may fall into the opposite trap of self-indulgence.

In daily life their negative pole can manifest in dreaminess and distraction. The boundary between reality and fantasy is always fluid to them and they can get carried away in an alternative life story. If they dream of climbing Mount Everest, they will believe in their self-image of a mountaineer even if they have trouble walking more than 50 yards from their car. Their heads in the clouds, they can daydream their life away in a world of make-believe. Unfortunately, reality has a nasty habit of suddenly catching up, which can be quite unpleasant. For example, compulsive fantasizing – which others more bluntly call lying – can get them into trouble. A talent for imitation which turns to forgery, manual dexterity put to use in becoming a card sharp or pickpocket, a fascination with the lives of others which leads to taking on a false identity or a fluid sense of intellectual property encompassing plagiarism can all end in a court of law. In the 1920s some love letters by Abraham Lincoln were exposed as forgeries. The actress responsible explained: 'The spirits of Ann and Abe were speaking through my mother to me, so that my gifts as a writer combined with her gifts as a medium could hand in something worthwhile to the world.' One of the biggest publishing sensations of the 1980s was the 'Hitler Diaries', which impressed people by the sheer scale of the scoop: 62 diaries supported by a vast archive of letters and documents. All were forged by a master con artist (*see page 253 for another dimension of this*). More recently an author who fabricated her memoirs apologized in an inimitable Artisan statement: 'The book is a story, it's my story. It's not the true reality, but it is my reality. There are times when I find it difficult to differentiate between reality and my inner world.'

Artisans find it hard to handle pressure, including the challenges of celebrity. They can easily lose the delicate thread of their inspiration and sometimes lose touch with reality and crack up. This has happened to some of the most talented artists, including Vincent van Gogh, and more recently in the music world to Syd Barrett (founder of Pink Floyd) and Kurt Cobain (Nirvana). The Romantic ideal of the artist has a dark side of self-destruction, which is sometimes glamorized but should be resisted. Kurt Cobain's suicide note read: 'It's better to burn out than to fade away.' But it is not romantic or fun to starve in a garret, get addicted to drugs and alcohol or suffer a mental breakdown. This is not bohemian free-spiritedness but delusion, the extreme form of the Artisan negative pole. It can happen to Artisans leading normal lives as well as to great artists. Fortunately most Artisans find methods to channel their imagination into creative projects before this happens.

The antidote is keeping it real. With practice and experience Artisans can learn to focus on the task at hand and move between the material and mental worlds without getting lost. This ability can be great fun if used consciously, which becomes easier at the relationship and philosophical Perspectives. An entertaining example is the rock band Porcupine Tree, which was originally created as a hoax, but the fabrication became so elaborate, the music so accomplished, that they ended up becoming a real and very successful band. Playing with the boundary between reality and imagination, creating gorgeous illusion, is the basis of art, and Artisans who have mastered this skill not only bring beauty to the world but help more 'earthbound' souls appreciate a more multi-dimensional reality.

How to Recognize an Artisan

Artisans can be either the easiest or the hardest Role to spot. When they are manifesting typically, you can spot them instantly across a crowded room by their bubbly personalities, buzzy energy, stylish or unusual outfits. But they are also mercurial, constantly shape-shifting. Sometimes they like to stand out and can be highly eccentric, but other times they prefer to blend in with their surroundings and the people they are with. In a marriage, they may take on the colour of their partner. Female Artisans are especially prone to this, reinforced by social conditioning, but men do it too. I once met a man who appeared to be a Scholar, like his formidably intellectual wife. It was only when he showed me a chair he had made that he came alive for the first time and I realized he was an Artisan in disguise. Flamboyant, extroverted Artisans can be mistaken for Sages, especially if they are also witty and good with words. Athletic Artisans can become bodybuilders or sportspeople and look like Warriors, including actors such as Brad Pitt who play tough guys. Quieter, more family-minded Artisans can look like Servers, since both Roles are ordinal and empathic. Occasionally religious or spiritual Artisans can seem like Priests, since both Roles are very high frequency and Artisans are always looking for inspiration.

Being a fluid and mercurial Role, their gender identity can be quite flexible, and they often enjoy bending the rigid categories of masculine and feminine. In particular, male Artisans can seem quite feminine or 'soft' compared to Warriors and Kings, though as businessmen or fitness trainers they may overcompensate by developing a macho persona. Artisan women often express the archetype of femininity with grace and panache, but some prefer to play with androgyny.

They are the Role most subject to moodiness, often inexplicably for others, as they hate explaining themselves.

When an Artisan feels happy, the mood of the whole group will lift, and vice versa. When they walk into a room, their antennae instantly pick up the emotional nuances and atmosphere and they can change it if they don't like it, consciously or unconsciously. Some describe themselves as chameleons:

> *'I don't exactly know what my personality is like to others, but for me it is a constant stream of change, growth and movement.'*
> DEBORAH, ARTIST/EDUCATOR/BODYWORKER

A Scholar described to me the experience of meeting an Artisan and not being able to tell if she was plain or pretty, intelligent or dumb, as his impressions kept changing. This is typical of the effect Artisans can have on others, like a trick of the light.

Another chameleon aspect of Artisans is that they can come across as either soft or sharp. This depends partly on them; they can be picky and discriminating or sweetly accepting. It also depends on your relationship with them and whether they find you sympathetic or not. Sages, Servers and Priests are more likely to bring out their softer side, while the 'solid' Roles (Kings, Warriors and Scholars) may threaten them into putting up their defences, stinging and needling.

Artisan Style

Of all the Roles, Artisans are typically the most stylish and best turned out, even without trying. They understand clothes as a medium to express, transform, reinvent themselves, enhance their best features, disguise their worst ones. They have naturally excellent taste, but may prefer the vitality of vulgarity. The most important thing for them is to look different, preferably unique, so even when they follow fashion they will introduce a new twist. Some have a signature style which everyone wants to copy, but nobody can do it with as much panache. By the time other people have figured it out, the Artisan has moved on to a new look. Like Sages, they see clothes as costume, but more to express a mood than a character.

'Artisans have a definite personal style, which may be very chic or very hippie or even very odd, but it will be unique to the person, and she/he will not feel comfortable if she/he has to dress differently for a job or because of unforeseen circumstances. I've always viewed dressing as costuming. I've got to be colour co-ordinated, and I must have my jewelry! Naked without it!'
CATHRYN, ARTIST/AROMATHERAPIST

Fashion is important to Artisans, but their attitude changes radically depending on their Perspective. At the competing Perspective, Artisan women are the ultimate clothes horses and fashion victims, addicted to designer labels, paying a fortune for the latest 'It' handbag. Their fascination with shoes borders on fetishism. Metrosexual Man is an Artisan, likely to moisturize, exfoliate and own an impressive collection of shoes, sunglasses, watches and cufflinks and all the latest gadgets and accessories.

At the relationship Perspective, Artisans may refuse to spend money on clothes or only wear fair-trade clothes made from organic materials. If they are interested in fashion, they will become avant-garde leaders rather than followers, sporting some of the wildest, weirdest combinations outside the catwalk. Even without money they have style. Their clothes will always look good on them, however casual (they are the masters of that difficult balance 'smart casual'). They are the enviable ones who look gorgeous in anything and are expert at mixing high street with designer items and a bit of vintage so the whole outfit looks stunning.

At the philosophical Perspective, Artisans display little interest in fashion or their appearance and are likely to dress more for comfort and convenience. Their enormous charm works better for them than any packaging and they become more interested in the inner than outer world. As a result, their creativity goes in a mental or spiritual direction. Even so, they are likely to have at least one unique item, perhaps a brooch or a watch, which displays their taste.

Most Artisans enjoy shopping, delighting in the challenge of creating a look out of thrift-shop items and bargain bins. The low cost enables them to buy more clothes and recycle them.

> *'I love to shop for bargains and get my biggest thrill shopping at discount stores where it is like a treasure hunt to find good-quality things hidden in the racks or shelves.'*
> MEREDITH, ATTORNEY/MEDIATOR

They are also good at making, mending or adapting their own clothes and unearthing original items from unusual sources. An Artisan is the best friend to go shopping with, as they are bound to pick out something that looks great on you but you'd never have noticed on the hanger. But you need to be thick skinned; normally hesitant to speak their mind, with clothes they will let you know with ruthless objectivity whether or not your look works.

Artisans are often beautiful or handsome, but even if not, they are skilled at enhancing their natural features, turning themselves into a triumph of style over physical perfection. They also have an enviable capacity to retain their looks. However, at the competing Perspective, when they are youth-obsessed, they are likely to be tempted by the transformative possibilities of cosmetic surgery. Both male and female Artisans like to use their skin as their canvas, which may end up covered in body paint, tattoos or piercings. The downside of their obsession with the perfect body is that health may be sacrificed to beauty in pursuit of the size zero or over-enthusiastic iron-pumping. They are natural make-up artists, using cosmetics like paint to create the most subtle or outrageous effects. Their hair is also an irresistible medium to play with; they may change colour and style on a whim, or suddenly decide to shave it all off.

Architects are mainly Artisans, and all Artisans appreciate a well-designed and well-built home, aesthetically pleasing as well as functional. Their homes can be havens of peace and harmony, though sometimes comfort is sacrificed to style – white empty space or spiky furniture. They may be fashion-plate perfect, an empty space with one strategically placed chair or casually but artfully bohemian.

The important thing is that the home reflects the Artisan's own taste and personality. They would rather buy a wreck than a beautifully decorated apartment and renovate it to their own vision. Although they enjoy spending money if they have it, they often respond with great panache to the challenge of poverty, creating a beautiful home out of the most unpromising materials. They enjoy rooting through builders' skips, seeking the perfect piece of discarded wood or metal to enhance a sculpture or decorate a room. Being sensitive to atmosphere, they love to change the mood of a room with lighting, splashes of colour and little touches that other people might not even notice.

Andy Warhol: An Artisan who Changed our Culture

The 1960s were glory days for Artisan culture. This era gave birth to an explosion of creative talent in all media and aspects of society. Artisans were in the vanguard of this cultural revolution, especially in the arts and media.

Andy Warhol was the most famous artist of the 1960s. He made art out of some of the most iconic brand images of mass culture and consumerism, including Coca-Cola bottles, dollar bills and the face of Marilyn Monroe. He was a far cry from the romantic image of the artist starving in a garret, and proved that artists could be both avant-garde and popular. Although he did not originate Pop Art, he made it the dominant aesthetic of the age, simultaneously inventing and parodying 1960s style.

Born ugly, gay and from a working-class immigrant background at a time when these were serious obstacles, his one advantage was his genius. Warhol began his career in advertising, which was the most glamorous profession in the 1950s. He shot to fame with his first exhibition, featuring his famous painting 'Campbell's Soup Cans', which literally reproduced all 32 varieties of the brand. This was the beginning of a controversial but highly successful career.

With his fine antennae and his unique mixture of camp and cool, Warhol became a prophet of modern life. He sensed that the fine-art values of abstract expressionism were becoming dated, while popular culture was vibrant and exciting. The critics and public took much longer to catch up, and his brash images were seen as an affront as well as a challenge, and widely attacked, which added to his fame. His response has since become a publicity truism: 'Don't pay any attention to what they write about you. Just measure it in inches.' He was the first artist to understand the power of image in the creation of celebrity and painted some of the most famous celebrities of his time, becoming a celebrity in his own right.

Warhol was a chameleon who created, manipulated and controlled his own image. He displayed the Artisan talent of enhancing unpromising material – his own looks – exaggerating his pasty paleness with trademark wigs and dark glasses to become an icon of cool. Artisans enjoy hiding behind masks, disguising, distorting and reinventing their image. Warhol's self-portraits presented a multiplicity of slippery selves, illegible outlines, shadows and self-parodies. His gender and sexuality were androgynous and fluid, and his paintings explored the subtleties of sexual desire, including transsexuality and homoerotic drawings. Behind the fame he was a lonely, enigmatic figure, quiet and shy, eventually reclusive, as often happens to sensitive Artisans in the bright glare of publicity. His sensitivity also drew him into negative-pole manifestations of neurosis, narcissism and hypochondria.

Warhol was adept in a variety of media which cross-fertilized each other, including film, television, performance art, photography, writing, fashion and music. His whole life work was a multimedia happening, mainly taking place on the stage of his famous New York studio 'The Factory', an alternative community of bohemians and freaks in which he created and nurtured 'superstars'. Typically of Artisans, words were his least favourite medium and he refused to explain his work, simply stating: 'If you want to know all about Andy Warhol, just look at the surface of my paintings and films and me, and there I am. There's nothing behind it.' He discovered and promoted one of the greatest 1960s bands, the Velvet Underground, designing the famous 'banana' sleeve of their first album. Both the band and Warhol himself were a major influence on the next generation of glam rock musicians, particularly David Bowie (another Artisan), who wrote a tribute song called 'Andy Warhol' and also played him in a film.

Warhol played with the boundary between the positive and negative poles of the Artisan Role, creativity and artifice. The whole glam movement was a reaction against the naturalism of the hippie movement, so artifice became a positive value. Warhol described himself as 'deeply superficial' and gloried in the artificiality of Hollywood. 'Everybody's plastic, but I love plastic. I want to be plastic.' Nowadays critics realize that Warhol's apparent shallowness and commerciality were in fact a brilliant mirror of the times and that he captured the zeitgeist of American culture in the 1970s. Artisans' fascination with surface can make them appear superficial, but more perceptive critics discerned the pathos and mysticism that underlay the vulgarity.

Like all Artisan artists, Warhol loved a blank canvas, and once quipped, 'I always thought I'd like my own tombstone to be blank. No epitaph, and no name.' The final but fitting irony is that the man whose most famous saying was 'In the future everyone will be famous for 15 minutes' became famous beyond his own time, attaining classic status. Although still a controversial figure, now his reputation is higher than ever and his paintings receive major retrospectives and sell for millions of dollars. His influence is pervasive in popular culture, being referenced and depicted in more songs, books, films and column inches than any other modern artist. It is hard to imagine contemporary artists like Damien Hirst and Tracey Emin without Andy Warhol.

The Artisan at Work

Artisans are very versatile in their creativity, so they have a lot of career options open to them. Arts and crafts are their natural activity; and most painters, sculptors, potters, weavers, hairdressers, tailors and graphic designers are Artisans, though other Roles are also found here. Artisans excel because of their ability to easily integrate their creative genius with impeccable technical prowess and an innate understanding of structure. They also love working with large, complex and challenging structures; and many architects and engineers are Artisans. There is an anonymous quote which sums up their search for the unique new thing (as well as the difference between Scholars and Artisans): 'A scientist studies what is, an engineer studies what never was.'

Artisans also predominate in the skilled trades. In a medieval village they would have been the blacksmiths, bakers and candlestick makers. Nowadays they make the best car mechanics, repairmen, decorators, plumbers and electricians – anything with a craft element, where their manual dexterity gives them an edge. They are also excellent at fixing broken gadgets and improvising solutions to mechanical problems. Such skills are always in high demand, and they can easily develop or fall back on them if deprived of other career opportunities. As makers and users of tools, displaying great mechanical aptitude and meticulous craftsmanship, they can be very focused when working on projects, in contrast to their dreamy image. This nimbleness can look quite magical to other Roles and they make the best conjurors and stage magicians.

The Sage–Artisan partnership is easy, successful and fun, and works brilliantly in the film industry. The Roles act well together, though Sages tend to prefer the stage while Artisans prefer movies, taking well to the minute subtleties of expression required by close-up camera work. Sages are usually the screenwriters and directors, though some of the artier directors are Artisans, including George Lucas. Artisans take care of the technical and creative aspects like wardrobes, sets and scenery. They particularly excel as cameramen, where their instinct for lighting and atmosphere produce magical effects. They love animation, with its multi-dimensional creative potential, and are continually striving to take this art to new heights of imaginative and technical perfection. They are at the cutting edge of multimedia, which they understand instinctively, inventing new technology to support it if they need to.

Competing Artisans love working in fashion as designers and models. Physically adept Artisans enjoy working in the performing arts as dancers, jugglers, mime and trapeze artists, as well as athletes and sportspeople. One of the greatest baseball players, Joe DiMaggio, was an Artisan who was renowned for the grace and elegance of his style on and off the pitch. The English footballer David Beckham is another Artisan, his creativity expressed in his footwork (and nowadays also in his outfits).

Artisans can also flourish in medicine and the healing arts as dentists, surgeons, bodyworkers, physiotherapists and aromatherapists. They prefer working with materials to words, which are the realm of Sages and Scholars. Being so attuned to subtle energies, Artisans find words clumsy in comparison.

'I have often thought that words can only lie, they are so defective and deficient a way to represent reality. Especially the spoken word, because I do not have time to ponder and craft my words for accuracy, thoroughness and clarity.'
PHILIP WITTMEYER, ENGINEER

They can turn their craftsmanship talents to wordsmithing, but may put more energy into the design of a book's cover than its contents. Having such fertile imaginations, however, they do well with imaginative writing such as fairy tales, fantasy and children's fiction. Lewis Carroll is an interesting example of an Artisan who could manipulate numbers adeptly as a mathematician but found his most famous expression in inventing wondrous worlds featuring fantastical, talking, shape-shifting creatures.

Artisans can also be excellent songwriters as well as singers, having a talent for expressing all the nuances of the human heart. They also do well in PR, advertising and marketing, working well with Sage copywriters since they are so skilled at getting under the skin of another person.

Several Artisans I know have the fantasy of opening a restaurant, and most of the best professional chefs are Artisans. They excel at creating ambience as well as great food, but have problems on the practical management side. Many don't succeed and the restaurant folds.

Other Artisans are florists or shopkeepers, preferably selling beautiful and original things such as antiques, fashion items and unusual gifts. They can even be fulfillled as shop assistants, if they are given some creative scope such as arranging shop windows and displays.

Leadership Style

Artisans are sometimes uncomfortable in the Warrior-dominated corporate world. Competing Artisans can be attracted to the power of big business, but will be happier in a design, publicity or marketing department. Relationship-oriented Artisans will be happier in a smaller, less ruthlessly commercial company with more emphasis on relationships and the quality of the product or service. They are a great asset to a business, as long as their creativity is valued. Their innovative vision can produce a never-ending stream of ideas, though it needs balancing with a more entrepreneurial Role to sort the commercial goers from the hare-brained schemes. Artisans are better at spending than making money and can easily get themselves or their business into debt. Routine stifles their spontaneity and they hate mindless, repetitive tasks like data entry. If they feel too bored and oppressed, they are likely to leave a job quite suddenly, whatever the consequences.

'I've had an extensive list of job titles. There is such an unending desire to express myself in new, creative and challenging ways that committing long term to one path feels unfathomable. I love getting entirely submerged in one point of view just long enough to shake it up a little and sprinkle in some new flavour, then move on to the next experience. Many of my short-term careers have centred around creative and/ or hands-on skills, from the renovation of Victorian homes to landscaping, painting murals, designing brochures, selling art, co-ordinating holiday events, and doing massage therapy, to name a few.'

CLEMENTINE, BODYWORKER

Like Scholars, Artisans tend to prefer working independently to being teamworkers or bosses, but they don't mind being employees or part of a team as long as they have some freedom to innovate. Of all the roles, they are the least interested in leadership, and can make problematic bosses if their talent gets them over-promoted. While generally having good social skills, they can be quirky and unpredictable, so colleagues can get confused, not knowing where they stand or what is expected of them. Artisans reserve the right to change their mind suddenly, which is tricky in a large corporation where the wheels grind slowly. They are also easily distracted, especially if the task in hand is a balance sheet or five-year plan, which they will do anything to avoid. On the other hand, they can bring an unusual flair to a public position, as illustrated by the mayor of Tirana in Albania, who sees the whole city as an art gallery and is making great efforts to bring his vision into reality.

Artisans can also make inspired leaders of creative enterprises such as an art studio, dance theatre, restaurant or fashion house, which can tolerate chaos as long as the end product works.

At the philosophical Perspective, they can be as practical, organized and focused as anyone, well able to handle the challenges of management and leadership in an area outside their normal comfort zone:

> '*I have had my own law firm for the past five years and two months. I love it. It is scary, fun, challenging, creative, and I have learned a ton. I am steadily doing better financially. The hardest part was when I started adding staff. Dealing with personnel issues has been a big challenge for me. I have relied a lot on my college teaching experience and my mothering experience (I have four grown children) to help me mentor my employees.. . .I love doing what I do for a living, which is negotiation and settlement, mediation, collaboration with another attorney outside of court to settle cases, and coaching people to represent themselves.*'
> MEREDITH, ATTORNEY/MEDIATOR

Communication Style

Language is not the favourite medium of Artisans, but as an expressive Role they can be very communicative. Some are social butterflies, capable of chattering non-stop for hours, sending streams of texts and emails, holding long telephone conversations and then calling back. In this case they need to be sensitive to other people's attention spans and busy schedules. Other Artisans are quiet and introverted, even reclusive, particularly when deep in a project. They can imagine '10,000 words in a cardboard box', while a Sage would let all the words out.

With their chameleon tendencies, many Artisans can flip between modes:

'In social settings, when with people I know, I am more extroverted. When with people I don't know, I am reserved and observant. It is in these situations that I can alter my behaviour so as to "fit in", or be included and "chosen". Problem is that I can't always remember who it is I'm supposed to be to be accepted. Not to be too hard on myself, though, I think that this was truer when I was younger. I do believe that as I get older and more comfortable in my own skin, I become more authentic ... in other words I am starting to like myself better as I have grown into who I really am.'
VIVIAN, LIFE COACH

Whether talkative or taciturn, public speaking is torture for most Artisans. Even professional entertainers tend to dry up if forced to address the audience rather than simply performing their art. They want their creation to be appreciated directly rather than mediated through words.

'Unlike Sages, their complementary Role, Artisans don't want attention on themselves. If they care to be acknowledged or remembered at all, it is that they want to be considered for their work's sake. In effect they say, "Here, look at this thing, not at me. See what I made. I am not of any consequence, except to the extent that I have created this thing of beauty and usefulness." Others should be careful about criticizing the Artisan's creations – that they take personally. Best leave it to them to be critical of their works.'

PHILIP WITTMEYER, ENGINEER

Artisans tend to take themselves seriously and are not renowned for their sense of humour, unless they have a Sage secondary Role, in which case they can be hilarious. Many comic writers and cartoonists have this combination, including Scott Adams, creator of *Dilbert*.

Artisans at the philosophical Perspective have a dry, wry, offbeat sense of humour. Their sharp eye for quirky foibles and gift for mimicry make them entertaining companions, enabling them to laugh at the comedy of life as well as their own and other people's pretensions.

'I definitely have a dry sense of humour that some people get and some don't. And as I've gotten older, I've found that a sense of humour about myself is indispensable to maintaining my sanity! I am aware that I am "creating" myself at all times and have developed the ability to watch myself from a

detached viewpoint (most of the time) and maintain a sense of the humour of it all, even when I am simultaneously suffering through some sort of negative-pole experience or the self-deception common to Artisans.'
CATHRYN, ARTIST/AROMATHERAPIST

Superficially it can be easy to communicate with Artisans, since they tend to be fluent conversationalists with good interpersonal skills – though with the chattier ones it can be hard to get a word in edgewise. Also, they can be so hyper-sensitive and thin skinned that it is easy to offend them or hurt their feelings. Coupled with their moody tendencies, this can sometimes make them prickly and abrasive as a defence. They have their own private codes of etiquette, which they imagine everyone else shares. You are expected to divine and intuit what they mean and how they feel, sometimes without any outer indication on their part. They will probably not confront you directly, but you will feel the room go cold, their mood darken, their energy withdraw; they may even stalk or storm off without you realizing what you've done to upset them. They can be even more shifty and manipulative than Sages, changing the rules of engagement without warning. It is therefore important to be as sensitive, intuitive and empathic as possible when you are with them. Be warm and open, listen and respond as empathically as possible. Also understand that if they seem distracted they are not necessarily bored but may be processing information on another level.

'Artisans are easily distracted from the outer world. Their quicksilver minds tend to slip back into their own rich inner

world of ideas, or plans for their current creative project, or whatever is puzzling them at the time.'
PHILIP WITTMEYER, ENGINEER

If Artisans like you and find you sympathetic, they can be delightful company – almost as entertaining as Sages, and more receptive, keeping you on your toes with their left-field perceptions and observations. As friends they are kind and generous, remembering your birthday and making you a personalized card or gift, entertaining you in style. They make wonderful cooks. Even the simplest meal is likely to be beautifully presented, pleasing the eye as well as the palate, and their dinner parties are a work of performance art. Some Artisans will spend days, even weeks, planning and putting together the perfect party – not just the food, but the whole ambience: flowers, candles, scents, playlists and of course their outfit.

The Artisan in Love

Like all the ordinal Roles, Artisans are generally excellent at one-to-one relationships. They are the most sensitive Role, so can easily tune in to what another person is thinking and feeling. Artisan women find it easy to attract a partner, transforming themselves into whatever fantasy you want to project onto them. They enjoy the game of flirtation and can give you the runaround. When one sets out to charm or seduce you, she is almost irresistible, to the irritation of other women.

On the other hand, Artisan men (and some women) can be very shy and introverted. They often have difficulty expressing themselves in words and keeping up a flow of banter and repartee like Sages. If they feel gauche, they can tie themselves up in knots and torture themselves over it. More confident male Artisans can be very suave, sometimes Casanovas. Women who prefer a new man to a cave man are attracted to their moody sensitivity, good grooming and style, charm and ability to tune in to them and talk to them.

Artisans invented the art of love and often make good lovers – playful, creative and technically adept. They are also skilled at creating a seductive, erotic environment for their lover, using light, scents, music, sensuous fabric and perfumed oils to enhance the experience. However, dating can be an ordeal for them as they are often highly discriminating and refined, so small flaws loom large. Someone with crude manners, who talks with their mouth full, laughs too loudly or wears the wrong shoes can be instantly rejected without being given a chance to redeem themselves. Placing such a high value on uniqueness, Artisans are often intolerant of ordinariness, in themselves and others.

They value commitment and look for it in a partner, but are not always the first to give it. Most Artisans want to be in a relationship, but they also 'want to be alone'. They need lots of space and respect for their boundaries. The more of a creative genius they are, the more space they need for their project, and their partner can end up playing second fiddle. The composer Delius said, 'No artist should ever marry . . . if ever you do have to marry, marry a girl who is more in love with your art than with you.' That said, Artisans can also make the most delightful and devoted partners with the right person.

In general, Artisans and Sages have the highest degree of mutual attraction, understanding and compatibility, being the ordinal and cardinal expression Roles. All Roles have something to offer an Artisan in a relationship, though Warriors and Kings make their most opposite and challenging partners. Servers will look after them beautifully, giving practical and emotional nourishment. Priests give them an ecstatic romantic experience and keep them inspired, though can be quite authoritarian. Scholars intrigue them as lovers but can be difficult partners, though each will respect the other's need for privacy and personal space. For a detailed description of the compatibilities between Artisans and other Roles, see Chapter 9.

Parents and Children

Artisans often love children and long to have their own, seeing parenting as a creative project. However, the reality of childcare can be difficult for them. Mothers at the competing Perspective are often cold, distant and neglectful. They don't want their figures ruined by pregnancy and breastfeeding, their clothes dirtied, homes disordered, social lives restricted. If they can afford it, they will hire nannies and send their children to boarding school at the first opportunity. While Artisans are more at ease with chaos than other Roles, they can find the relentless routine and drudgery of childcare distracting from their other projects, seeing 'the pram in the hall' as the enemy of creativity. They may find one child is enough and struggle to cope with looking after stepchildren and extended families. They are the Role least well equipped to set boundaries and discipline, so will find it hard to deal with naughty or difficult children. Some Artisan parents treat their children as a blank slate to mould or overwrite with their own tastes, less a child than a malleable Mini-Me – a temptation better resisted. However, since they usually possess excellent taste and style, they can help children develop these qualities. At the relationship and philosophical Perspectives they delight in their children and can make the most loving, affectionate parents. Since they are usually in touch with their own Inner Child – spontaneity, inventiveness, playfulness – they can easily enter into a child's imaginative world and be good friends with them.

As children, Artisans often show artistic or creative ability from an early age and are happy – and usually quiet – if you provide them with paper and crayons. However, they see any surface as fair game, to the annoyance of the Scholar siblings whose books they deface. They enjoy stories and games of make-believe, and girls love a dressing-up box. Both girls and boys can be extremely cute and charming; their winning ways make them adored and spoiled by the whole family. If over-indulged, however, they can become manipulative and brattish, learning to use their charm to twist adults around their little fingers.

Both girls and boys are sensitive, picking up easily on emotional undercurrents, and may even display psychic abilities. This means they easily become confused and scared if adults are not honest with them, or with each other. They are prone to daydreaming and fantasy, having a rich imaginative life, and will retreat into a dream world if unhappy in daily life. If loved and encouraged, however, they will become confident and popular.

Self-expression is more important to them than knowledge, so they may not enjoy school unless there is a strong emphasis on arts and crafts. They can suffer from attention disorders or dreaminess, especially if they get bored, preferring to dismantle their watches than learn maths. Girls are usually popular at school, expressing the feminine ideal that all girls aspire to: pretty, cute, fashion conscious, charming. All the other girls will want to be friends with them and join their clique. Boys can find it hard, especially in a rough school where the culture is macho or military, and can be bullied if they display too much sensitivity. They need to find a way to stand up for themselves, or get befriended by a Warrior, or excel at sports. In a liberal school, however, they will usually be fine.

As teenagers, they are the moodiest of the Roles, torn between the pressure of their peer group to blend in and their own need for uniqueness. In search of their individuality they rebel against conformity – and their parents – more intensely than any other Role. Song and album titles like 'I'm Not Like Everybody Else' and *Whatever People Say I Am, That's What I'm Not* express their attitude at this or indeed any age. Boys are likely to react against parental pressure to get a sensible job or learn a profession, particularly if they hear the calling of their muse. The upside is that both boys and girls are often the cool kids – stylish, popular and objects of romantic yearning for the whole class.

Artisan Archetypes in Myth, Fiction and Film

Artisans seek beauty, and the ideal of beauty was Helen of Troy, the face that launched a thousand ships. Look at the image of the most iconically beautiful woman of any age and there you see Helen – in fairy-tale princesses, great royal courtesans, southern belles, artists' and poets' muses, *femmes fatales*, 'It' girls, screen sirens and supermodels. The male equivalent is the Greek god Adonis, celebrated as Prince Charming in fairy tales and the matinée-idol hero of romantic movies.

In myths and sacred stories, the world begins as an act of creation: God the Potter shapes human beings out of clay. Changing Woman is the Navajo goddess of creation, shape-shifting with the seasons. The Sun fell in love with her, married her and built her a house, which pleased her so much that she danced a joyful dance of creation, creating rain, plants, animals and beautiful fabrics and jewels.

Hephaestus (Vulcan) was the Graeco-Roman Artisan god of technology, patron of craftsmen, artisans, sculptors and blacksmiths. A master craftsman himself, one of his main jobs was to make armour for the other gods, including Hermes's winged helmet and sandals. Perhaps his most impressive creation was life itself in the form of the beautiful woman Pandora, the gods' gift to humanity.

Another mythical Artisan was the Greek sculptor Pygmalion, who fell in love with his own creation, the statue of a beautiful woman. Venus took pity on him and brought the statue to life. This is perhaps the secret fantasy of all artists. The story resonated down the ages and was adapted into a play, *Pygmalion*, by George Bernard Shaw, then into the film *My Fair Lady*.

The character of Neo in *The Matrix* (played by Artisan Keanu Reeves) is an excellent depiction of Artisan imagination and inventiveness, playing with alternate realities and drawing from many sources, from *Alice in Wonderland* to cyberpunk.

Artists are not well portrayed in movies, often being shown as mad, self-destructive geniuses, but Artisan Colin Firth does a good job of playing the Dutch artist Vermeer in *Girl with a Pearl Earring*, while *Goya's Ghosts* shows the artist surviving in a cruel, unstable world by focusing on his art and staying out of politics.

How to Fulfill Your Artisan Potential

'I feel divinely privileged to be an Artisan, able to see beauty in anything irrespective of the vision of those around me.'
CLEMENTINE, BODYWORKER

Artisans keep the world evolving through daily acts of creation. They are fortunate in that it is relatively easy for them to be happy and fulfillled, since life throws up so many opportunities for creative expression. It is important for them to recognize their creativity rather than take it for granted, and find what works best for them, whether painting, playing an instrument, baking cakes, fixing appliances, arranging flowers or making jewellery – all equally valid. This section summarizes how Role and Perspective work together for growth and fulfillment.

Competing Artisans are highly aspirational, snobbish, obsessed with style, glamour and celebrity. The label is everything. I once watched a 'reality' television show in which a family had to give up all their expensive brands for a month and live cheaply. Afterwards, when asked about their experience, the woman said of her husband, 'Without his expensive watch and clothes, he's nothing.'

At this Perspective, Artisans are driven to succeed and win, and their favourite arenas are showbiz, fashion or anything giving them the opportunity to realize their highest aspiration: to become a celebrity. Success is also about a fabulous champagne-fuelled lifestyle. These Artisans are style icons, party animals and scenesters, piling on the bling, adorning the pages of the fashion and lifestyle magazines and occupying the top tables of hip restaurants and nightclubs. Wealth is important, though they are less likely to make it than marry it, as trophy wives and husbands, even gold-diggers. Those who succeed are gorgeous, glittering, unattainable, but the less successful can at least read the magazines, copy the style and dream of entering the charmed circle.

At this Perspective it is easy for them to get stuck in their negative pole of artifice, but they can at least imitate and reproduce to the highest quality, which will please customers at the same Perspective. Their clothes are fun, their songs and films entertaining. Their restless drive for innovation keeps wheels turning and the world changing and evolving. They often work in dream factories, churning out fantasies for starry-eyed consumers, but the mass production of glamour fulfills a valid need even if it is not the end of the story.

At the relationship Perspective, Artisans see through the illusions of fame, wealth and glamour and reject that world as shallow and unfulfillling. They are sensitive and empathic, shocked to realize the wastage and slave labour conditions underpinning the fashion trade, and turning to ethical fashion and more humane endeavours. They understand that their own creativity can guide them into a more authentic and interesting individuality than reliance on celebrity-endorsed brands. As a result, they begin to pick up on and lead the zeitgeist intuitively, turning away from easy routes to success and rejecting demands for commercial entertainment or products. They would rather carve beautiful chairs in obscurity than make a fortune out of mass producing reproduction antiques. They may still hunger for recognition, but on their own terms, and may refuse to show or sell their work to non-connoisseurs. They suffer greatly if forced to vulgarize their artistic vision for popular consumption and commercial gain, and find it much harder to handle the pressure.

Resolving the conflict between outer and inner values is the challenge of this Perspective. Their relationships are extremely important, but filled with drama and sometimes tragedy. If it all becomes too painful, psychotherapy and counselling can help. Artisans take well to analysis, as long as they are not labelled, preferring a more open, soul-searching approach. Art therapy is now a recognized approach, and art itself can become a healing process for Artisans at this Perspective. It's also important to be surrounded with like-minded friends and colleagues as far as possible, not to mention a loving, committed partner, to avoid the energy-sapping confusion of dealing with conflicting values. Once they have passed through this dark night of the soul, Artisans themselves make good counsellors and therapists, seeing psychotherapy as a craft. The lesson for them to integrate with this Perspective is that being your own person rather than trying to become someone else is essential for creativity. It is better to fail in originality than succeed in imitation.

At the philosophical Perspective, Artisans are delightful company, being warm, witty, relaxed and self-accepting. Their creativity now expands to take in the bigger picture. They no longer require a material medium, since their whole life becomes the canvas. They lose interest in producing finished works of art, though still enjoy coming up with ideas and projects. As a result, their studios are full of unfinished masterpieces, some still in their head.

Yoga and meditation are excellent practices to enable them to slow down and become calmer, more centred and grounded. They enjoy visual meditations and have no trouble envisaging every petal of the thousand-petalled lotus as well as the most elaborate mandalas. The Zen koan 'Form is emptiness, emptiness is form' is intuitively understood by Artisans at this Perspective. They are attracted to spiritual paths that embrace sensory and artistic methods of reaching the divine; and they themselves create the inspiring atmosphere of a church or temple by mixing the incense, painting the icons and murals and composing the sacred music.

'I need alone time for recharging my batteries, indulging in true rest. And I need introspection. I set aside about an hour a day for self-communion, and give myself some honest evaluation, some recontextualizing of my thoughts, feelings and beliefs, and some self-love and forgiveness. And I need true play (some humour, singing and dancing, beauty); true work (doing

something that is fulfillling); and true study (finding something truly interesting to direct my attention to).'

CATHRYN, ARTIST/AROMATHERAPIST

◆◆◆◆◆◆

The formula for success, happiness and self-mastery in this system is a simple but powerful three-step process:

1. *Discover your Role.*

2. *Integrate it with your Perspective.*

3. *Operate from their positive poles.*

I hope by now you recognize whether you are an Artisan or whether it is your secondary Role. Identifying your Role is the first step on a lifelong journey of self-discovery. The insight needs to be confirmed and applied in daily life on an ongoing basis for best results, so requires commitment, but with practice it becomes second nature. The reward of self-transformation is well worth the effort.

Secondary Role Influences for Artisans

One of the most important factors influencing the personality variations between people who share the same Role is the secondary Role. This colours, flavours and generally modifies your personality. The combination works like an omelette:

your primary Role is the egg, while your secondary Role is the added ingredient – cheese, mushroom, tomato. Sometimes the flavour is subtle, sometimes it overpowers the egg. Similarly, the secondary Role can manifest more strongly than the primary Role, particularly if it corresponds with your profession. Some people have the same Role in both the primary and secondary position, so will conform more closely with the Role archetype. If this is your case, you will probably recognize yourself quite easily. This section summarizes the influence of the other six Roles on Artisans.

Sage-Artisans

These will be highly expressive and more flamboyant, communicative and wittier than the average Artisan. As artists, their work is often witty and humorous, like that of Salvador Dali, and they make brilliant cartoonists. They also do well in the performing arts, including acting, film animation or directing and theatrical costume. They excel in advertising and marketing, having a greater than usual facility with words as well as style and flair. They are enormous fun and a big draw at parties and other social events, but may be quite flighty and ungrounded.

Server-Artisans

Softer and gentler than the typical Artisan, they will want their art to serve others in some way. They will also enjoy creating a beautiful environment for their loved ones. A man I know with this combination is a house husband who is continually redecorating the house, embellishing the garden and serving up gourmet dinners for guests. Server-Artisans will want to please others as much as themselves in their style, including dress and conversation. Women with this combination are the ideal girlfriend or wife for many men, the one who intuitively knows how to please him and make him feel good. (These qualities can be quite appealing in a guy too.)

Priest-Artisans

Their creativity is likely to be spiritual in flavour, often in the service of a higher cause such as religion.

'There is a strong sense for me that my role as an artist in the world needs to be driven by a divine purpose. The work I do as an artist is layered with images using divine proportion, meditative figures and eastern religious imagery.'
DEBORAH, ARTIST/EDUCATOR/BODYWORKER

They build churches and temples, paint icons, make stained-glass windows and compose religious music. As secular artists, they are likely to donate work or put on shows for charity. They are attracted to ritual and brilliant at devising unique, colourful and fun ceremonies. They may be very ungrounded, uncomfortable in their bodies and the material world, so need to exercise and do other physical work to stay on the planet. A statement by the poet-artist William Blake expresses this combination perfectly: 'If the doors of perception were cleansed, everything would appear to man as it is, infinite!'

Warrior-Artisans

This is a difficult combination to handle, as these Roles are so opposite in every respect. Warrior-Artisans are more confrontational and abrasive than most Artisans, which can make both them and others uncomfortable. It needs a lot of practice and experience to integrate the energies. On the plus side, these Artisans are more comfortable in their bodies than many others and excel at physical activities like dance and sport. The baseball player Joe DiMaggio and martial arts actor Bruce Lee are good examples of this. They also make good aromatherapists, being highly attuned to the subtle aspects of plants and flowers as well as good at massage. I suspect that the German playwright Bertolt Brecht had this combination: 'Art is not a mirror held up to reality, but a hammer with which to shape it.'

King-Artisans

This is another tricky combination, but with great potential. King influence lends the Artisan not only more groundedness and gravitas but also a grandeur of vision which enables them to take on large projects. People who meet them will be impressed by a quality of magnetic power and charisma, and will often defer to them. They might become film directors, architects designing public buildings or a whole city, or directors of a fashion empire or a restaurant chain. They can catch others off guard by suddenly coming on with Kingly authority and silencing their critics or opponents, and do not take kindly to teasing. They are often regarded as a good catch, but need to be treated with great care, as regal dignity added to Artisan sensitivity makes them quite touchy. Generally, though, they will handle power and responsibility more successfully than most Artisans. Johnny Cash had this combination, making him a charismatic king of country music.

Scholar-Artisans

Again this needs careful handling, as it combines very different energies, but done well can lead to great originality. Many inventors have this combination, which makes them well equipped to research and test their prototypes. It is also good for engineering, IT, science or any career that requires both creativity and intellectual prowess. Albert Einstein is the most famous example, while in a different sphere Ry Cooder is a musician who studies and absorbs the style of musicians from very different global cultures and then reproduces it perfectly with a fresh twist. The combination is also good for writing.

'I enjoy writing papers in which I can creatively integrate poignant construction with playful discourse. My Scholar secondary Role assists in a certain quality of organized thinking. It also provides for versatility. Not all Roles appreciate my Artisan-like flair, but in a culture that often champions intellect, drawing on the Scholar influence comes in handy. Employers tend to value my logical approach with an ability to innovate.'

CLEMENTINE, BODYWORKER

Famous Artisans

Michelangelo, Botticelli, Rembrandt, William Blake, Joseph Turner, Claude Monet, Henri Matisse, Salvador Dali, Francis Bacon, James McNeill Whistler, Man Ray, Jackson Pollock, Andy Warhol, Damien Hirst, Tracey Emin, Christopher Wren, Buckminster Fuller, Frank Lloyd Wright, Le Corbusier,

Thomas Edison, Nikola Tesla, Albert Einstein, Queen Marie Antoinette, T. E. Lawrence ('Lawrence of Arabia'), Coco Chanel, Yves St Laurent, Giorgio Armani, Twiggy, Naomi Campbell, Claudia Schiffer, Kate Moss, Joe DiMaggio, Bruce Lee, David Beckham, Victoria Beckham, Walt Disney, George Lucas, Francis Ford Coppola, Ang Lee, Stanley Kubrick, Tim Burton, Marlene Dietrich, Marilyn Monroe, Brigitte Bardot, Audrey Hepburn, Nicole Kidman, Brad Pitt, Johnny Depp, George Clooney, Catherine Deneuve, Juliette Binoche, Daniel Day-Lewis, Leonardo DiCaprio, Keanu Reeves, Lewis Carroll, Anaïs Nin, Kazuo Ishiguro, J. K. Rowling, Martha Graham, Maria Callas, Luciano Pavarotti, Edith Piaf, Billie Holiday, Elvis Presley, Johnny Cash, Paul McCartney, Syd Barrett, David Bowie, Michael Jackson, Kurt Cobain, Björk, Amy Winehouse

CHAPTER 3

The Sage

'Laughter without a twinge of philosophy is but a sneeze of humor. Genuine humor is replete with wisdom.'
MARK TWAIN

The Sage Personality

The Sage is the cardinal expression Role. The key to this personality is communication, which Sages do exceptionally well, mainly through words but also through performance. They are the storytellers of the tribe, with a built-in flair for drama and comedy and the ability to use words with wit, style and originality. Loving the limelight, they come alive in front of an audience and are often good raconteurs who regale their friends and anybody else in earshot with jokes and anecdotes and can keep a dinner party entertained for the whole evening. They believe, along with the Sage dramatist Shakespeare; 'All the world's a stage, and all the men and women merely players' – with themselves in the starring role.

The paradox of this Role is that it has two quite different though related facets or modes of expression: wit and wisdom. Humour is a Sage's lifeblood. Everything that happens to them, however unlikely or unpromising, can be turned into a joke or amusing story. They are great improvisers who can invent new jokes or embellish old ones on the spot and never fluff the punchline. However, they also have a more serious, philosophical side. *Sage* literally means 'wise one', as in 'sagacious', which the dictionary defines as 'mentally penetrating, gifted with discernment, having practical wisdom'. So Sages can have gravitas, particularly at the relationship or philosophical Perspectives, and may turn their excellent minds to writing, teaching and exploring the human condition. They value knowledge not for its own sake but as a means to wisdom. Most would agree with the biblical proverb that 'the price of wisdom is above rubies.'

There is an integral connection between these apparent opposites, which come together when Sages are operating from their positive pole: communication. Everybody communicates, but for Sages it is their speciality and one which they can develop to the highest degree. Whether telling a story, declaiming from a soapbox, acting on stage, making an after-dinner speech, teaching a class, selling a used car or defending a client in court, they have the gift of gab. It is not just about talking but sharing and disseminating their wit and wisdom, getting from 'me' to 'we'. They delight in charming, swaying and enlightening their audience, winning their love and applause.

Sage satirists hold a mirror up to society in which to see the distortions, pretensions and vanities of the age. Their function is to break up habits of thought and language and fixed ways of thinking and being, and to help us see things through new eyes. In particular, they have an irresistible urge to make fun of a wiseacre by pricking the balloon of their pomposity and self-importance. As Lords of Misrule they break boundaries and taboos, thereby advancing the progress of the species – humour being the most uniquely human form of expression. In this way they serve as a counterbalance to the authoritarian tendencies and seriousness of some of the other Roles, showing them how to laugh at themselves and take life less seriously.

'I think that Sages can go either way, from being a lightweight joker ("You can't get a serious word out of that man!") to being full of insightful, astute observations about life; usually, they are a combination. One way to bring enlightenment is to lighten things up. The core of humour is the surprise that causes us to look at something in a new way and gain insight about it, releasing tension and perhaps letting the air out of a false assumption. I find some of the most astute political insight in political cartoons: they can succinctly say a great deal.'
SHEPHERD HOODWIN, AUTHOR/TEACHER

Sages are also the arbiters of society, making, breaking and changing the rules while having a broad vision of etiquette as a civilizing force. They are acutely aware of the differences between trivial, arbitrary rules, which are class-based, snobbish and used to humiliate outsiders who don't know which fork to use, and true good manners which show respect and consideration for others. However, they have no compunction about bending the rules themselves. Understanding that greed is not good, they will position themselves by the kitchen door at a cocktail party and consume vast quantities of canapés, hoping that nobody will notice, then nibble a lettuce leaf at dinner but expect a share of their partner's dessert. They will proclaim it's rude to brag and boast, but will master the art of pseudo self-deprecation to broadcast their achievements acceptably. Such habits can give them a reputation for phoniness, but they also have an acute sense of the difference between genuine and ersatz expression. They therefore tend to condemn over-familiarity, such as the growing tendency to sign off business emails with hugs and kisses.

Sages comprise around 10 percent of the population. They are often cultured, urbane people who feel most at home in an environment as sophisticated and metropolitan as possible. They may enjoy occasional country visits for weekend parties, sporting events and recharging their batteries, but quickly get bored and return to town. They are irresistibly drawn to capital cities, particularly if these are also entertainment centres. For this reason, American Sages tend to prefer New York or Los Angeles to Washington, DC, with Broadway and Hollywood being their Mecca. London is also a favourite as one of the world's top capital cities with thriving entertainment and fashion industries and many opportunities in journalism and politics. Sages flourish on the buzz, the hustle, noise, colour and general animation. As *bons viveurs*, they also enjoy the restaurants, bars and nightclubs.

The Challenge of the Negative Pole

Sages are the golden girls and boys, good-humoured, charming and urbane, and on first meeting them it is hard to imagine they have any flaws. If you get to know them, though, you will quickly discover that like all the Roles they have a negative pole, which is verbosity. Sages have a motor-mouth and can easily get carried away with their wit, the sound of their own voice, the sheer joy of performing to an audience. Proverbially, they can talk the hind legs off a donkey, till the cows come home and deep into the night – if there is anyone left awake to listen. Born talking, they wake up in the morning with their mouth moving, get on a roll and can't or won't stop. Quantity overrides quality and point and plot are lost in a tide of words. On and on and on they go, hardly pausing for breath, so nobody else can get a word in edgewise. It is not a conversation but a long-winded monologue, and the response of their audience switches from delight to restlessness, irritation and finally exhaustion.

As well as being orally fixated, Sages are often vain and narcissistic. They need to sparkle more brilliantly than anyone else in the room and will try to outshine anyone in their orbit. This is a form of greed, wanting all the attention on themselves, hogging the limelight, commanding centre stage in their one-man show and refusing anyone else even a bit part.

The darker side of their negative pole is the razzle-dazzle factor. Any performance has an element of illusion, requiring a suspension of disbelief to work its magic. The audience has to be open to the storyteller's art, which makes them vulnerable. So it is easy for Sages to become unscrupulous, carry their skill at spinning a line into their relationships and business dealings and take advantage of people's trust with their gift of the gab, selling and promotional abilities. These are the used-car and snake-oil salesmen, the hucksters and shysters, grifters and swindlers, conmen and carpetbaggers, unscrupulous lawyers and politicians, the spin doctors who are 'economical with the truth' (which they see as a fluid phenomenon) to the point of outright deception and dishonesty.

> *'Sages are usually rather shrewd and clever, being concerned as they are with wisdom. In their selfish manifestation, they believe the world owes them a living just because they are attractive and charming. They expect others to give them gifts of appreciation, to throw money at their feet for a great performance. Less honorable or malevolent Sages may think that they are justified in taking advantage of other people and that fools are fair game if they can talk them out of their money. By looking and sounding good, they dupe gullible people into buying into their get-rich-quick schemes.'*
> PHILIP WITTMEYER, ENGINEER

The negative pole manifests most crudely and starkly at the competing Perspective, when Sages are insensitive to the needs and even the existence of other people. They have a sharp tongue, sometimes accompanied by a quick temper, which can make them aggressive, bullying, even abusive, particularly to their social and professional 'inferiors' and sometimes to their families.

At the relationship Perspective, they become much more empathic and capable of listening, enjoying the give and take of conversation and discussion.

'The years have taught me the value of knowing when to stop talking.'
Lydia

At the philosophical Perspective, they become more understanding and accepting of their protean nature. The urge to be the star of the show is still strong and they are always liable to get carried away given any encouragement. However, the dividing line between communication and verbosity manifests more subtly; and they find it much easier to channel their need for admiration and applause into projects and causes that lead to wisdom and true happiness.

How to Recognize a Sage

Sages are often the easiest Role to spot, having larger-than-life personalities, loud voices and a flamboyant style which makes them stand out in any group. Many are bubbly extroverts – or shameless exhibitionists, depending on your attitude. They love parties and are often the life and soul of them. As hosts, they give the best parties; as guests, they are much in demand. Gregarious and outgoing, they cultivate their friendship networks assiduously and are often to be found holding forth in the middle of a large group of friends. Their popularity and sophistication can make them quite intimidating to less confident people, though relationship-oriented and philosophical Sages are warmer and more approachable.

Sometimes Sages can be mistaken for Artisans when you first meet them, especially if they are creative and artistic, since both expression Roles tend to come across socially as bright, vivacious, chatty and fun. Artisans can also be witty, but the superior quality of Sages' wit and language skills, as well as their more cardinal personality, usually comes through quite fast. Intellectual Sages can look like Scholars, particularly if they are working in education or academia, but whereas Scholars put their emphasis on facts, information and evidence, Sages are more concerned with presenting their knowledge dramatically, revealing the moral of the story. Religious and spiritually inclined Sages can also be mistaken for Priests, both being cardinal Roles, though they will never display the missionary zeal of a Priest in full flow.

Sages tend to have sunny personalities, look on the bright side, see the best in a person or situation and view the glass as half full – unless they are cynics, in which case they make the best gallows humour out of pessimism. They know how to enjoy themselves and have fun, and their light-heartedness is their gift to the world, helping others lighten up and enjoy life more. Nonetheless, Sages can suffer as much as anyone, even if they feel compelled to put on a happy face. This is the classic 'tears of a clown' syndrome. Sages can become trapped by others' expectations of them to be the entertainer and always merry, believing this is the only way to be loved. In fact, disclosure of their more emotional, raw and real inner self makes them even more lovable. Their challenge is to live and express themselves authentically rather than perform.

Sage Style

Artisans are the ultimate clothes horses, but Sages run a close second. Their sense of style is not as subtle and finely tuned as that of Artisans, but they can be even more chic. They see clothes as theatrical costume and dress for effect, to project a certain persona or self-image, or simply to draw attention to themselves. To this end they are also liable to throw taste to the winds, favouring leopard-print, bold patterns and neon-bright colours. Male Sages make the most of men's restricted opportunities for sartorial self-expression, often possessing a particular way with hats. One of my Sage friends used to stroll through London's premier shopping streets in shorts in the middle of winter to show off his tanned legs. Another, a university professor, wears Hawaiian shirts. However wildly or eccentrically dressed, Sages are usually immaculately groomed as part of their urbane, polished image, though occasionally they rebel into extreme scruffiness. Competing Sages are wild about designer labels, but relationship-oriented and philosophical Sages get bored with fashion fascism and do their own thing in a relaxed way, though they can still enjoy glamming up now and again. They love vintage shops, dressing-up boxes and fancy-dress parties. Female Sages enjoy shopping and need no excuse for it – after all, a girl's got to have some new clothes.

Sages love to be the centre of attention and their appearance is often eye-catching. Physically they tend to extremes, often being toweringly tall or tiny, stick-thin or obese. Comedy duos often team up as physical opposites for maximum impact. Sages are often strikingly good-looking, but would prefer to be dramatically ugly than plain ordinary. They attract attention with their animated faces and twinkling eyes, and are skilful at compensating for any deficiencies of appearance through style, wit and charm. They are photogenic, always aware of their best angles. Regardless of looks, Sage men often pride themselves on their ability to laugh a woman into bed. Older Sages may well prefer to retain their laughter lines than resort to the surgeon's knife and lose their facial expressivity.

Sages are prone to excess and indulgence, which can lead to health problems in later life. They are particularly susceptible to colds (sometimes relabelled as 'flu), which can be a means of avoiding a difficult situation. They don't mind being 'just ill enough' to rest for a while, and know how to make the recuperation enjoyable. When a Sage is seriously ill, it is often flamboyantly expressed, but can also give them the space for self-examination leading to wisdom. Their cheerful disposition is a safeguard against stress-related illness. They instinctively understand the preventive and curative power of a sense of humour for both mental and physical disorders. Medical research is now providing evidence that laughter can indeed lower stress hormones in the body and boost the immune system. Sages also use laughter to heal other people. An unusual example is a group of clowns who entertain hospital patients by acting out parodies of medical procedure 'to give it some laughter, to give it some intrigue, to give it something that they can contact and play with'.

Laurence Olivier: An Immortal Sage Actor

'There's no business like show business,' and Sages are its stars. The theatre is the Sage's natural habitat, so much so that they turn any public event and arena into a stage – courtroom, church service, lecture, party or political campaign. Most of the great theatrical actors and many movie stars, dramatists, directors and producers are Sages. They are more drawn to theatre than film because of the interaction with the audience and the reward of the applause, though film offers them a worldwide audience and greater fame. Performing is energizing for Sages, and they have a magical-seeming ability to act while simultaneously hearing themselves speak, connecting with their fellow actors and checking the audience's reaction.

> *'The song or performance wells up inside you, is expressed and offered to the audience. You then tune into their enjoyment, which comes back to you as an energy which lifts your performance to new heights. On a good night this feedback loop continues till both performer and audience reach euphoria.'*
>
> JULIE, ACTRESS

Laurence Olivier was the greatest actor of the twentieth century as well as a brilliant director and producer. Intensely competitive, his fierce determination to succeed took him to the top of his profession; his many awards included two Oscars (14 nominations), five Emmys and three Golden Globes. Despite being first and foremost a classical stage actor, he was placed at #14 on the American Film Institute's list of the greatest male movie stars of all time. As a Sage, he saw performance as fundamental to personality: 'We have all, at one time or another, been performers, and many of us still are – politicians, playboys, cardinals and kings.'

Olivier was born in 1907 into a strict and repressive religious family. Despite this disadvantage, he manifested his Role from an early age in school drama, debuting to rapturous applause at age 15. As a result he was allowed to go to drama school and never looked back. While he worked hard to perfect his technique, acting came naturally to him: 'Surely we have always acted; it is an instinct inherent in all of us. Some of us are better at it than others, but we all do it.'

In the 1930s he burst onto the London theatre scene already a legend. His matinée-idol looks made him a star of drawing-room comedy, but he found true glory as the leading Shakespearean actor of his time, shining equally in comic and tragic roles, as heroes and villains. Being the greatest Sage dramatist, Shakespeare remains the benchmark for any actor aspiring to true greatness. However, Olivier did have competition. His breakthrough role was in a production of *Romeo and Juliet* with the highly successful gimmick of alternating the role of Romeo between Olivier and John Gielgud. Sages often thrive on vying with and upstaging each other, and this was the beginning of a lifelong rivalry, sometimes embittered but leavened with mutual admiration.

Olivier's charismatic acting and handsome looks soon attracted interest from movie producers and eventually, though reluctantly, he succumbed to the lure of Hollywood, becoming a heart-throb in such Golden Age classics as *Wuthering Heights*, *Pride and Prejudice* and *Rebecca*. A great communicator and popularizer, he was the first person to make Shakespeare work on film, directing and starring in a string of award-winning adaptations that are still admired today. In World War II he entertained troops and civilians with his swashbuckling heroics, most memorably his Oscar-nominated Henry V. However, his star waned in the 1950s; he found himself out of vogue and washed up, his acting style considered mannered, hammy and lacking the emotional expressiveness demanded by the new era. Always unpredictable, he solved the problem spectacularly by starring in a play written for him by the most fashionable Angry Young Man dramatist, John Osborne. As Archie in *The Entertainer*, he bravely played a caricature of himself – a has-been vaudeville comedian – which earned him rave reviews. From then onwards, he was rarely off the stage or screen, latterly in small but lucrative cameos which brought cachet to the movie, even if some of his performances were substandard. He achieved success as a stage as well as movie director, most impressively as a founder and the first director of the National Theatre, London's newest and biggest theatre, which showcased the talents of the greatest actors and directors of the new generation.

Like many Sages, Olivier was adored by his public but had difficulties in his personal life. Most alive in his acting, he was given his identity by his audience. His third wife, Joan Plowright, said: 'There were times when he said, "I don't think I know who I am when I'm not acting." He wasn't quite sure of that person who was not required to do anything to impress an audience.'

While his verbosity was mostly channelled into his acting, Olivier often displayed the monstrous ego of a Sage in the negative pole, with the accompanying flaws of vanity, narcissism, addiction to applause and selfishness. His private life became as much of an entertainment as his acting, particularly his relationship with his second wife, Vivien Leigh (an Artisan), the most beautiful and glamorous actress of her generation, who starred as Scarlett O'Hara in *Gone with the Wind*. Their romance began on a film set and was enacted in a succession of stage and screen love affairs that were much publicized in the media. They were the highest-profile celebrity couple of their day, carving out a niche later filled by another Sage–Artisan couple, Richard Burton and Elizabeth Taylor. Their relationship was highly dramatic, glamorous in public but tempestuous in private, full of explosive rows and bouts of madness in which they screamed, sobbed, swore and occasionally slapped each other, had affairs and then made up. He once said, 'Living is strife and torment, disappointment and love and sacrifice, golden sunsets and black storms,' which well describes his own life.

'Lord Larry' was awarded a special Oscar for the full body of his work, his unique achievement and contribution to the art of film. His 120 stage roles and 60 movies made him a truly international star whose talent belonged to all nations. He summed up his art: 'There is a spirit in us that makes our brass to blare and our cymbals crash – all, of course, supported by the practicalities of trained lung power, throat, heart, guts.' This spirit carried him through many years of severe illness in which he transformed his disability into an asset, particularly in a stunning performance as the ravaged King Lear. It seems fitting that when he finally died in 1989, he was buried in London's Westminster Abbey between the Shakespeare Memorial and the hero he had portrayed so brilliantly: King Henry V.

The Sage at Work

Acting is the archetypal Sage profession, but they excel in any occupation based on communication, particularly through words. As playwrights and screenwriters, they have the ability to imagine themselves acting all the roles. They love working in television, especially as presenters, ideally hosting their own comedy or chat shows. They are among the best singers, particularly of opera and musicals, which combine their acting and singing talents. The more physically adept performers can become clowns, acrobats, dancers and sometimes sporting champions. The Sage Muhammad Ali was the greatest boxer of all time and voted the greatest sportsman of the 20th century. As a child, he was a practical joker and prankster, and retained his merriment into adulthood. He breezed into the ponderous Warrior world of heavyweight boxing saying: 'I float like a butterfly, but sting like a bee.' His most unorthodox but effective weapon was to wear down his opponent by keeping up a continual barrage of comments, insults and putdowns throughout the fight. Never lost for a soundbite, his talent for self-promotion, ability to wisecrack and compose and improvise rhymes on the spot made him a great celebrity as well as a sporting champion.

Sages are natural storytellers and writers and are among the world's best novelists, poets and dramatists. To adapt the words of Shakespeare: 'As imagination bodies forth the forms of things unknown, the [Sage's] pen turns them to shapes, and gives to airy nothing a local habitation and a name.' Sages also write most of the humour books, satire, sagas, comic novels, plays and film scripts. They are natural self-promoters, sometimes enjoying the publicity circuit and parties more than the hard grind of writing a book. Most journalists are either Scholars or Sages. While Scholars tend to write the serious comment pieces, Sages often prefer humorous 'me-columns' where they can bring in anecdotes, witticisms and sparkling insights, sometimes relying on straw polls and rent-a-quotes rather than substantial research. They enjoy the challenge of making something entertaining out of unpromising material, for example as political correspondents who can expose hidden agendas or put an amusing spin or twist on the dullest government proceedings. Comedian-columnist Will Rogers quipped: 'I don't make jokes. I just watch the government and report the facts.'

Sages are excellent teachers, able to impart knowledge pleasurably and entertainingly and keep a whole class riveted without needing to resort to more brutal disciplinary measures. This ability makes them the most popular teachers. One remembers how he handled a music class as a substitute teacher in a tough school:

> 'The kids exchanged instruments, and when I started to conduct them, it sounded as dreadful as you might imagine. Afterwards, they expected me to get angry; instead, I said dramatically, with tears in my eyes, "Guys, that was so beautiful!" They laughed, and were then on my side (as I was on theirs).'
>
> SHEPHERD HOODWIN, AUTHOR/TEACHER

Sages also flourish in academia, where they are loved by their students though sometimes mistrusted or disparaged as lightweights by more scholarly peers. They are more drawn to the arts and humanities than science, particularly to their *forte* of philosophy. Jacques Derrida was a French

Sage philosopher who shot to international fame by upstaging famous philosophers at a conference. He was dashingly handsome and cultivated his charisma and mystery. His lectures and writings were peppered with puns, neologisms, rhymes and enigmatic pronouncements. He criticized other philosophers for prioritizing 'serious' uses of language at the expense of humorous and playful usage. He was often dismissed as a poseur or 'celebrity philosopher', but his entertaining lectures, delivered with a comedian's impeccable timing, aimed to provoke students into a fresh understanding of meaning.

Sages enjoy the cut and thrust of public life on a real-world stage. They bring showbiz talents to the hustings and the courtroom, using their skill at rhetoric and acting to sway voters and juries and spin a case for the media. They enjoy pressing the flesh more than most other Roles and excel at the communication and PR aspects as press secretaries and spin doctors. In public life and business they make good negotiators and diplomats. An alternative stage is the pulpit. Rule-bound and competing Sage preachers can conjure up the horrors of hellfire as effectively as Priests, while relationship-oriented ones will make religion entertaining and keep their congregation awake. Less intellectual Sages may become loud-voiced and entertaining market traders, tour guides and auctioneers.

Leadership Style

Whatever their choice of profession, it is vital for Sages to find that it is fun and gives them lots of space to communicate and express themselves. They make great entrepreneurs and salespeople, and do well in any business that requires wheeling and dealing and a combination of charm and ruthlessness. They may be agents and managers in the entertainment and sport industries and can even be happy as accountants if they can spend more time lunching with clients and sorting out the office politics than poring over figures. However, as Shepherd Hoodwin warns, 'stuck in a job that gives them little opportunity to express themselves, they may resort to loud, empty chatter or inappropriate humor'.

Sages find it hard to work alone, preferring the companionship and drama of a busy office. They are fine as teamworkers as long as they have opportunities to stand out and make a splash. Despite their cardinality, unlike Kings and Priests, they don't need to be the boss or leader – and may even prefer not to be if the post comes with grindingly long hours, heavy responsibilities and not enough perks and playtime built in. As bosses they tend to be brilliant but unreliable, blowing hot and cold and panicking or disappearing in a crisis. Their favourite position is a starring role with lots of opportunity for self-expression, fun and interaction in a non-routinized environment with good pay. PR, publicity, sales and marketing fulfill these requirements well.

One Sage who has found fulfillment in the business world describes his work, which in some ways bucks the stereotype of this Role:

'I usually take the number-two role in the businesses for whom I consult. This allows me to give my input, make decisions or help others in making decisions and not have to have the

responsibility for the overall running of the show. I am good at
seeing the overview of the business and the business owner's
(and sometimes their employees') individual needs. My mind
is detail-oriented, quick and processes a lot. Being a cardinal
Role, leadership comes easily to me. I also provide facilitation
services for people. This allows me to utilize my gift for
"speaking the truth" as well as to listen and follow the deeper
threads that run through all of our individual lives. Finding the
thread and guiding people to it, what a wonderful experience
for me!'

MICHAEL, BUSINESS MANAGER

Communication Style

Sages are the greatest communicators, sharing their wit and wisdom with all and sundry. Their ideal audience is large and rapturously appreciative, but at a pinch anyone will do, even a stranger on a train or, if all else fails, the cat. They are born raconteurs who can keep an audience enthralled well past their bedtime.

If deprived of words, they are ingenious at creating other forms of communication. Mime artists are often Sages, as were some of the greatest stars of silent comedy such as Harpo Marx. Sign languages were doubtless invented by Sages, including the elaborate system developed by Trappist monks to evade their vow of silence. One of the most moving and impressive examples of a Sage triumphing against all odds was Jean-Dominique Bauby, a French magazine editor who at the age of 43 suffered a stroke that paralyzed his entire body, except his left eye. Using that eye to blink out his memoir *The Diving Bell and the Butterfly*, Bauby eloquently described the aspects of his interior world, from the psychological torment of being trapped inside his body to his imagined stories from lands he'd only visited in his mind. Both book and movie adaptation were impressive testaments to his courage.

Sages have a multi-dimensional ability to talk, listen and process impressions simultaneously, which facilitates their performing skills. It also enables them to easily carry on a conversation at a party or in a restaurant while listening to another conversation. They find it easier to split their attention than to focus. This may explain their habit of channel-hopping while watching television, which does not always endear them to the rest of the family (the Sage always controls the remote control). This ability is invaluable on the stage, though, and also for public speaking, which they can often do easily and without notes. However, preparation and rehearsal are important safeguards against one of their worst fears: stage fright.

Once they have started to speak, many find it works better to relax and let the words flow without interference. Being quick-witted and able to think fast on their feet, they are quite capable of winging it, making it up as they go along and dealing confidently with questions and even heckles.

'I feel that I'm turned on talking in front of a group. In a group, ideas stream out of my mouth that I've never even thought of before (some good, some better left unsaid, but oops, I've already said it now).'
DONNA, HEALTH CONSULTANT

One of Sages' most important functions is to revitalize the language, coining new words, creating metaphors and inventing slogans and labels. This makes them good copywriters and journalists, expressing the zeitgeist in fresh language. Their quality of communication is (mostly) high and they expect the same from others, getting irritated with sloppy usage, poor grammar, exhausted clichés, clumsy phrasing, impenetrable business jargon, tortured metaphors, meaningless gush, bad puns, stale jokes or – the latest horror – emoticons. They will feel an irresistible urge to correct such peccadilloes, at least in their head but sometimes aloud too, maybe with a withering putdown.

Sages and Scholars are the two Roles best at discussion and argument, but while a Scholar is focused on making a point and getting at the truth, a Sage enjoys the whole process of communication, the exchange, drama, cut and thrust. Sages are sometimes happy to switch sides in an argument just to make the process more stimulating. They make the most successful debaters in a debating society, able to gauge the mood of the audience as well as score points.

Sage humour can take any form: clowning and slapstick, stand-up comedy, drawing-room repartee, the rudest jokes and the wittiest insults, wisecracks and wordplay, riddles, the blackest comedy and the bitterest satire. Any Role can tell a joke, but Sages can update and embellish them and create new ones on the spot, telling them with panache and impeccable timing and mimicking voices, facial expressions and gestures, sometimes with cruelly comic exaggeration. They particularly enjoy subtle or obscure jokes which only the quick-witted will get, leaving slower wits scratching their heads in puzzlement. Scholars are good at puns, but Sages invent the wildest ones. The rhymes of the satirical singer-songwriter Tom Lehrer are one of the most brilliant examples of this ability, including such rhymes as try an' hide/cyanide and Oedipus/duck-billed platypus.

Sages also like to tease and play practical jokes on people, especially if they feel they are pompous or pretentious and need lightening up. They are able to take a joke themselves, and don't mind playing the fool as long as people laugh.

If you are communicating with a Sage, you need to be an appreciative audience, listening attentively, laughing at their jokes and applauding their best lines.

> 'My experience is that Sages are acutely aware of their audience, unless they are in the negative pole of verbosity. A Sage's worst fear is feeling unheard or misunderstood.'
> GLENN, MUSICIAN/ARTIST

Most Sages are fun to listen to, but it's hard to receive the same attention in return. They are the best talkers but sometimes poor listeners. 'But enough about me' should be their watchword, and not ironically. They hate being interrupted, so you need to be firm and determined to get a word in, if necessary telling them to shut up. Being quick-tempered as well as quick-witted, they can easily flare up if you provoke or annoy them. However, like a frog or a puffer fish, their aggression is mostly for show and can easily be deflated if you stand up to them firmly.

You'll get a better response if you open with a compliment. If you want them to enjoy your conversation, you need to raise your game to their level of verbal sophistication. Be wary of engaging in a war of words, since their ability to twist and manipulate language gives them a clear advantage.

Sages at the relationship Perspective can be very attentive and empathic, especially if they are fond of you and find you interesting. They'll also pay you the most gratifyingly fulsome compliments of anyone, though it's better to take these with a pinch of salt. If you are seeking a more intimate connection, both you and they will have to work hard to get behind the performance to a deeper, authentic level of communication.

At the philosophical Perspective, they are compassionate listeners whose wisdom is healing and inspiring as well as entertaining.

The Sage in Love

Both male and female Sages enjoy the drama of dating and can put on a good show to attract, dazzle and seduce their date. The most important thing for them on a date is to make each other laugh. Of all the Roles, they seem to get the best results from online dating, enjoying composing their résumé and playing different parts with each person they meet. They improvise the best pick-up lines and also the best rejections of bad ones.

Most Sages are attractive, urbane and witty enough to succeed at the game of love, but Sage women can sometimes find their personalities are too powerful for more reserved men. Both male and female Sages will act out romance with their usual panache. Moonlight and candlelight become them well, especially accompanied by champagne and roses. Not that they would turn in a clichéd performance, but they know how to tune into your romantic fantasies, satisfy your longing for heightened experience and whisk you off in a sports car to dinner and adventure. They enjoy sex, but like to lead up to it with an elaborate seduction scenario and an exchange of repartee, including *double-entendres*. Words for them are often the most stimulating foreplay. They are the Role most likely to play out their love life in the glare of publicity and to 'kiss and tell' if it goes wrong, even if the scandal rebounds on them when their sex life is plastered all over the tabloid press.

The Sage's challenge is to love sincerely, authentically from the heart, rather than performing movie-style. Novelty is always fun for them, bringing the thrill of wooing a new audience, but the question is whether once the excitement of courtship and seduction have worn off they can find ways of keeping it fresh and experiencing genuine emotion and connection. They value commitment but may find it hard to give, preferring to move on to greener pastures. Their performing skills work brilliantly for them at parties and other social events, but can get in the way of true intimacy in romance, particularly if they try to turn their partner into an admiring audience. Their partner may fall for it on the first date, but will get frustrated if they cannot get behind the façade as the relationship progresses.

'Strange as it may seem to other Roles, Sages find it easier to express their innermost intimate thoughts and feelings with a public audience than with their "significant other", if they have

one. Typically they are so full of themselves that they do not really listen to the other.'

PHILIP WITTMEYER, ENGINEER

Sages can even act their whole lives away without ever experiencing true feeling. Introspection can bring fear that they have no real self or soul, but instead an echoing, all-consuming blankness.

As marriage partners it becomes harder still, as the routine side of life often bores them. A Sage husband is the least likely of all Roles to take out the rubbish for you and can come up with a never-ending stream of ingenious excuses for not doing household chores. The singer Peggy Lee would rarely have dinner on the table when her husband came home, but would instead present him with her latest lyric – hardly the ideal 1950s housewife.

However, Sages are adept at talking and charming their way out of trouble. The technique often works, and is a more civilized way of resolving conflict than some other options. But faced with serious emotional or financial issues they can find themselves out of their depth. Loyalty is not their strongest virtue and if the jokes stop working they may panic and run off to a more inviting audience or even walk out altogether.

They are also subject to moods, including anger and depression, tending to indulge their darker side at home while maintaining their happy face in public. The inevitable backlash when they become tired, depressed or run out of steam hits with a vengeance in their more intimate relationships, particularly with their family, who bear the brunt of the Sage's darker moods. Of course everyone gets these, but Sages, with their dramatizing tendency, can exaggerate the effects and wear out the patience of their family with their histrionics. The rage or depression usually passes quite quickly, but is a dragon that needs to be tamed. But the bright side of loving a Sage is that they will always make you laugh and once they emerge from their moods are likely to charm you into forgiving them. You need to allow them a lot of space to hold the floor in public and to control your jealousy, as Sages deprived of the opportunity to play with other people will be miserable. But if they love you, it will go no further.

Sages are often most attracted to and compatible with Artisans. They have a lot of fun with other Sages as friends and colleagues, but as lovers can spend more energy upstaging each other than relating. Servers are the Role best equipped to give the care, nurturing and support that will enable the Sage to shine and enjoy themselves while doing the minimum of household chores. Scholars share their interest in language and communication, and these two will keep each other interested and mentally stimulated, though both Roles can find the emotional side tricky. Priests and Kings are highly charismatic, so will often attract Sages, but two cardinal Roles in a relationship will compete for limelight and leadership. Sages can have fun with Warriors as friends, but have very different energies and values, particularly around loyalty. For a detailed description of the compatibilities between Sages and other Roles, see Chapter 9.

Parents and Children

Sages often get on well with children, being in touch with their own Inner Child. Children have short attention spans, but a Sage can keep them entertained for hours with stories, jokes, acting games and treats. They give their children lots of treats and holidays and encourage them to express themselves. However, they don't enjoy the messier and more routine aspects of childcare, preferring to leave that to a more nurturing partner or professional caregiver.

Also, while being delightful playmates when they're in the mood, they expect to be left in peace when they're working or otherwise occupied and can get quite angry if disturbed at these times. In fact, temper can be one of their parenting problems. This is partly because they have strong ideas about parenting, including the need for good manners, but find it hard to set up and police boundaries. The result is a tendency to veer between indulgence and sudden flare-ups, leaving children confused. It's important for them to convey to their children an understanding about moods, as well as being clear around rules and expectations. The good news is that their anger evaporates quickly, as they prefer to have fun.

Sage children learn to talk early and will impress adults by coming out with proper words, whole sentences and thoughtful questions. They are natural show-offs who enjoy and actively need the attention of an adult audience and are good at getting it by being cute and charming or playing the clown. If all else fails, they will seek attention by throwing tantrums or getting into trouble. As the oldest child, a

Sage will expect to maintain their position as special and privileged. If younger, they will compete hard to win attention away from their elder siblings. They desperately want to be Daddy's or Mummy's favourite little boy or girl (usually the opposite-sex parent is preferred), and will be very indignant and unhappy if they don't achieve this position. In fact, they may spend the rest of their lives ensuring they compensate for any early-life deficit of favouritism.

Sage parents value academic achievement but set more store by creative self-expression. They'd rather their child was one of the cool kids than getting straight A's, and Sage children agree. At school, they are generally smart and fast learners, but easily bored. They are likely to do exceptionally well as long as they are enjoyably taught and can achieve the results painlessly, without interfering too much with their fun. If they are understimulated or feel they are 'too kool for skool', they will switch off, act up or be chronic underachievers – to the despair of their teachers, who can see their potential. But a smart teacher can wake them up to the consequences – for example by marking them down for talking too much – and set them straight. The more physically adept Sage children will enjoy sports, particularly the kudos of being a sporting champion. Generally, they are more likely to enjoy the creative and expressive subjects of the curriculum, particularly drama, and are bound to end up in the starring roles. In fact, they are likely to spend a lot of time daydreaming of stardom.

At school, as at home, Sages are adept at using humour to get attention. They often become the class clown or at least popular by keeping their fellow students entertained. Sage boys are not naturally macho, so in a rough school their wit can become an essential tactic to gain confidence, deflect anger and fend off bullies. They will usually end up leading their own gang, though it's more likely to be composed of smart and cool kids than thugs. Girls tend to be more interested in being pretty and popular than working towards academic or sporting achievements, but can overcome any perceived deficiencies in the prettiness stakes through personality and charm. If they are also pretty, they may well end up being the most popular girl in the class.

Sage Archetypes in Myth, Fiction and Film

Dionysos (Bacchus) is the most Sage-like of the Greek deities: fun-loving god of wine, inspirer of ritual madness and ecstasy and patron saint of parties. Exceptionally attractive, he often wore leopard skin (a favourite Sage accessory) and his chariot was drawn by panthers.

Hermes (Mercury) represents Sages as the god of literature, oratory and wit. His caduceus, a staff entwined with serpents, is a symbol of wisdom. He was as smooth-tongued as quicksilver, suave yet treacherous, messenger of the gods, symbol of eloquence and patron saint of communication. One story is that he stole Apollo's cattle and when Apollo confronted him played his lyre so sweetly that Apollo was enchanted and let him keep the cattle in exchange for the lyre.

Wisdom is highly revered in the Bible and the most famous exemplar of Sage wisdom is King Solomon. He is best remembered for his resourceful judgement, which saved the life of a baby while teaching an important lesson. His dalliance with the exotic Queen of Sheba is legendary, immortalized in the great biblical love poem *The Song of Solomon*.

The trickster is also a Sage archetype in myth and folklore: a god, spirit, human or anthropomorphic animal who plays tricks on people to raise their consciousness. The greatest trickster hero in classical literature was Odysseus (Ulysses), created by Homer, a Sage poet. He is often referred to as 'Wily Odysseus' and he lived on his wits during the Trojan wars and his long odyssey home. Myths and fairy tales are full of tricksters, often disguised as animals, including Coyote, Brer Rabbit, Bugs Bunny, Reynard the Fox and Puss in Boots. Kokopelli is a Native American trickster known as the Don Juan of the Southwest. Venerated as a fertility deity, he seduces the maidens he meets on his travels with his flute playing.

In folklore, the mischievous spirit Puck was another Sage trickster, immortalized in *A Midsummer Night's Dream*. Being a Sage dramatist, Shakespeare filled his plays with great Sage characters. Falstaff in *Henry IV* is the most substantial comic character ever invented, the clownish but witty drinking companion to Prince Hal, who is 'bewitched with the rogue's company'. Falstaff's wisecrack when accused of gluttony and villainy is 'If sack [sherry] and sugar be a fault, God help the wicked! If to be old and merry be a sin, then many an old host that I know is damned!'

Scheherazade, legendary Persian queen and narrator of *One Thousand and One Nights*, is the greatest fictional example of a Sage storyteller. 'Pleasant and polite, wise and witty', she uses her storytelling skills to save her life by entertainingly educating the king into kindness and morality so that a thousand stories later he makes her his queen instead of beheading her.

Mark Twain's creation Huckleberry Finn is a quick-witted, lovable and engaging hero. After faking his own death, he sets off on a life of adventure and reveals himself as a trickster who outmanoeuvres seasoned grifters, creating his own rules and reaching his own philosophical conclusions.

Broadway and Hollywood provide many larger-than-life Sage personalities, such as Max Bialystock, producer of *Springtime for Hitler* in *The Producers*, and Billy Flynn, sharp lawyer anti-hero of *Chicago*. Both are deeply flawed hucksters, but their wit and entertainment value make them sympathetic against the odds.

One of the best examples of a Sage brilliantly expressing wit and wisdom is the movie *Borat*, written by and starring Sacha Baron Cohen (a Sage). It seamlessly weaves many strands of comedy into a multi-level satire. Borat releases his Inner Idiot in the broadest farce and slapstick, lets loose his trickster in hilarious sitcom sketches and strings the narrative along with visual and verbal wit. The result is great entertainment that is also a morality tale exposing the folly, self-deception and prejudice of modern society.

How to Fulfill Your Sage Potential

Sages are in many ways the most attractive Role. They give the most pleasure to others and have the most fun, all summer long and through the winter too. Many people who study this personality system would like to be a Sage, but it is harder to play the Role well than at first appears. It requires more work, self-examination and commitment than many Sages are willing to give, since it is easier to reap the rewards of pleasing an audience than to seek authenticity. This section summarizes how Role and Perspective can work together for growth and fulfillment.

Competing Sages live the high life as big spenders, high rollers, dandies and divas, inhabiting the grandest mansions (filled with priceless art treasures, tiger-skin rugs and all the latest gadgets), throwing spectacular parties, spending fortunes in nightclubs and casinos and featuring in the pages of lifestyle magazines and gossip columns. They revel in conspicuous consumption and ostentatious display. Hollywood is their Mecca, but any profession that offers opportunities for celebrity and stardom will appeal, particularly PR and politics. Sales is another popular area, though at this Perspective there is a strong temptation to become hucksters or con artists.

Winning and getting top billing are competing Sages' top priorities, though dissing their rivals is a close second. Romance for them is all about beauty, glamour and status. They prefer to marry a trophy wife or husband, or a wealthy one to bankroll their success. If the relationship fails, they will blame their partner and move on, choosing another in the same mould. In their positive pole they have great determination and resilience and can pick themselves up after a fall and try again. Frank Sinatra's song 'My Way' is their anthem. They can also provide enormous pleasure and entertainment to their audiences, putting on the most spectacular entertainment as actors, singers, directors and producers and giving their audiences great enjoyment as well as much-needed escape from grim daily reality in the best Hollywood movies, Broadway musicals, top 10 albums and popular fiction.

Relationship-oriented Sages express the angst of the conflict between outer and inner, worldly and spiritual values, through biting satire and sweeping tragedy. Their relationships will become much more emotionally engaging, full of soap-opera drama and sometimes tragedy. Their wit becomes quirkier, sharper edged, and is turned on themselves as much as others. They use their communication skills for good causes and campaigns, for example lawyers who expose corporate malpractice or defend poor clients for reduced fees. Many are successful, since they are attuned to the zeitgeist and there is a vast audience at the relationship perspective, hungry to have these values expressed in the arts. However, they pursue success less ruthlessly than competing Sages and are likely to forego the easy route to fame to be true to their own artistic integrity. This will bring them more discerning appreciation, which they will value more than mass acclaim (though still sometimes hankering for this and suffering if less talented but more popular performers do better than them).

As with all the Roles, psychotherapy and counselling can help them, turning their attention away from their audience and towards their own mental and emotional processes, needs, desires and motivations. They need a therapist whose insights they respect and who is empathic enough to be trusted with their real feelings. Otherwise they are likely to get bored and leave, preferring to play than 'grow'. Some find going on retreat helpful to get away from the stimulus and distractions of daily life and reach deeper experience and higher insight. If they can stick with this sometimes painful process, they will find new sources of inspiration to enrich and deepen their communication and explore more deeply the mysteries of the universe and the human organism.

Philosophically oriented Sages are much more relaxed and self-accepting, which enables them to enjoy and communicate the comedy of life. Some use their roguish charm and well-honed entrepreneurial skills to take advantage of others, though more out of laziness than real criminality. They will probably not be high achievers, lacking motivation to finish a project. However, if they do have something to communicate it will be very well worth hearing and can often gain them a public position or even fame.

Meditation and yoga can help them to glimpse an interdependent reality beyond their emotional dramas, and are helpful to ground and integrate body, mind and spirit. They may also benefit from advanced spiritual practices to guide them through the potentially terrifying vastness of inner space. Being natural philosophers, they are easily drawn to metaphysics, and usually prefer their path to have a valid and stimulating intellectual dimension. More emotionally oriented Sages will get more from an approach offering emotional fulfillment or spectacular psychic experiences. They naturally prefer a laughing Buddha to a suffering Jesus and expect their co-religionists to relax sometimes from their serious devotions and have a laugh. Their challenge is to become truly authentic, which will enable them to reach the deepest wellsprings of their wisdom.

◆◆◆◆◆◆

The formula for success, happiness and self-mastery in this system is a simple but powerful three-step process:

1. *Discover your Role.*

2. *Integrate it with your Perspective.*

3. *Operate from their positive poles.*

I hope by now you recognize whether you are a Sage or whether it is your secondary Role. Identifying your Role is the first step on a lifelong journey of self-discovery. The insight needs to be confirmed and applied in daily life on an ongoing basis for best results, so requires commitment, but with practice it becomes second nature. The reward of self-transformation is well worth the effort.

Secondary Role Influences for Sages

One of the most important factors influencing the personality variations between people who share the same Role is the secondary Role. This colours, flavours and generally modifies your personality. The combination works like an omelette: your primary Role is the egg, while your secondary Role is the added ingredient – cheese, mushroom, tomato. Sometimes the flavour is subtle, sometimes it overpowers the egg. Similarly, the secondary Role can manifest more strongly than the primary Role, particularly if it corresponds with your profession. Some people have the same Role in both the primary and secondary position, so will conform more closely with the Role archetype. If this is your case, you will probably recognize yourself quite easily. This section summarizes the influence of the other six Roles on Sages.

Artisan-Sages

This combination is the most creatively expressive and innovative. These Sages have the most dramatic, sometimes tragic, love affairs of all time, but may find it hard to get intimate in a relationship. They are almost as comfortable with chaos as Artisans:

'Humour is emotional chaos remembered in tranquility.'
JAMES THURBER

but it is an ungrounded combination, so they may have trouble filling in their tax returns on time. These people usually have several outlets for their talents, sometimes combined, such as the cartoonist who integrates a satirical wit with graphic skills, theatrical dress designers, circus performers and TV presenters. They are at the forefront of multimedia developments, which they use to the maximum.

'While I've always had a facility for verbal communication, music is the thing that really excites my soul. I have numerous songs, paintings and recipes under way, along with outlines and notes for at least three books. Lately, my focus has been on painting, as if music, cooking and theatre weren't enough.'
GLENN, MUSICIAN/ARTIST

Server-Sages

More low key and quieter than the average Sage, these are also gentler and easier to get along with on a one-to-one basis. They are also easier to be married to, as they are more likely to shoulder their share of domestic and childcare responsibilities and be generally more caring and emotionally engaged.

One Server-Sage who works as a travel agent describes very articulately how this combination is expressed positively in her work:

'The Sage/Server in me likes to jolly the people up a bit. I like to interject a human quality into their experience with me. The reality is that while we are on a phone we are all human beings, not machines, and I am usually able to create a human connection between us. I like to jog them out of their role as "client" and into the role of an adult talking to another real-life adult, having the two of us being as kind and realistic with one another as possible on our brief journey together. I like to get off the phone feeling like their day is a little better for having experienced a few moments with me, and that they have been given their best chance to be their best self.'
MARY, TRAVEL AGENT

Priest-Sages

This is one of the most charismatic combinations. These Sages are wonderfully entertaining and imaginative, and their art is likely to have an inspirational, other-worldly flavour. They may be unsure whether the stage or the pulpit is the better platform to express their genius, and many will become preachers, drawing large crowds with their entertaining sermons. Actors with this combination will enjoy roles with some spiritual or inspirational dimension. In general they will be keen for their communication to advance a humanitarian cause or do some good in the world. Their communication with friends is less about wit for wit's sake and more about looking for the moral or an illuminating insight.

Warrior-Sages

Less diplomatic, more aggressive and confrontational than most Sages, these will be more likely to express themselves in an active way such as through the performing arts and athletics rather than sedentary professions like writing. They make good stand-up comics, for example Michael Moore, who also uses his good ol' boy appearance to gain access for satirical purposes. It's a good combination for both political and tabloid journalism. These Sages make excellent entrepreneurs and salespeople, as they are more productive and able to get their projects up and running than most Sages. They are at home in their bodies and likely to take good care of them, enjoying sport and exercise, although the more hedonistic ones are as likely to be found in the bar as the gym. The champion boxer Muhammad Ali is an excellent example. This is one of the sexiest combinations, producing Byronic lovers and *femmes fatales* who unite Sage charm and seductive skills with Warrior energy and sexual prowess. They make fun parents, being more physically expressive than most Sages and playing games with their children as well as giving them treats.

King-Sages

This is one of the most cardinal combinations, so these Sages will have more grandeur and gravitas than usual and will be taken more seriously. They are likely to be attracted to the bigger stage of politics or public life. If they work in the media, they are more likely to be directors or producers than solo performers, needing a lot of power and being well able to handle it. They may be writers, and their imposing presence will earn them much respect, sometimes beyond their talent. The novelist Kingsley Amis used his nickname, 'the King', in a book, *The King's English*, whose punning title contains a secondary accuracy. Someone described her son with this combination as 'great at managing projects and getting others to work with him, which is the King influence. He's very social and has a large network of friends and contacts, and is the one telling stories or jokes at a party. That's the Sage part of his personality.'

Scholar-Sages

A superb combination for writing, especially of a more serious or philosophical bent. As journalists, these Sages will be able to process data and information, do proper research and have a firm grasp of the facts to give a solid basis to their work. Some of the greatest novelists have this combination, including Salman Rushdie, as does the immensely cultured and learned playwright Tom Stoppard. Many of the finest minds in academia also have it. They are more likely to be on the arts and humanities than scientific side, and their writings will be more accessible, polished and entertaining than those of the average academic, as they won't be able to resist inserting a few jokes and puns even in an academic paper. Simon Schama is a historian with this combination. His television presentations blend a higher than average intellectual content with maximum entertainment, without using talking heads, mime shows or special effects and relying solely on his charisma and communication skills.

Famous Sages

Harpo Marx, Charlie Chaplin, Lenny Bruce, Lucille Ball, Laurence Olivier, John Gielgud, Alec Guinness, Richard Burton, Clark Gable, Peter Sellers, Whoopi Goldberg, Jack Nicholson, Richard Pryor, Mel Brooks, Jeff Goldblum, Geoffrey Rush, Bill Murray, Barry Humphries, Michael Moore, Sacha Baron Cohen, Noël Coward, Steven Spielberg, Francis Ford Coppola, Federico Fellini, Werner Herzog, Tom Stoppard, Homer, Geoffrey Chaucer, William Shakespeare, Miguel de Cervantes, Molière, Jonathan Swift, Alexander Pope, Lord Byron, Charles Dickens, Oscar Wilde, Rudyard Kipling, Mark Twain, William Faulkner, Joseph Heller, Philip Roth, Kingsley Amis, Salman Rushdie, Douglas Adams, Ken Kesey, Jonathan Franzen, Zadie Smith, Umberto Eco, Dorothy Parker, David Letterman, Jerry Springer, Johnny Carson, Steve Allen, Larry King, Jay Leno, Jacques Derrida, Christopher Hitchens, Giacomo Puccini, Cole Porter, George Gershwin, Fred Astaire, Louis Armstrong, Bing Crosby, Frank Sinatra, Tom Lehrer, Chuck Berry, Mick Jagger, Elton John, Missy Elliott, Muhammad Ali, Cleopatra, Anne Boleyn, Benjamin Disraeli, Mussolini, Franklin D. Roosevelt, Ronald Reagan, Bill Clinton

CHAPTER 4

The Server

'If I can stop one heart from breaking,
I shall not live in vain.
If I can ease one life the aching,
Or cool one pain,
Or help one fainting robin
Unto his nest again,
I shall not live in vain.'
EMILY DICKINSON

The Server Personality

Servers are the ordinal inspiration Role, bringing inspiration into every aspect of daily life. They have excellent relationship skills and can motivate other people through their cheerfulness and tireless support. This ability is invaluable in keeping projects going when difficulties are encountered or enthusiasm is waning. It seems almost like magic – hard to define, but wonderful to see.

Just as other Roles get inspiration from Servers, so they in turn love to give it out in any way they can, particularly in the forms of practical service, comfort and nurturing. They are enablers who put others' needs before their own, working behind the scenes to take care of everyone and everything. Servers have the widest range of opportunities in life to find personal fulfillment; in the process they make the world a happier place and are much loved.

The term 'server' originally meant someone who assisted a priest. It is appropriate to this personality system, as Servers are often happiest working with and supporting Priests in both religious and secular contexts. In the modern world they are found wherever service and support are needed – which means everywhere. Their strongest connection is with the helping professions, particularly social work and medicine. The Role and job are not identical and other Roles also contribute greatly, but Servers are in their element and predominate in these areas. They are naturally Good Samaritans. 'How may I help you?' is their favourite question.

Service is the positive pole of the Server Role. Servers have the best emotional intelligence and strongest interpersonal skills of all the Roles. They can handle difficult people better than anyone else and are able to alert others when they see something devious or unpleasant in a stranger. Nevertheless, they like to treat strangers as their honoured guests, at least until they show they don't deserve this (and sometimes even then). They are extremely insightful and shrewd when assessing someone and alert to small changes in mood and behaviour that other Roles would miss. They notice when you're tired, offer to help or bring you an aspirin and glass of water and tell you to go and lie down, without being prompted. Their motto is often 'Life is other people.' They are wired up to be helpful and supportive, so will volunteer for the unpopular job without being asked, offer to do overtime or cover for a sick colleague, give you a lift to the airport and feed your cat while you're away. However, being on the inspiration axis, their motivation needs to be voluntary and come from their heart.

'Servers do like to be inspired to serve. It doesn't take much inspiration on one's part and a little will go a long way. It may simply be that I like your looks or there's something about you that inspires me. I have found with certain people I have bent over backwards and wondered what made me so willing to work so hard for that person. I usually conclude that it was my choice and not some personality flaw on my part.'

JEAN, NURSE

Although Servers' helpfulness is mainly directed at individuals, they also have a broader purpose. Their aim in life is to facilitate and support the common good, which they interpret in different ways, but it usually involves bringing people together as a community. This can be their family, neighbourhood or the company they work for. They look after their immediate family devotedly, often shouldering all the childcare. While the family is watching television, they will get up to fetch a blanket for Grandmother, attend to the baby crying upstairs, then make tea for the rest of the family. They also care for the extended family, remembering everyone's birthdays, arranging get-togethers and being on hand to provide childcare or nursing services, patch up troubled marriages and look after aged relatives.

People often bemoan the lack of community spirit in the modern world, but what little is left is mostly kept going by Servers. In our London apartment block, many of the busy professionals don't know each other's names and are in too much of a hurry to even say good morning. However, the Servers know everyone's names, business and sometimes secrets. They run the residents' committee, email everyone with news, find babysitters, organize parties, pass on gossip and paint the hallway. This is on an unpaid voluntary basis, which is typical. However, they also use their power to combine self-interest with public spiritedness, which does not always equate with the benefit of their fellow residents. In the wider neighbourhood, most of the shopkeepers are Servers, and all know each other and their customers by name and chat with them. Even outside their core community, Servers extend the hand of friendship. They are true do-gooders, always the first to give up their seat on the bus, pick up whatever you've dropped or rush to help you if you fall in the street.

> 'When Servers are in their positive pole, you'll probably find many of them to behave like "covert magicians". Their inspiration often consists of the elements of "surprise" in their acts of love and common good services.'
>
> JOE

It should be said that there is a negative side to the kind of small, close-knit community that Servers favour. There is enormous pressure to conform to the conventional norms of behaviour that Servers see as holding the community together but freer spirits find stifling. Servers can be extremely nosy and are very good at finding out everyone's business and unearthing secrets. They are the suburban curtain twitchers, keeping a sharp eye on their neighbours and gossiping about any signs of scandal. At the rule-bound and competing Perspectives, they can make life a misery for 'dissidents' like single mothers, homosexuals, hippies and communists, who may come under pressure to step back in line or be hounded out of town. A Japanese proverb expresses this attitude: 'The nail that sticks out must be hammered down.' From a distance such a community may have a certain charm, but close up it can remind us why many of us are happier in more anonymous but liberated urban societies.

As Servers are the most numerous of the Roles (approximately 30 percent of the population), it is unsurprising that there are many societies around the world which are based on the ideal of serving the common good. Developing countries such as India and China need selfless service in building their infrastructure, and Servers may be more appreciated there than in the West. The inspirational ethos permeates Indian culture; the quality of service, its loving kindness and dignity, are a rewarding experience for those who come from more competitive and self-reliant cultures. In the West, Servers congregate in more traditional rural communities and small towns, where there are more opportunities for community building. They are less common in big cities, where commerce and culture are considered more important. They are the bedrock of society – a well-grounded Role with both feet firmly planted on the earth – but one eye is always fixed on the common good and how it may best be served.

The Challenge of the Negative Pole

With all this helpfulness and good-heartedness, it is hard to see that Servers have any flaws. But like all Roles they have their negative pole, which is bondage. It is easy for them to slide into bondage, because on the one hand their capacity for hard work and selfless service makes them neglect their own needs and on the other hand other people are prone to exploiting their goodwill.

Part of the problem is that being so unobtrusive, Servers can be taken for granted and overloaded with extra duties, which they feel obliged to carry out. It may begin as a voluntary process but easily decline into drudgery and servitude. Servers then feel that their whole life is filled with one obligatory chore after another, like that of a slave in the ancient world. Nowadays they are the downtrodden housewives and exploited workers. In bondage, their inspiration turns sour, their wellspring dries up and instead of a support they become a painful, guilt-inducing burden to others. They usually go on doing their duty, but with bad grace, a scowl rather than a smile. As with all Roles, the negative pole manifests most damagingly at the rule-bound and competing Perspectives, from where Servers can end up joyless, crabbed and bitter.

Servers' negative pole can also manifest actively as a need to control. So strong is their desire to serve that they often feel they need to take over the whole process and will fret if they think that they are not in complete control of all the details. They can be busybodies who meddle and interfere, nose out all the gossip and use it to gain unfair advantage and power over people. In the family they can manipulate their children and any other relatives who allow them to control their lives. In the workplace they can become less supportive and more self-serving. If they feel undervalued and mistreated, they can become very resentful and turn nasty, rapidly becoming an obstacle and a liability. At the competing Perspective they will take revenge on the culprit by undermining them or even stabbing them in the back. The victim may not know where it comes from, as Servers are so well plugged into all the networks that they can spread rumours and gossip, start whispering campaigns, implant suspicions. Being ordinal, they have less widespread destructive impact, but they can sometimes cause great annoyance and distress to individuals, divert the course of justice and undermine plans that they disapprove of.

Relationship-oriented Servers' need to control is less destructively manipulative and more about manoeuvring others into serving a good cause, whether helping an unfortunate friend or supporting a campaign. They are the 'charity muggers' who accost you for money in the street. In the family or workplace they take on more responsibility than they can handle and become workaholics – exhausted and eventually ill. They also get into intense emotional dramas which can end up bringing everything crashing down around them. Before this happens, family, friends or bosses need to step in and help to rescue them from themselves.

At the philosophical Perspective, their negative pole manifests much more subtly, if at all. Here they are capable of enormous selfless devotion to a person or cause, but need to take care to stay in balance by factoring in their own needs.

How to Recognize a Server

The first thing you notice on meeting a Server in the positive pole is their warm, welcoming smile, which immediately makes you feel at ease. Their eyes are soft and sympathetic. Even if they are not classically beautiful, their inspirational friendliness gives them an inner glow, though this can become dulled if they are disappointed in life. Their appeal is simple and natural, without the need for artificial enhancement or airs and graces. They do not have the charisma of the more cardinal Roles or the style of Artisans, but their warmth makes them more approachable. Both men and women tend to be small in stature, sometimes smaller than their siblings. Male Servers are less macho than average unless they have a King or Warrior secondary Role, but their social skills usually make them well liked and accepted in male company. Female Servers conform naturally to the feminine ideal and often display the quiet confidence of fitting in easily with social expectations.

These characteristics usually make it quite easy to recognize the Role. If their inspiration takes a more elevated or spiritual direction, however, particularly if they have a confident, outgoing personality, they can be mistaken for Priests. Intellectual Servers can look like Scholars, especially those working in education; both Roles are gentle, unassuming and low key. Servers with a bubblier, more vivacious personality working in a creative field can look like Artisans, since both are ordinal Roles. Male Servers working in business or the army can be mistaken for Warriors, since they can blend in well and both Roles are ordinal, dutiful and hardworking.

Server Style

Fashion-wise, Servers are the least adventurous of the Roles, dressing for convenience, comfort and practicality, so they can look dowdy or frumpish. They are happy in functional outfits where they don't stand out, including uniforms. Their favourite colours are the more neutral shades, particularly grey (which at the time of writing is the most fashionable colour, but the point is clear). In the workplace men are the grey suits, while women usually dress in the style of their boss, which gets them points. Women Servers do not usually go in for make-up unless it is required by their job or social group, and then it will be discreet. Dressing for high-profile occasions can be problematic, as they don't do glamour and prefer to look modest rather than sexy. However, they like to dress up for big family and community occasions, which are high points in their lives, so can sometimes surprise people by turning up for a wedding in a flattering suit and hat which get them lots of attention. Shopping can be a stressful experience, as they find it hard to receive rather than give service and will sometimes end up doing the shop assistants' job for them: picking up clothes from the floor and hanging them up, tidying piles of T-shirts, replacing items on the shelves. They tend to shop at chain or thrift stores and pride themselves on spending very little.

They are extremely house-proud and their homes are immaculately cleaned (usually by themselves even if they can afford a cleaner), well maintained, comfortable but not opulent or stylish, warm and welcoming. Generally they are happy to make a hobby out of activities that could be seen as maintenance, like cookery, sewing and gardening. They delight in extending hospitality to their friends and will look after their guests beautifully. They usually have moderate appetites and are also moderate drinkers, if not teetotalers. More hedonistic partners may find this difficult. It can be awkward to go out for a banquet in a top French restaurant if your spouse just orders an omelette.

Servers have a tendency to ignore their bodies and even despise them, except as engines of service. Their health disorders often spring from this attitude combined with overwork. They will wear themselves out staying up all night with a sick patient or a dying family pet. They are therefore more prone to catching contagious illnesses than some other Roles. Conversely, their sense of duty may bring them into work when they have the flu, so they give it to others. They have an unfortunate tendency to ignore their symptoms, refusing to go to the doctor till they have to. If the prognosis is bad, they may keep it to themselves so as not to upset their loved ones. They don't like complaining, since they feel that this would impose obligations on others and make them seem less in control. Philosophically oriented Servers become well balanced, understanding the need to take care of themselves and keep fit, out of respect for the body as well as in order to carry out their duties more effectively.

The Life Story of a Server

This is the true life story of a Server which illustrates how they can live happily and positively even with a difficult start in life. This man was born during World War I into a family of modest means. He was always helpful and co-operative as a child, assisting with the housework and other tasks. While he was still a child his father died suddenly, so in addition to his schooling he went out to work in order to help support the family. Though clever, he gave up school soon afterwards to learn a profession and bring in money. He excelled at this, until World War II scuppered his plans. But he had a 'good war'. In the army he volunteered for the front line and gained rapid promotion from the ranks to an officer (appropriately in the service corps), mainly because he had made himself indispensable in critical areas. He organized social events, entertained the troops with his piano playing and stories, and was a popular figure in the mess. This shows how Servers can flourish even in a macho military environment, though some soldiers found him over-fussy and a bit too concerned for their welfare – after all, they were in the army and at war.

After the war, he returned to his profession and took his family to South America, working for a large multinational company. He became a personnel manager, which suited his Server talents well. He decided to found a Protestant church, since there was none in the country, and took the initiative. In doing this, he was very active in raising money and promoting support, but stayed out of the limelight, letting others do the high-profile work. It was a success and still flourishes, a model for other Protestant churches in South America. Moving on around the world, he loved organizing concerts, plays and social events, being useful and available for anyone needing help.

On the downside, he became something of a martyr, showing the effects of devoting his life to the service of others while neglecting his own needs. Perhaps also his tough childhood had left its scars, which he had pushed aside. The result was that underneath the surface there was an angry person, out of view from most people, but apparent to friends and family. Worse, it was bottled-up anger, seldom openly expressed but leading to long bouts of sulking. To his credit, he admitted that he was prone to this problem and tried to find ways of dealing with it.

Typically for a Server, he knew everyone in the neighbourhood and heard and shared all the gossip, but knew when to curb it before it became harmful. Later in life, when his arthritis (which he never complained about) prevented him from being of service any more, he suddenly died of pneumonia.

His life story illustrates how a person's Role informs and guides them through their lifetime choices. Fortunately, this Server was able to fulfill his Role throughout his life.

The church-founding episode illustrates something that many Servers believe: that a shared spirituality is an important prerequisite for a cohesive community life. In almost any church, mosque or temple there will be a band of Servers who are the backbone of the place of worship and who perform all the practical tasks needed to keep it functioning smoothly. In our secular age, many Servers perform these tasks in golf clubs, the Boy Scouts, amateur dramatic societies, Freemasons' Lodges and countless other voluntary organizations. The need to be of community service is the motivating force.

The Server at Work

Their capacity for hard work, administrative and interpersonal skills and general helpfulness make Servers invaluable employees in any organization. They can do well in any field, but will feel most fulfillled in jobs that enable them to combine these qualities and provide a good service for a cause they approve of. Servers are the mainstay of charities and voluntary organizations, happy to work long hours unpaid or underpaid for a good cause. Most offices have a Server going around with large volumes of papers and a bulging diary in hand, doing the unpopular tasks and believing that they alone are holding the show together. They may be the secretary, the manager or anyone in between, but will always see themselves as the vital support for the organization's front-line workers. They generally don't want to be in the limelight themselves, but do like being appreciated. Servers also like to support one particular person whom they see as being especially important in advancing the common good. In the workplace, the classic example of this is the secretary–boss relationship, where as often as not the secretary holds together the reputation and effectiveness of the boss.

Since Servers are fulfillled by playing a supporting role in a good cause, they are often drawn to the helping professions, including teaching, medicine and the social services. Here they team up well with Priests, the Role with whom they share the greatest compatibility. Hospitals and social work departments have a strong Server ethos and atmosphere. Servers make the most sympathetic family doctors, with an excellent bedside manner and a healing presence. A visit to one will make you feel better just by itself and they also make good healers in complementary medicine, where this quality counts for more. Their interpersonal skills also make them good diplomats, mediators and facilitators. They are popular as family lawyers and accountants, good at reassuring and calming people in stressful situations.

'My greatest pleasure is getting people out of trouble.'
HOWARD, ACCOUNTANT

Servers are modest, gentle and unassuming, but this never stops them from being highly effective and getting results. Of all the Roles, they get the most satisfaction doing so-called menial work as cleaners, bus drivers, waiters and shop assistants. You seldom get surly, resentful or inadequate service from them (unless they're in an exceptionally bad mood). Their service will come with a smile and a little touch that makes you feel nurtured. These are qualities that can get overlooked in a wealthy society and yet are so important not just to its smooth functioning but also to its civilized values. At times of crisis and in poorer countries, Servers come to the forefront and their community-building skills hold the fabric of society together.

Servers have no objection to starting at the bottom of a company, however low paid the position. They are the fabled tortoises who proceed slowly and methodically, unnoticed at first. Sooner or later, though, their general helpfulness, efficiency and willingness to take on extra tasks will be noted and rewarded. One result is that they will be the last employees to be laid off. However, their usefulness may either make it hard for them to rise through the ranks, since managers want to hang on to a good assistant, or they get promoted out of their depth. If they are working for somebody as a PA or deputy or reporting to them, they will discreetly take on much of that person's workload, including the tedious bits, without making a big point of it or claiming credit. With their ability to find out all the gossip, they will keep their boss well informed and supported, and soon become indispensable.

In business they often do well as personnel officers, where they enjoy the opportunities to know everything that's going on in a company and pull strings behind the scenes. They particularly excel at customer service, being good at dealing with irate customers face to face or on the phone, attending to any problems and leaving people feeling soothed and satisfied.

For some Servers it is enough simply to have that level of power and control, though others will expect more concrete appreciation eventually, e.g., a pay raise or promotion. Their helpfulness is sometimes exploited and can turn to resentment if not appreciated. The culprit may then find themselves on the Server's invisibility list, unhelped and even obstructed. Conversely, Servers can overestimate their interpersonal skills and not realize that they are annoying others and encroaching on their domain by being too controlling and manipulative. However, it really is important for Servers to have a fair amount of control over their working environment – they can become miserable if this need is not met, as they will also in a situation where they can't serve the common good.

Leadership Style

Servers are rarely happy working alone, preferring to collaborate as teamworkers. Generally they are happy as employees, even at the bottom of the pecking order, and would rather work behind the scenes than be exposed in a leadership position. More ambitious Servers aim to become assistant or deputy to the boss.

As employers, they are apt to impose their idea of the common good on their employees, which may include working late, doing overtime and taking on other people's work if they are sick or on holiday. Unless you can persuade a Server that your dedication is equal to theirs, even if expressed in a different way, and validate their own vision, assuring them of how inspired you are by it, then you will probably be pressurized into doing a lot more than you want to. However, in their positive pole they make popular bosses who can put a human face on a soulless corporation. They nurture their staff and are likely to remember their birthdays and the names of their children.

One Server who attained the world's top job is Jimmy Carter. Although his domestic and foreign policies as President of the USA were not highly rated, he was widely admired for his moral leadership, humane values and decent, modest personality. While not a great speech maker, he was respected for softening his public rhetoric with humility. Like many Servers, he was a workaholic, but also a devoted family man. Significantly, the Carter family's life at the White House was much more low key than usual, with little of the pomp and ceremony of their predecessors; the king-sized limousine and presidential yacht were abandoned. Carter's simple, folksy manner endeared him to the electorate. Unusually for such a high-ranking public figure he seemed to prefer to help than be helped – as he still does – reportedly to the extent of handling his own luggage at airports. As President, his humanitarian and peacekeeping efforts stood out, particularly his mediation of a peace agreement between Israel and Egypt at Camp David. For this achievement among others, he is considered a worthy recipient of the Nobel Peace Prize. He certainly went a long way in his stated goal of making government 'competent and compassionate'. Typically of a true Server, much of his energy nowadays is devoted to voluntary work and charitable causes, including teaching Sunday school, a favourite occupation of devout Servers. His work and vision are continued in the Carter Center, whose goal is to advance human rights and alleviate suffering, including the eradication of major diseases and the improvement of global health.

Communication Style

Servers talk to everyone, without inhibition. They are quite happy to fall into conversation with strangers, whoever they happen to be standing next to in line. Often the content is quite bland – about the weather, the lateness of the train, the slow service, their ailments. It doesn't matter; they just want a response and exchange. They are the Role most likely to greet you when you pass them on a hike, even if you are deep in conversation, and to talk to you on the bus or train, even if you're reading. This can be irritating to people who value their privacy, so it's important for Servers not to let their community-building instinct intrude into other people's lives where it is not desired or appropriate. Their aim, though, is to reach out to people, put them at ease, affirm a common humanity, and accept them as part of the larger community, which is most welcome when done sensitively.

As the most ordinal of the seven Roles, Servers are the best at personal relationships. They excel in any one-to-one interaction, with children, friends, colleagues, anyone.

Situations that would be stressful for many people are easy for them, such as meeting strangers, making small talk, exchanging pleasantries with shopkeepers and giving orders humanely. However, they find it very difficult to function well in groups if they have to play a prominent or leadership role. Public speaking can be a nightmare in which their inspirational flow dries up. Their best technique, if they have to address a large meeting, is to imagine the audience as a small group of friends.

Humour is not their *forte*, unless they have a strong Sage influence. They appreciate the power of humour to bring laughter and joy, though, and will laugh at other people's jokes even if they don't understand them. They generally prefer those jokes to be clean and kind – a tall order – so will probably enjoy a family entertainer more than black comedy or satire.

The best way to communicate with a Server is to be as warm, friendly and open as possible, qualities which they value and respond to better than wit or cleverness. Even intellectual Servers display high emotional intelligence and tend to be more interested in how you feel than what you think about a subject. They usually prefer talking about people – their relationships, problems, achievements – or practical issues rather than abstract ideas. Allow them to help and look after you; tell them what they can do to support you. Above all, show your appreciation and don't take them for granted. At the philosophical Perspective they can enjoy talking about their cause or values, but like the discussion to be grounded in practical and emotional realities rather than theory.

The Server in Love

When Servers fall in love, they can't do enough for the object of their love. They are the Role most genuinely devoted to others. Kindness to others is their default mode, unless you have done something to really annoy them. While an Artisan will make themselves more beautiful and alluring to win your love, a Server will shower you with attention and gifts – thoughtful ones, just for you. They prefer giving to receiving compliments, but will glow under the spell of true love. Server women are often very feminine, sometimes in quite traditional ways, which can make them very popular with men tired of competing with more assertive women.

Sexuality is not always a Server's strongest card. They are inclined to see sex as a way of serving and sometimes healing their partners, but may participate more virtuously than passionately as a 'marital duty'. Like Priests, they can have an ambivalent attitude to the body, seeing its natural demands for food, sex and sensual pleasure as being selfish and inimical to the ultimate goal of serving the common good. When these instinctual drives become too strong, the Server may feel guilty and look for ways of atoning.

The qualities of Server women make them very marriageable, and they often surprise their family and friends by making a match to high-profile men who may have dated more glamorous girlfriends but see Servers as potentially good wives and mothers. Similarly, Server men have an understated charm and sweetness which can sometimes win a girl's heart more surely than the sophisticated graces of a Prince Charming. Paradoxically, Servers can be quite calculating, understand their own appeal and know how to use it in the dating market.

They make the most devoted wives and husbands, taking care of their partner beautifully, catering to all their needs and taking on more than their fair share of the domestic duties. As husbands they are well domesticated, understanding that washing up includes cleaning up and leaving the kitchen spotless. They are happier than most men to stay home as house husbands if their wife has a demanding job.

Servers should be highly appreciated as wives and husbands, but may be taken advantage of. They will put up with a lot of exploitation and even abuse, sometimes including infidelity, particularly if they are stuck in their negative pole of bondage. Alternatively, they can become overly controlling. Both the downtrodden doormat and the nagging shrew are sides of the negative Server wife, while Server men can become henpecked husbands. More positive, well-balanced Servers will eventually issue an ultimatum – and walk out if it is not observed. This will provoke shock, disbelief and grief in their partner, who did not believe them capable of such independent action and will live to regret their loss. It is vital that Servers learn to stand up for themselves, state their needs clearly and take steps to get them met before the relationship reaches crisis point.

Generally, Servers and Priests have the highest degree of mutual attraction, understanding and compatibility, being the ordinal and cardinal inspiration Roles. Servers get on well together and will be mutually devoted, as long as each is happy to receive as well as give. Servers and Warriors work well together, both Roles being dutiful and hardworking, but both male and female Servers are liable to get bossed and bullied in marriage to a Warrior. This can be worse with a King, but Servers feel highly honoured to have a King partner and will look after them with total dedication. They prefer to be with a more cardinal partner, so Sages can be more inspiring for them than Artisans. However, Artisans and Servers are often good friends, both being excellent at one-to-one relationships. Servers can live happily with Scholars; they may find scholarly reserve challenging, but if they can get through emotionally this can be a very satisfying relationship for both partners. For a detailed description of the compatibilities between Servers and other Roles, see Chapter 9.

Parents and Children

Servers usually love children and enjoy the nitty-gritty process of childcare more than any of the other Roles. They do it well as parents and grandparents and extend the same warm, nurturing skills to other people's children. If childless, they will put boundless nurturing energies into their nephews and nieces as well, or into looking after aged parents. Anna Freud's lifelong devotion to her famous psychologist father, continuing beyond his death, is an iconic example that also exemplifies a Server–Priest relationship. Charles Dickens's heroine Little Dorrit is a good fictional example.

There are only two general criticisms that could be made about Servers' parenting skills. First, their need to control can make them annoyingly manipulative and interfering with their children, wanting to know every detail of their inner and outer lives. Secondly, they can allow themselves to become a doormat to a pushy and demanding child, which won't help either of them. Server mothers can get trapped in the childcare role, slaving away but being taken for granted, in contrast to a more glamorous father who gives the treats. They are the Role most likely to suffer from empty-nest syndrome when the children finally leave home, so should prepare for this stage well in advance.

Server babies and children are sweet and adorable. From the earliest age they seem to be programmed not to give trouble, so they are the babies least likely to cry, throw tantrums or keep their parents awake all night. They are obedient and helpful – Mother's little helper – and will benefit from being encouraged to help in the house and given their own tasks. It is important to encourage their nurturing instincts by letting them help with looking after their younger siblings, which they will enjoy. They go through their teens with less outward show of rebellion than most other Roles.

At school they are likely to be teacher's pet, not necessarily for their academic prowess – though they can do well if they set their minds to it and are academically inclined – but more because they are likeable children who always turn in their homework on time, pay attention and resist joining in the troublemaking of the Sage and Warrior children. They will happily be class monitor and perform any other duties. Boys can sometimes be bullied, especially in rough schools, but are often adept at using their relationship skills to find themselves a Warrior or King protector. Girls are often popular with their fellow pupils because of their kindness and friendliness, and they usually make friends easily. In their teens, pretty Artisan and Sage girls sometimes choose them as their best friend, since they will be more uncomplainingly accepting of the role of plainer friend than other Roles. But they can sometimes turn the tables and a boy may end up choosing the Server over her prettier friend because of her sweet disposition. And of course, they can be as pretty or handsome as any other Role.

Server Archetypes in Myth, Fiction and Film

In the Warrior culture of the classical world, service was an underrated value, so there are few role models from that period. In Christianity, however, service became elevated to the primary spiritual virtue. Mary the mother of Jesus exemplifies the highest level of service in her acceptance of the Annunciation: 'I am the Lord's servant. May it be done to me as you have said.' Mary comes into the narrative of Jesus's life at important points, particularly his birth and death, but always in the background as an emblem of selfless devotion. One of her titles is the New Eve, her obedience contrasting with Eve's disobedience. Her song, the Magnificat, celebrates her humility as the Lord's Handmaiden and is a favourite prayer of peasants, whose social function is service.

Cinderella was a Server heroine who overcame her bondage to her ugly sisters and won the hand of Prince Charming – a success story that is often emulated by Server women. Cinderella was aided by her fairy godmother, an important Server archetype in fairy tales who supports and protects her protégées.

Both Meg and Beth March in *Little Women* are Servers. Meg is the older sister, responsibly running the household and protecting the youngest (Artisan) sister Amy from their (Warrior) sister Jo. Beth is sweet, kind and selfless. Her aim is to look after others and make them happy, and she sacrifices her health looking after a poor family. The heroine of *Rebecca* is a Server, unnamed and overshadowed by the unseen but more sophisticated Sage Rebecca, but whose long-suffering devotion finally brings her happiness.

There are fewer famous fictional figures representing the male Server, but the master–servant relationship is entertainingly depicted in P. G. Wodehouse's stories, where the Server valet Jeeves skilfully maintains the reputation of his bungling employer Bertie Wooster through many tricky situations. The controlling negative pole is wittily portrayed in the self-serving civil servant Sir Humphrey in the TV sitcom *Yes, Minister*. In film, Hoke Colburn, the chauffeur in *Driving Miss Daisy* (played by Morgan Freeman), is an excellent representation of a positive Server, devotedly looking after an employer who gives him very little in return but truly needs his help.

How to Fulfill your Server Potential

Servers have a great advantage because they have more opportunities to find fulfillment than any other Role. Every life situation requires service and so they play a vital role in society, underpinning family life, the workplace and the wider community. At their best, they are the world's unsung heroes or heroines, true saints. However, at their worst they become exhausted drudges, or alternatively like spiders, manipulating and trapping other people in their web. This section summarizes how Role and Perspective can work together for growth and fulfillment.

Competing Servers want to be winners, though they tend to succeed by attaching themselves to a winner rather than competing directly. They may marry a great artist or leader. The wealth and support of Denis Thatcher, a Server, was an essential ingredient in his Scholar wife Margaret Thatcher's rise to become the first female prime minister of Britain.

Servers may join a successful company, political party or religious movement, their tireless support helping them become deputy, the power behind the throne and occasionally top dog. In their negative pole they are not always very discriminating in their choice of cause and can end up supporting corrupt leaders. They will be devastated if their husband turns out to be a criminal, their boss a financial fraud or their guru a charlatan, and suffer with them if they are exposed and disgraced. If they have not bothered to investigate the values and ethics of the person or cause too closely, they will have to face up to the part they have played in the débâcle. Their tendency to carry out orders unquestioningly can lead them into immoral, dishonest or criminal actions, which cannot by any stretch be said to support the common good. In their positive pole, however, they are well equipped to soften and humanize the aggressive 'winner-takes-all' ethos of the corporate world, thus creating a much more pleasant as well as smooth-functioning environment. Their challenge at this Perspective is to learn discrimination and ally themselves to people and causes which really do advance the common good, so that they can enjoy a clean win.

Servers are more comfortable at the relationship Perspective than some other Roles, because their whole being is attuned to other people and their needs, whereas to more self-centred Roles it is like visiting a new planet. The challenge for Servers here is to go beyond their simple instinct to comfort and nurture and take into account all the different needs, viewpoints and complexities of a situation or relationship.

Psychotherapy is helpful for all Roles at this stage. Servers are more advanced emotionally than most people, but can benefit from an analytical or cognitive approach. They can find it difficult to receive rather than give help and may avoid their own problems by trying to help the therapist instead. It's really important for the Server (and their therapist) to resist this game and focus on clarifying the Server's inner processes and integrating their kind hearts with a more discriminating mind, leading to more genuinely effective service. They also need to ask for and receive back from their partners and families the loving support they so gladly give. If they can stick with the sometimes painful process of inner exploration, they will find deeper sources of inspiration to take their own inspiration to a higher level. They will also learn to help people in non-material ways such as supporting them through emotional crises.

Philosophically oriented Servers are a great blessing wherever they are found. They integrate their devotion and practical skills with a philosophical outlook that can take into account broader social and spiritual issues. As a result they are greatly loved, totally trusted and frequently consulted. In other words, the control they seek at the competing Perspective now comes to them naturally, but they will not abuse it.

Philosophically oriented Servers are naturally drawn to religion and spirituality, preferring paths of prayer and devotional service. Meditation is less appealing, as they are prone to see it as self-centred, but it can prove tremendously beneficial in helping them to glimpse an interdependent reality beyond their microcosmic concerns.

One of the most famous real-life examples of a Server living from the positive pole of service was Mother Teresa. She is widely considered the archetypal saint of the modern world, despite various criticisms. Her outlook expresses Server values in an elevated, spiritualized yet accessible form. One of her many sayings that sum up her inspiration is: 'In this life we cannot do great things. We can only do small things with great love. Love begins by taking care of the closest ones – the ones at home.'

However, at this Perspective Servers can begin to function more confidently in groups and on the world stage, as spiritual teachers and peacemakers. Nelson Mandela is one of the most successful and uplifting examples, promoting a compassionate but practical political vision: 'If you want to make peace with your enemy, you have to work with your enemy. Then he becomes your partner.' He speaks from the heart, connecting with his fellow human beings in words forged out of the bitterest experience transformed into loving kindness.

◆◆◆◆◆◆

The formula for success, happiness and self-mastery in this system is a simple but powerful three-step process:

1. *Discover your Role.*

2. *Integrate it with your Perspective.*

3. *Operate from their positive poles.*

I hope by now you recognize whether you are a Server or whether it is your secondary Role. Identifying your Role is the first step on a lifelong journey of self-discovery. The insight needs to be confirmed and applied in daily life on an ongoing basis for best results, so requires commitment, but with practice it becomes second nature. The reward of self-transformation is well worth the effort.

Secondary Role Influences for Servers

One of the most important factors influencing the personality variations between people who share the same Role is the secondary Role. This colours, flavours and generally modifies your personality. The combination works like an omelette: your primary Role is the egg, while your secondary Role is the added ingredient – cheese, mushroom, tomato. Sometimes the flavour is subtle, sometimes it overpowers the egg. Similarly, the secondary Role can manifest more strongly than the primary Role, particularly if it corresponds with your profession. Some people have the same Role in both the primary and secondary position, so will conform more closely with the Role archetype. If this is your case, you will probably recognize yourself quite easily. This section summarizes the influence of the other six Roles on Servers.

Artisan-Servers

These will be more creative and dress with more style and flair than usual. Their preferred areas of service will offer more scope for creativity through making or fixing things. Domestically, they would rather cook, sew or garden than clean, and their homes will be tasteful and beautiful as well as welcoming. They may work in the arts, like actresses Laura Dern and Mariel Hemingway. They can be quite animated and talkative, and are popular as friends and colleagues. Women with this combination are the ideal girlfriend or wife for many men, looking good and being sweet and feminine.

Sage-Servers

They will be more colourful and communicative than most Servers, having a way with words and a ready wit. They require a more theatrical appreciation of their efforts on your behalf; clasped hands and gasps of amazed pleasure will go down well. In the workplace, they will organize parties and outings. They are the mainstay of amateur dramatic and choral societies and may take to the stage professionally. They make excellent psychotherapists, combining Server empathy and skill at relating one to one with the Sage gift for expressing their insights. Both Roles have a gift for friendship, so they will be extremely popular with their friends and colleagues.

Priest-Servers

More cardinal and charismatic than usual, their inspiration will shine through brightly in everything they do, from the most mundane to the most exalted task. They are likely to be drawn to religious and spiritual people and causes and to become ministers or teachers or involved in a profession where service values are prominent. They will be more confident in groups than usual and may have a high profile and public platform if they see their position as enabling the common good. Mother Teresa and Archbishop Tutu are good examples of this. They can also display the manipulative tendencies of both Roles, however, and become control freaks. If they stay positive, they will be greatly loved by everyone whose path they cross.

Warrior-Servers

These Roles are very different, almost opposed energies, therefore hard to integrate smoothly. At their best, these Servers are extremely active, practical and hardworking in their service and will achieve a tremendous amount. They are an asset to any cause or project, doing the work of two or three normal workers, and will thrive in a corporate environment. They will be more loyal than usual, likely to stick with a job through thick and thin. Similarly, as marriage partners they will stand by their man or woman. They also find it easier than other Servers to stand up for themselves and not get taken for granted or treated as doormats. However, they can be quite prickly and abrasive and find it hard to handle the more aggressive side of their personality, especially if provoked.

King-Servers

These Servers will have a powerful, charismatic presence

and are unlikely to be ignored or overlooked. Instead, they are likely to rise to the top of any organization and hold down the job well. Kingly perfectionism with Server control makes them efficient but potentially difficult bosses. More positively, King leadership qualities integrated with Server interpersonal skills are an excellent combination for leadership, especially in a democratic society favouring flat management structures and consultative government. Kings ultimately lead in order to serve, so this combination is perfect for that goal, Jimmy Carter and Nelson Mandela being much admired political leader examples. These Servers are also likely to be the leading force in their family, intervening in all the issues and dramas and getting their way in all the important decisions.

Scholar-Servers

These will be more intellectually oriented than usual. As children, they do well at school; as adults, they excel in any profession requiring a good brain and administrative and interpersonal skills. In relationships they can provide intellectual companionship as well as looking after their partner immaculately. They make ideal librarians, being patient and helpful in handling enquiries as well as good with the books. They are also excellent teachers, particularly of young children, kind and patient with slow learners and understanding the importance of pastoral care as well as intellectual development. As pharmacists, they combine knowledge with helpful advice and a friendly, comforting manner. They can also flourish in academia, their interpersonal skills enabling them to manoeuvre themselves up the ladder better than more introverted Scholars. The Dalai Lama has this combination; his inspiration shines through as the world's most admired spiritual and political leader and also an excellent teacher.

Famous Servers

Florence Nightingale, Albert Schweitzer, St Thérèse of Lisieux, Meher Baba, Mother Teresa, Archbishop Tutu, Ram Dass, the Dalai Lama, Thich Nhat Hanh, Catherine of Aragon, Queen Victoria, Queen Elizabeth II, Prince Charles, Neville Chamberlain, Clementine Churchill, John Major, Eleanor Roosevelt, Jimmy Carter, John Kerry, Tipper Gore, Barbara Bush, Denis Thatcher, Nelson Mandela, Emily Post, Linda McCartney, Phil Donahue, Ingrid Bergman, Doris Day, Laura Dern, Mariel Hemingway, Mia Farrow, Emily Dickinson, Pearl Buck, Alice B. Toklas, John Steinbeck

CHAPTER 5

The Priest

'I have a dream that one day this nation will rise up and live out the true meaning of its creed: "We hold these truths to be self evident: that all men are created equal."'
MARTIN LUTHER KING, JR

The Priest Personality

Priests are the cardinal inspiration Role, responsible for values, morals and ethics in society. They are visionaries who provide charismatic leadership to groups of people, uniting them in an enterprise, cause or belief system. Wherever they work, they want to make a difference. They are adept at converting confusion into clarity, fear into faith. Their own faith is boundless. They believe in miracles and understand the power of love and positive thinking in making dreams come true. Priests see your best possibilities and can inspire, goad and motivate you to achieve your goals. Their sights are set on a better world and they can see what needs to be done to achieve that mission. Whatever their political beliefs, most would agree with the message of (Priest) President Barack Obama: 'It's only when you hitch your wagon to something larger than yourself that you will realize your true potential.'

Since the word 'priest' has such strong religious associations, it's important to understand that the Role is not identical with the spiritual function. There is an archetypal connection, because Priests founded and led most of the world's religions as well as the institution of priesthood, and they naturally possess the qualities and skills for this work. But all the Roles can be good priests and ministers. Conversely, most Priests nowadays do not work in a religious context, especially in the West, where the scientific worldview is dominant. Psychiatry has taken over from religion as the authority for mental and spiritual health, with Freud and Jung as its 'High Priests', and many Priests work as psychotherapists and counsellors. They can be equally inspirational as political and military leaders, motivational coaches, community activists, healers, musicians or in any walk of life.

The goal of this system is to live from the positive pole of your Role, which for Priests is compassion. They are filled with compassion for suffering humanity and want to take care of all the sad, lonely, troubled and hungry people in the world. They feel your pain, have a fine instinct for seeing where you're stuck in your life and want to help you grow to become your best self. People often spontaneously unburden their souls and pour out their most intimate problems to them, treating them like counsellors or confessors.

'It is my greatest joy to have those rare moments when I can offer insight into a relationship issue to someone and see that it makes an important difference.'
MIKE, ELECTRICAL ENGINEER

They may not have as much skill at identifying their own problems; self-criticism is always much harder. However, at their best they offer a quality of perception, diagnosis and advice which is unparalleled.

Like Servers, Priests are motivated by a desire to be of service to humanity. Whereas Servers like to look after people's comfort and practical needs, Priests are concerned with their development or spiritual needs. Servers comfort, Priests bless. Servers are concerned with the common good, Priests seek the higher good. They often feel connected or plugged in to a higher power, which is the source of their inspiration. For religious Priests, this is God or Spirit, but others can experience it as Reason, Nature, Art (or their Muse) and above all Love. Some simply follow their own intuition, an inner knowing of what to do and say in a situation, how to move forward. They have a permanent dual consciousness, divided between everyday and ideal reality. Their higher good may not always be uppermost in their minds but is a permanent undercurrent in their daily life. Their challenge is to integrate the two levels of reality and they may feel guilty if they can't do so.

Every Priest needs a mission to give their life meaning and purpose:

'I have always had a very strong sense of mission, that there is something I have come into this life to do and it is imperative that I do that, I complete that.'
TARIN, HOUSEWIFE

They may struggle to find it, especially if they are in an unsympathetic environment like an office where the goal is simply to get the job done and go home, but they will not rest or feel fulfillled till they have found it. Some have to struggle against inner disincentives:

'My challenge is that the body type I have would love to lie on the couch and eat bon-bons, but my insides say full steam ahead on changing and healing the world.'
CATERINA, LIFE COACH/COUNSELLOR

but once they find a cause that really stirs them, they gain confidence and can rapidly be propelled from obscurity into an influential leadership position.

A Priest's mission usually involves helping or healing people. It can be a local campaign or stretch to encompass a dream of a better society or an exalted vision of salvation or enlightenment. Priests love grand gestures, but also see that one small step in the right direction can be the beginning of major transformation. Their message may be uniquely their own or (perhaps more often) it can be the active promotion of an existing cause. They rarely initiate a new ideology – Scholars normally do this – but they create the movement around the cause. It follows that they are quite likely to encounter resistance and opposition to their ideas, and as a result they have developed strong political skills to counter objections. In fact, they are the most politically astute of all the Roles and prefer dealing with hostility to complacent indifference.

Both Servers and Priests are community minded, but while Servers like to connect with individuals and attend to practical needs, Priests create and lead the communities. In order to fulfill their mission, they need to engage the support of other people. To spread the word, they need a platform and a following from which to reach out. These could be called a pulpit and a congregation respectively (to keep the ecclesiastical flavour), although lectern and supporters would be the modern equivalents. Priests are very successful at motivating people to support a cause, collecting signatures for a petition, setting up a campaign, putting on a benefit gig. If they find themselves leading an army, they can rally the troops brilliantly, like Joan of Arc and Napoleon. Even the most modest Priest will have a devoted following among their friends and colleagues.

Although comprising only a small fraction of the population (around 5 percent), Priests have a disproportionate impact and can shape the culture and beliefs of entire nations. Hedonistic, materialistic Western culture currently does not offer them many opportunities, since they flourish and are most appreciated when times are hard and people need messages of hope and inspiration. That may be about to change, but meanwhile there are some major issues attracting them. In the mid-20th century the civil rights movement was their great cause. Nowadays many Priests see the interfaith movement, which seeks to bring about reconciliation between different religions, as being of supreme importance. Notably, former British prime minister Tony Blair says that he is dedicating his life to this cause. Since he has many other attractive options open to him, this is a significant choice. The environmental movement was established by Scholars like James Lovelock, but many of its current standard bearers are Priests, such as the co-founder of Greenpeace, Robert Hunter. The business world offers many opportunities, particularly to competing Priests who may make prosperity or organizational change their higher good, investing capitalist principles with a mystical glow and preaching synergy between money and God. Relationship-oriented Priests are often involved in ethical business or using the power of capitalism to help developing countries. Looking towards the future, much of the world's wealth is accumulating into fewer and fewer hands, driving the population into poverty. This imbalance offers an opportunity for Priests to lead a movement for social justice and the redistribution of wealth.

The Challenge of the Negative Pole

It is easy to see the appeal of being a Priest as a Role conferring charisma, power and glamour. But like all Roles they have a negative pole, which is zeal. It arises out of their sincere desire to help people, improve their lives or save their souls. The intensity and drive that fuel their mission make it easy for them to tip over into zeal or fanaticism when they are stressed. Some less attractive forms this takes – as noted by some of the Priests I interviewed – include being self-righteous or holier-than-thou, puritanical, moralistic, didactic, narrow-minded, sanctimonious or hypocritical. When they fall into zeal, they become totally convinced that they know what's best for you, but there are always strings attached. Whether or not you want their help, they will hammer away till you accept their point of view or tell them to get lost. Most Priests simply do not realize that their attempts at helping people may be very unwelcome to the person on the other end of their missionary zeal. All Priests have a tendency to believe that they have a direct hotline to God, or whatever they believe to be the source of good and authority. This can appear an extraordinary claim to other roles, particularly when it manifests as a guru complex or messianic delusion. If they are wise, at this point the flock will decide to part company with their shepherd.

Their negative pole manifests most fanatically at the rule-bound and competing Perspectives. At the rule-bound Perspective, Priests are inflexibly conservative as fundamentalist preachers, condemning sinners to all the torments of hellfire. At the competing Perspective their zeal can be triggered by any questioning of or resistance to their ideas, which they feel as a threat to themselves, their ideology and their congregation. They rule by promoting fear and superstition in order to control people, making them feel guilty and unworthy. They brand their critics as heretics, punish them and in extreme cases put them to death. Examples are the Holy Inquisition and Crusades in medieval Europe, the witch trials in Salem, the communist purges of the USSR and the anti-communist excesses of McCarthyism. Yet even the most malevolent, fanatical Priest can show small moments of compassion. Adolf Hitler's first act on becoming Chancellor of Germany was to ban the live boiling of lobsters in Germany.

At the relationship Perspective, Priests become more sophisticated and softer in their approach. They may campaign zealously and self-righteously for social reform and goad all their friends into joining their cause, but at least the cause will be good. They can help friends or clients with their crises skilfully and compassionately, but if zeal takes hold they will come across as overly intense, preachy and probing. Most Priests are unaware of this effect on people and saddened that their well-meant efforts to be of service are not appreciated, but they can also get angry if you don't take their advice.

At the philosophical Perspective, they are much less likely to fall into zeal. If they do, it will be much more subtle and typically fuelled by a belief in their own enlightenment. Whoever is the focus of their attention will feel fortunate, even blessed. However, Priests tend to move on to someone else as soon as they've finished with you, which can leave you feeling abandoned, as if you've just been signed up for a cause but the recruiter has rushed off to sign the next person. This should not necessarily be held against them, since they perceive their mission as more important than bonding with one person. One Priest at the philosophical Perspective explained how the negative pole manifests and how she deals with it:

'The over-zealousness is driven by fear – fear that I won't be able to fulfill my mission. I have had to acknowledge that fear, face it, surrender it to Spirit and let it be transformed into deep faith. That's how the negative pole of Priest is transformed into compassion. When I'm coming from True Self, I naturally, spontaneously and effortlessly connect with people heart to heart. People feel drawn to me and they feel safe to "confess their sins", because they are received with no judgement, only acceptance, love and compassion.'

TARIN, HOUSEWIFE

How to Recognize a Priest

Often the first thing you notice about a Priest is their energy – dynamic, high octane, always speeding away on an urgent mission. Priests have a charismatic presence and find it hard to go unnoticed in public, even if they want to be anonymous. Modest Priests may be quite unaware of their effect on people, but their friends, colleagues and even strangers will feel it and be drawn to them. Even if they are not classically beautiful, Priests have an inner radiance that makes them highly attractive to other people. Women in particular often have a soulful or ethereal quality, like a madonna or muse. Their eyes are typically very bright, intense and penetrating – glowing with compassion or burning with zeal. When they look at you, you feel they're gazing into your soul, or maybe that they have designs on you.

Priests in full flow are easy to recognize, particularly if they are spiritually oriented. Less confident, lower-key Priests can be mistaken for Servers, though even without a public mission their personality is more imposing. (*See the case history on page 118 for an example of this.*) When you first meet a Priest they can look like an Artisan, particularly if they are stylish and artistic, since both Roles have a buzzy, high-frequency energy and can be very talkative. Intellectual Priests can sometimes seem like Scholars, especially if they are lower frequency and work in education, though their inspiration usually shines through quickly. If they hold a responsible position in government, business or the army, where action is more important than inspiration, they can seem more solid, like Kings or Warriors. Some Priests communicate their message as entertainers, so can initially seem like Sages, though their performance is more intense. The differences between Priest Bob Dylan and Sage Mick Jagger make this clear.

Priest Style

Priests tend to be uninterested in clothes, since their sights are set on higher aims. If they do enjoy fashion, they need to justify their interest as a requirement to 'honour your inner Goddess'. They are likely to be aware of the ethical implications of shopping, buy fair-trade clothing and encourage others to do the same. Their taste tends to veer more towards the bohemian, favouring natural fabrics, soft textures, loose and flowing shapes. However, they are happy to 'power dress' if they need to impress at a business meeting. They often feel very comfortable in a robe.

'At work, I always wear a jacket. I used to think that it was because I got cold easily until I heard that Priests liked to wear robes and that really hit home with me. I love jackets that feel like robes.'

JOSEPHINA, MANAGEMENT CONSULTANT

Priests are also attuned to the symbolism and energies of colour, favouring black (authority), white (purity) and purple (ecclesiastical). More sophisticated Priests like Martin Luther King Jr see beyond abstract symbolism to the reality of people's greater needs: 'It's all right to talk about "long white robes over yonder", in all of its symbolism. But ultimately people want some suits and dresses and shoes to wear down here.'

Even if they are not fashion conscious, Priests are aware of the power of image to influence people and are skilled at controlling and presenting their image to maximize their popular appeal. President Barack Obama is a Priest, and commentators have noted his success in projecting an image that skilfully combines Kennedy-era classicism with a more contemporary youthful appeal. He has been idolized as a matinée idol and claimed as a muse by top designers. But his appeal is considered to go beyond youthful vigour, handsomeness, fresh ideas and even inspiring rhetoric, residing in his uniquely charismatic luminosity.

Being more attuned to the spiritual than earthly realm, Priests sometimes have difficulty adapting to life in a body, feeling pulled down by it. Priests in the competing Perspective, prone to extremism, are liable to condemn the body as sinful in its sexuality and mortify it with fasting and flagellation. Their challenge is to be compassionate towards the body as well as the soul. In the relationship and philosophical Perspectives, they come to terms with their physicality, viewing the body as a temple to be kept clean and pure, and experimenting with purifying practices and faddy diets like veganism, detoxing, breatharianism and colonic irrigation.

Priests may see their home as just a base from which to run their mission. They are not usually interested in home decoration, preferring simplicity, but they do like spaciousness and high ceilings. Many Priests have an open-house policy like a vicar, welcoming callers at all hours, especially those in distress. They often feel more at home in a place of worship – church, synagogue, mosque or temple – than a house, even if they are not formally religious. One described looking for a place to stay in an unknown town, being drawn to a bed-and-breakfast place and discovering that it had originally been a small church:

'When I got there, I had such a feeling of "coming home" and felt really at peace.'

JOSEPHINA, MANAGEMENT CONSULTANT

At the philosophical perspective, Priests' sense of sacred space extends beyond religious buildings into nature. Groves of trees become their cathedral, springs and wells their holy water.

'Pretty much as far back as I can remember, I have always had "special places" out in nature where I would go to be alone and just commune with Spirit. As an adult this practice became more conscious and deliberate. I would go out into the mountains and find my "power spot", then visit that same place over and over again when I had free time. I would go there to sit quietly for meditation and prayer and communion with Spirit. These days I have a place very near my home I go to daily for spiritual practices.'

TARIN, HOUSEWIFE

Diana: People's Princess and Priest

Diana, Princess of Wales, may seem an unlikely choice to illustrate the Role of Priest, but inspiration can take many forms. Priests are adept at using attributes like fame, glamour and beauty to attract people's attention and make them more receptive to a deeper message. Dig a little deeper beneath the media images and Diana's inspiration shines through. Her beauty was dazzling but soulful, with unforgettably sparkling eyes. She captured the spirit of the age, putting more faith in psychics than politicians and embodying many powerful archetypes, from fairy-tale princess to wounded healer, from superstar to saint.

In her youth she struggled to find her mission, being expected only to make a good marriage, which she certainly achieved. Her marriage to Prince Charles launched her as the biggest female celebrity since Jackie Kennedy. However, this was only her public persona, expressing her Artisan secondary Role. All that was required of the Princess of Wales was to produce heirs (preferably male) and turn up at functions. Instead, she turned a routine job into a high-profile mission: to modernize and humanize the archaic institution of the royal family.

Instinctively sensing her cardinal leadership potential, in contrast to her ordinal Server husband, she found it hard to take a back seat. Her first independent step was to remove a symbolic barrier: the gloves that royal functionaries were expected to wear. She also quickly discarded many routine aspects of the job in favour of charities of her own choice. Her support for AIDS patients at a time when the illness was viewed with tremendous fear is considered one of the most important turning points in public opinion, while her support for the victims of landmines was an important influence in their abolition. These were controversial choices for a princess, but made her an inspirational role model for millions of people, particularly the misfits and rejects of society. She said: 'Nothing gives me more happiness than to try to aid the most vulnerable of this society. Whoever is in distress who calls me, I will come running.'

Priests often exemplify the archetype of the wounded healer, having the ability to transform their own sufferings into compassion towards others' suffering. Diana was a classic example. She had an unhappy childhood, which taught her empathy. She said, 'I understand people's suffering, people's pain, more than you will ever know yourself.' People felt better if she sat on their bed and held their hands, simply from the healing power of her presence.

Unfortunately, once she left the royal family after her divorce she could not sustain her mission. Then her negative pole emerged in self-righteousness, paranoid conspiracy theories, counter-plots and revenge tactics. However, she was able to switch back to the positive pole of compassion through finding a new, broader mission: 'Helping people in need is a good and essential part of my life, a kind of destiny.'

Like many high-profile Priests, she was a controversial figure who polarized public opinion. Widely adored, she was also sharply criticized as a 'loose cannon' and an attention-seeking, self-serving, scheming narcissist. Her Priestly unpredictability was part of her fascination: 'I'm a free spirit.' In her adroit negotiations concerning her position and her dealings with the media she displayed (but denied) finely tuned political skills. Some felt that her courting of media attention did not help her children and brought into disrepute the institution she represented, but she used the publicity to draw attention to her favourite causes.

Despite her flaws, many people loved Diana as a victim who spoke for their own woundedness. Women in particular saw their own concerns, passions and pains mirrored in her sufferings, which were typical of millions in unhappy marriages. The combination of beauty and glamour with the sufferings of a wronged wife made it easy for them to worship her and forgive her 'sin' of adultery. The then prime minister Tony Blair called her the 'People's Princess', a name that stuck. Her own self-selected title was 'Queen of Hearts'. In the same television interview she proclaimed, 'I think people need someone in public life to give affection, make them feel important, give them light in their dark tunnels.'

While the original fairy tale of a Cinderella ('Shy Di') who married her prince turned sour, the tragic ending of her life story took her to legendary status. It is a strange fact about Priests that many die young, through burning the candle at both ends, pursuing dangerous causes regardless of personal safety and sometimes a desire for martyrdom. Early death has the effect of raising their reputation to iconic, sometimes saintly status. Some examples are Joan of Arc, St Thomas à Becket, Martin Luther King, Che Guevara and John Lennon. At the time of Diana's death, her reputation was at its lowest ebb, but it turned around overnight. In his funeral eulogy her brother Lord Spencer described her as 'the very essence of compassion', i.e., exemplifying the positive pole of her Role. The so-called Diana effect heralded the end of 'selfish' 1980s materialism and the start of a much looser, caring, self-disclosing, feminized society. She did not initiate this change, which had been going on since the 1960s, but as a royal superstar she made it acceptable. This is her wider legacy and impact on popular culture and public life.

The Priest at Work

Priests are found in all jobs and professions, but are happiest in a job where they can use their inspiration to be of service. Servers and Priests share this motivation and so work well together. Both Roles predominate in the helping and healing professions, including teaching, the social services and medicine, often working in teams led by a Priest. Their natural healing talent helps them excel in any work concerned with health and wellbeing, though they are more drawn to the spiritual than physical aspects. They respond well to crisis, being unfazed by suffering, which brings out the best in them, and are often unafraid of death. They therefore prefer to work in something like bereavement counselling or with the critically ill rather than the worried well.

Priests are at home in a religious setting, ministering to their congregations as pastors, rabbis, mullahs, bishops and popes. It's been observed that one of the most iconic figures in American history is the travelling preacher, who is an archetypal Priest. Today's preachers are televangelists like Billy Graham and Oral Roberts, who command a national congregation. Priests fervently believe that faith is the way forward and can work miracles: 'Only believe!' Nowadays they are often more drawn to become therapists, psychiatrists or healers, since most people are more open to spiritual healing from these sources. As counsellors they are extremely inspiring, but often reluctant to get embroiled in the nitty-gritty of a personal issue, urging people to move on. Generally they prefer working with groups of people, but can work one to one in the counselling relationship as a short, temporary interaction with boundaries allowing some distance between the two people. They like to maintain a certain mystique, a bit like papal infallibility – a very Priestly doctrine.

'I think most Priests find it awkward to deal with others in a very personal sense. I think we are much more comfortable in a professional or non-personal relationship. It seems Priests like to stay looking like Priests as much of the time as possible.'

PATRICIA

When Priests commit their vision to writing, they produce some of the world's most inspirational and brilliant literature. Many of the most sublime poets were Priests, including Dante, Milton and all the best Romantic poets. Some of the greatest novelists have also been Priests, though such Priests are unlikely to remain desk-bound and more likely to use their writing in the service of some greater social or religious vision, as did Leo Tolstoy and D. H. Lawrence. Priests also write many of the most inspiring self-help books with motivational titles like *How to Win Friends and Influence People* or *Feel the Fear and Do It Anyway*.

Science may not seem their most likely career, but there are Priest scientists, including Richard Dawkins. Nicknamed 'Darwin's Rottweiler' by the media, he may appear more like a Warrior (as Thomas Huxley, 'Darwin's Bulldog', certainly was), but he is viewed as an 'evangelical atheist' who has created a counter-religion out of Darwinism and evolutionary biology. Many people feel Dawkins is doing a great service to humanity in his mission to eradicate the superstition typical of the rule-bound Perspective that predominates in conservative schools which attempt to control the minds of children by only teaching creationism.

Music is often seen as bringing people closer to God than anything except prayer and some of the most uplifting classical composers have been Priests, for example Richard Wagner. They are also drawn to popular music. "Amazing Grace," the favourite gospel song, was written by a slave trader turned abolitionist and minister (in a dramatic Priestly conversion), and the best version is sung by a Priest (Mahalia Jackson). Perhaps surprisingly, many rock stars are also Priests. Bob Dylan has repeatedly stated his belief that he has a purpose and mission, and he was seen as the messiah of the civil rights movement. His music is deeply imbued with religious and spiritual imagery, from 'The Times They Are a-Changin'' to 'Spirit on the Water'. Another rock god/ Priest was Jimi Hendrix, whose most iconic moment was the ceremonial burning of his guitar at Woodstock: 'The time I burned my guitar it was like a sacrifice.' Another dramatic example of a Priest using music for a higher cause was Sinead O'Connor singing 'War' by Bob Marley (another Priest) on television and exhorting her audience to fight against evil as she tore up a photograph of the pope.

Many Priests flourish in business. Anita Roddick was a Priest entrepreneur who created a global brand (The Body Shop) out of a small shop. Her motto was 'Business is more powerful than politics, and it's more powerful than religion,' and she proved it by successfully campaigning for ethical business practice and human rights. Priests are also excellent motivational coaches and corporate trainers who can galvanize a workforce and transform a whole organization with their vision, enthusiasm, positive thinking and can-do attitude.

The jobs a Priest will feel most comfortable with are ones that involve interfacing with as many people as possible. Sales and marketing offer excellent opportunities for this, and most Priests enjoy the process of going out, meeting strangers and persuading them to buy a service or product. Personnel management can be a good choice; better still, corporate training. Priests can also be found as financial advisors with a mission to help their clients against the corporate world or preaching 'prosperity consciousness':

'My ministry is the business world. People have told me that I'm a good person to work for. I know a few other Priests that I've heard their employees rave about. I think it's because we tend to care about people and can really focus on helping them get ahead or find what they need to be successful. To me, there's nothing more satisfying than seeing someone become a success after I've worked with them or coached them.

JOSEPHINA, MANAGEMENT CONSULTANT

Leadership Style

Priests are excellent leaders whose political instincts and skills will get them into the top job if they believe that is where they are meant to be. Once they achieve power, their cardinality enables them to see the bigger picture and ways through difficulties that other people have missed. They always feel they are the ones who can make a difference, turn the company around. Unlike Kings, though, attention to detail is not one of their talents. This is fine if they can delegate to an efficient Warrior or Server, otherwise it can undermine the success of their plan, though by that time the Priest has either moved on or found some way not to be held accountable.

It can be hard for Priests to recognize and accept their leadership skills if they do not receive encouragement and opportunities, and this is particularly true of women. Here is a case study of a woman in Finland who achieved success once she had validated her Priest Role, which enabled her to take on a leadership function with confidence. Her story is equally relevant to men lacking confidence.

> Heidi used to be a hardworking restaurant worker with no real career ambitions, afraid of standing in front of a crowd. She managed to get promoted to HR manager, but felt stuck and distressed, sensing a clash of values with the company she worked for. Just after her new appointment, all managers in the company were introduced to a new leadership and communication training course, Keys to Balance, directed by a Priest (*see Resources section*). Heidi at first clung to the belief that she was a Server, but when the Priest Role was clearly explained, it suddenly hit her that this was her true type. She loved giving advice, and people were naturally drawn to her for counselling, though she found it hard to believe that Priests loved being leaders and standing in front of people, as this still terrified her. Nevertheless the revelation of her Role was a true turning point in her life. She actively grew into the Role and became more balanced, taking on leadership issues. She discovered her mission: to transform the workplace into a more humane environment for everyone. She succeeded in

many ways, becoming a real asset as a moral leader. However, she felt something important was missing: not being able to really live according to her values and operate on a broader scale.

Eventually, after over 15 years of service in the restaurant business, Heidi took on the challenge of a new job in a different area. She is now responsible for leadership and management programmes in a big training institute. What really excites her is helping people develop their leadership skills in other companies. She plans and facilitates the leadership programmes and now really enjoys speaking up, as she loves her new work. Heidi has never had doubts about her job change, having found her mission: helping people by giving advice and waking them up. It's now possible for her to share the values of her workplace, influencing many leaders and companies with great training programmes and also helping develop more branches. The work is very rewarding, as it's long-term planning and she can see the change taking place in people.

Communication Style

As with everything they do, Priests' communication has a higher purpose. Being cardinal, they feel more comfortable talking to and working with large numbers of people than in one-to-one relationships. Those who have found their mission are gifted public speakers, preachers, prophets and propagandists. Rarely relying on scripts and notes, they are easily able to sway an audience to tears of joy or rage, leading to belief or action. Some of history's greatest orators have been Priests rallying their congregation behind a cause, like

Martin Luther, Martin Luther King or Barack Obama, rallying the troops like Julius Caesar, Joan of Arc or Napoleon, and uplifting people to ecstasy – and action – through poetry and music like Milton or Shelley, Bob Marley or Bob Dylan.

Other Roles can find it hard to understand Priests and see the vision that is so very clear to them, since we live in a rational age. Priests persuade through sheer force of charisma and belief, unworried about self-contradiction or getting facts wrong as long as the moral point is right. A Priest motivational trainer faced with a barrage of criticism shouted back at the audience, 'I don't want your critiques, just give me your emotions!' Priests will be interested in information that supports and furthers their cause but likely to discard any inconvenient facts that cast doubt on it. Their justifications can be obscure and impenetrable, but by the time you've discovered the lack of substance, the Priest has moved on and will dismiss your objections as old news. This cavalier attitude towards truth is infuriating to more literal-minded people, particularly Scholars, who are the Role most likely to challenge a Priest, demanding evidence and proof. Despite their good case, they may lose, as Priests are so slippery and adept at changing the ground rules and counter-attacking.

Sages are more likely to respond with wit, mercilessly deflating and debunking Priests' more arcane claims and pretensions. Some years ago, for example, a very senior British police officer announced to the press that he had been communicating with God. This received widespread publicity, as he was controversial anyway. It is seen as acceptable, if eccentric, to talk to God in a religious context, but highly inappropriate for a policeman dealing with high-level sensitive matters to bypass his superiors' orders in favour of personal revelation. A satirical magazine called *Private Eye*, run of course by Sages, broke the story, headlined 'Inspector Knacker Talks to God'. There followed a hilarious commentary on what God might say to a policeman, complete with cartoons of a cop talking to a bearded figure.

Life is very serious to a high-minded Priest and they are not renowned for their sense of humour, unless they have a Sage secondary Role. More sophisticated Priests understand the power of humour and how it can open and relax people, get them on their side and make them more receptive to their message. They can learn to use it quite effectively as a tool or weapon in their campaign and are not averse to undermining their enemies' position with ridicule.

Priests are always on the lookout for new methods of communication to spread the word and have taken enthusiastically to the internet. They forward petitions and inspirational circulars regularly unless pulled up for spamming. Many have a website and send out regular missives to rally their flock. These websites often host a forum, charismatically moderated, on which posters are encouraged to interact with each other and become a community. These web-centred communities can become large and influential and be used as powerful campaigning tools.

There is something about a Priest that is decidedly intense and extreme – and that can be hard for others to handle. People either love them or hate them, or feel confused and ambivalent because they sense something self-serving or sanctimonious but can't put their finger on it as Priests are so skilled at evading criticism. It is generally easier to admire and be inspired by them from a distance than to be intimate with them. This is equally frustrating for Priests themselves:

'It can be challenging [to be a Priest] because it is certainly not "the norm" or mainstream. I tend to see things very differently to others. I seek out depth, see things symbolically, am very moved by many things that inspire me. I feel great passion about making a difference in this world and bringing out the best in others. It can be lonely because Priests are a low percentage of the population.'

CATERINA, LIFE COACH/COUNSELLOR

It is hard to communicate with Priests at the competing Perspective except by becoming a follower or supporter. At the relationship Perspective they work hard to improve their interpersonal skills. In social situations they are uninterested in small talk, preferring soul-to-soul communication. This is wonderfully uplifting, but can make people uncomfortable if it happens too fast, particularly as Priests are not always willing to be open and forthcoming in return. It's hard for them to be just good friends rather than your confessor or counsellor. Friends sometimes get annoyed by their tendency to sermonize and preach, though if made aware of this effect, most Priests will back off a bit. However, you do need to actively support them and their causes if you want to stay friends with them. At the philosophical Perspective they become much more tolerant and accepting of people as they are and so can sustain an equal relationship in which their communication abilities can flourish.

'Ever since I was a little girl, people have told me their problems. One of the things I've learned over the years is how to temper my Priestly tendency to tell other people what I see about them or how I feel about them. Most people, in my experience, really are not ready to have someone point out their faults and how they can fix them, or tell them how they can get their life back on track. I've learned to be much softer in my comments. It's made me a better person and a much better counsellor and consultant to those I work with – in the business world or in personal situations.'

JOSEPHINA, MANAGEMENT CONSULTANT

The Priest in Love

Priests are adept at using their charm and charisma to attract and seduce a lover. Even without Priests trying, people will naturally gravitate into their orbit and be captivated, but may also misinterpret their compassion as romantic interest or exaggerate the degree of attachment the Priest really feels towards them. As a result, Priests tend to leave a trail of broken hearts behind them, however unintentionally. One says: 'For me, when I'm in love, I am the most caring person, totally focused on the person I'm with, surrounding them with love and joy. When the "glow" wears off, it can get pretty nasty.'

They have a strong sex drive, which helps ground them in their bodies. They tend to go to extremes with it, either multiple partners (sometimes promiscuity) or celibacy. However, they can be monogamous if they find the partner who can fulfill all their needs. Sex can also be used inspirationally by them to nourish, heal or express compassion and mercy.

Priests are irresistible at the courtship stage, sweeping you off your feet, taking you to ecstatic heights of romance, putting you on a pedestal and idolizing you as their god or goddess. Once the initial courtship is over and both come down to earth, they can be quite tough on their partners, expecting perfection but not giving much in return.

'I had to work on being realistic in my expectations and not expecting the ideal from a partner.'
CATERINA, LIFE COACH/COUNSELLOR

Their challenge in relationship is to help their partners open their hearts and feel good by inspiring them to grow, rather than making them feel guilty for not achieving their own high standards.

Priests themselves often value independence more than personal relationships. As a result it can be said that nobody owns a Priest, even those who are married to one. They may give you their heart, but rarely their soul. Commitment doesn't always come easily to them:

'I think Priests are prone to a modicum of self-deception; if they do not honour that commitment, they tend to justify not doing so with a lofty reason.'
PATRICIA

In marriage, the dream can fade rapidly for both partners. Priests find it hard to make one person the recipient of their inspiration and once the novelty wears off their spouse can easily be relegated to the background of their lives and expected to keep the home fires burning while they charge off on a new mission. Ultimately their mission comes first, and if you want to continue to be an important part of their life you need to share their cause.

'My challenge is that I have an incredibly strong drive to be "out there" making a difference. A partner has to understand that and be willing to work with that.'
CATERINA, LIFE COACH/COUNSELLOR

If you try and force a Priest to choose between their cause and you, you are likely to be the loser. This can mean celebrating your birthday alone, being abandoned on Valentine's Day or having plans changed at the last minute. The good news is that with minimal effort they can continue to inspire their partners, even without realizing it.

'In my marriage I don't feel particularly inspiring – more like a dud. When I asked my wife about this, she said I had inspired her to look at things in different ways and do a good job of clarifying spiritual ideas.'
MIKE, ELECTRICAL ENGINEER

In general, Priests and Servers have the highest degree of mutual attraction, understanding and compatibility, being the cardinal and ordinal inspiration Roles. When two Priests come together they may feel they have found a soulmate, but each will want to be the leader so may find it hard to give way to their partner. Kings and Sages will also compete with Priests for leadership and limelight. Relationships with these other cardinal Roles usually work better in the workplace or as friends. Priests are often strongly attracted to the earthy sexuality of Warriors and vice versa, but they can clash over boundaries and end up fighting each other. Artisans and Priests can have a magical, ecstatic romance, but find it hard to achieve long-term stability. Scholars understand Priests better than most people, but Priests can find Scholars too analytical and critical, while Scholars find them flaky, so they are liable to fall out over ideas and beliefs. For a detailed description of the compatibilities between Priests and other Roles, see Chapter 9.

Parents and Children

Priests have divergent attitudes to children, depending on their Perspective. At the rule-bound Perspective, they see them as sinners and are prepared to use the rod to redeem them. At the competing Perspective, they will try and indoctrinate them into their own beliefs and rope them into their mission. Ironically, Priests are the Role most resistant to being indoctrinated, so if their children are also Priests their efforts will be wasted. At the relationship and philosophical Perspectives, they see them as gifts from God, precious young lives to be cherished and guided. However, they are rarely hands-on parents and once the novelty has worn off may not give them enough time and attention.

'It seems Priests tend to be a little distant (not necessarily cold) as parents. They do have expectations in their minds about their children, even if that expectation is that the children have to figure out how their own life should be lived – that still is an expectation of the child (albeit a high-minded one).'
PATRICIA

156

Parenting may take second place to their mission, which seems more urgent. Home is a place they may visit rarely, and more to recharge than anything else. They may be so busy saving the world, crusading for other people's children, that they forget about their own or treat them as ideological symbols. Family life usually works best for them if their partner is willing to do most of the hands-on childcare. Despite absence, Priests are likely to be adored by their children, sometimes to the annoyance of the parent doing all the work. However, the relationship is likely to become problematic later.

At the philosophical Perspective, Priests become exemplary parents, showering their children with love but also offering them the gift of freedom. They will guide their children into the best path for their growth and happiness – but only if asked, as they will respect their right to make their own choices.

As children, Priests often manifest their Role at a very young age, revealing a strong, independent character and a sensitivity to suffering which can make them very loving. It is important to offer them respect and sympathetic guidance and allow them as much freedom as possible to find their own path. They may take religion very seriously, imposing penances on themselves like burning their teddy bear. Even if they are born into non-religious homes, they often have a sense of spirit or God in their lives.

'I can remember at a very young age knowing that Jesus was sitting next to me, feeling his presence, and when I went to church, I knew the minister was not telling the truth about how

things really were. I knew that there were other friendly and protective spirits with me at many times in my life.'
JOSEPHINA, MANAGEMENT CONSULTANT

At school Priests can find it hard to fit in with their fellow students, being more serious and high-minded and less inclined to childish pursuits. They tend to be very service oriented, kind and helpful, which makes them popular with teachers. However, they have a strong sense of justice from an early age and if they feel something is wrong will have no hesitation in speaking up, carrying their complaint to the head teacher if necessary. Unless they are quite intellectually inclined, they are likely to be uninterested in lessons and dreamy, their minds already on higher things, but can also be quite precocious. They are likely to abandon their studies to go on a protest march.

As teenagers, they may have difficulties on the dating scene if they are not conventionally good-looking, combined with difficulties in one-to-one relationships. Most Priests quickly discover how to use their charm and charisma, though, and can become practised seducers from early on. They may skip further education unless they see it as useful to their mission or haven't found one yet. Until they do, they can be lost souls, feeling they are just marking time. Many, though, have an urgent sense of destiny which they want to follow as soon as possible, and will often make their mark very fast.

Priest Archetypes in Myth, Fiction and Film

The Greek gods were not a Priestly pantheon. It was an age in which reason predominated over faith, action over inspiration. The Bible, however, is a rich source of Priestly archetypes, particularly the Prophets. Moses is the greatest Prophet and liberator of his people. He may or may not have literally existed and led the Children of Israel out of the land of Egypt, but his cry 'Let my people go!' resonates down the ages both spiritually and politically. He represents both the positive and negative poles of the Role. The seven plagues are a truly terrible punishment of sin, and Moses preached and ranted interminably at his flock. However, he has some of the best stories and the Ten Commandments are one of the greatest ethical codes. Moses's charismatic leadership, rallying the Hebrews into courage and rebellion and boldly leading them out of slavery to freedom, has inspired many rebellions against social injustice, particularly slavery. It is understandable that black slaves related to the Exodus myth more than any other biblical story, as celebrated in gospel music, and Martin Luther King can be seen as a latter-day Moses.

There are surprisingly few fictional Priests who stand out, perhaps because Priest novelists tend to use their characters as mouthpieces to promote their vision or cause rather than reveal their personality. Wagner's operatic hero Siegfried, however, is a Priestly protagonist on an epic scale. The Ring Cycle is a grand saga based on Norse mythology, dramatizing Priestly themes of redemption, salvation and transfiguration through death. Wagner saw himself as a child of destiny with a mission to regenerate German nationalism and redeem the German soul through his operas. The philosopher Friedrich Nietzsche, another Priest, was originally a great fan of Wagner's music and part of his inner circle, but fell out with him over his misuse of philosophy for political ends. Zarathustra (Nietzsche's Superman) is an idealized Priest hero who exemplifies a vision of human potential and redemption that has been highly influential in Western culture.

Film is a more revelatory medium than literature for depicting the Priest personality, including mythologized historical characters like Joan of Arc, the subject of many movies. The great Hollywood epics *Ben-Hur* and *Spartacus* depict Priestly heroes from the heroic age of ancient Rome. Spartacus is particularly inspirational as the leader of a slave revolt in the tradition of Moses. The *Star Wars* series shows a formulaic representation of positive versus negative Priests in Luke Skywalker and Darth Vader, who both manipulate the Force for different ends. On a more touching, human scale, Cole Sear, the boy hero of *The Sixth Sense*, played by the Priest actor Haley Joel Osment, gives a vivid portrayal of what it is like for a Priest child to have psychic powers and learn to handle them.

How to Fulfill your Priest Potential

It is a great privilege and blessing to be a Priest, but it is also the hardest Role to do well. At their best, Priests can move you to tears, spark hope when you are most depressed, motivate you to fulfill your highest potential. At their worst, they can inflict great cruelty – sacrificing your body to save your soul. This section summarizes how Role and Perspective work together for growth and fulfillment.

Competing Priests are driven to succeed and win in the wider world, like all Roles at this Perspective. Their ambition knows no bounds and in the negative pole they wield their political skills ruthlessly to reach the top of their profession. They are less likely than other Roles to admit their desire to win, wanting to be seen as the good guys. They are convinced of their own righteousness, which can make them not just zealous but fanatical. Representing the beliefs of the prevailing culture, they can't tolerate difference or dissent. They become missionaries, crusaders, inquisitors or fierce nationalists rousing the masses to patriotic fervour with their oratory and hatred of foreigners. It is very hard for them to remain compassionate at this Perspective and easy for them to become deluded that their fanaticism is in the best interests of their cause, that it is acceptable to kill people just because they do not share your beliefs.

In the positive pole, their charismatic leadership can have enormous impact for political, social and religious change. They can also be effective leaders and motivators in the business world, where competing values predominate. Here they can get amazing results, galvanizing a workforce or an entire organization to become more successful and go beyond their limitations. Their lesson at this perspective is that no cause justifies the infliction of suffering on a person and that compassion will win people to their cause far more effectively.

Adjusting to the relationship perspective can be very challenging for Priests, as it involves introspection, which does not come easily to them. They often become social misfits, whether defiant or revelling in this position, perhaps as protest singers. Being marginalized is particularly painful for them because of their need for connection. The suffering can, however, be a therapeutic process which opens their hearts and softens their attitudes to others and to themselves. They feel compelled to spend more time and energy on their families, even though such a small arena feels restricting, and are rewarded with the comfort and joy of family life. Psychotherapy can also be a tremendous help to their inner search, though they find it hard to be on the receiving end.

Confusion is the biggest challenge of this Perspective, but Priests work hard and rapidly become insightful. Therapy may become their mission, and they make some of the best counsellors and psychiatrists. Since they feel so at home in a spiritual environment, they may prefer a contemplative period or even spend their whole life in a retreat centre or monastery, and are better able to benefit from the discipline than some of the other Roles. Eventually they will find a broader mission again, but it will be a more genuinely ethical or spiritual cause, and they will be equipped to become compassionate and effective leaders for the higher good of humanity.

At the philosophical Perspective, self-righteousness finally becomes true righteousness as Priests relax into their own being. This changes their attitude from the belief that they always know what's best for another person to the understanding that everyone needs to be free to find their own way and learn their own lessons, including making their own mistakes.

'I have come to believe that everyone offers their best contribution by being who they truly are, not by trying to do anything.'
MIKE, ELECTRICAL ENGINEER

Then they are able to help people achieve their potential in a much gentler, more respectful way. Their spiritual practice will deepen and can take unusual forms, such as living on a mountain for years learning occult practices. They can become the most inspirational spiritual leaders and gurus, usually outside an organized religion, since they no longer need these trappings. Instead they rely on their own inner radiance to shine through them as a guiding light to anyone attracted to their vision. They also become wise and compassionate leaders in the workplace:

'My inspiration in the workplace comes from being a catalyst for positive change, seeing positive culture change happen when people can grow to be the best they can be, when they can excel at something, when they can learn to work together, when productivity happens, when conflict becomes teamwork. I get to nurture and coach so many people and see the results. When a plan comes together and an entirely new system goes into place, it is a thing of beauty to behold. When people who are shy and unsure of themselves grow into excellent employees or competent managers, it's a true joy to watch. When the light comes on in someone's mind as they comprehend how they can accomplish a goal, my heart sings and my soul is nourished.'
JOSEPHINA, MANAGEMENT CONSULTANT

The formula for success, happiness and self-mastery in this system is a simple but powerful three-step process:

1. Discover your Role.

2. Integrate it with your Perspective.

3. Operate from their positive poles.

I hope by now you recognize whether you are a Priest or whether it is your secondary Role. Identifying your Role is the first step on a lifelong journey of self-discovery. The insight needs to be confirmed and applied in daily life on an ongoing basis for best results, so requires commitment, but with practice it becomes second nature. The reward of self-transformation is well worth the effort.

Secondary Role Influences for Priests

One of the most important factors influencing the personality variations between people who share the same Role is the secondary Role. This colours, flavours and generally modifies your personality. The combination works like an omelette: your primary Role is the egg, while your secondary Role is the added ingredient – cheese, mushroom, tomato. Sometimes the flavour is subtle, sometimes it overpowers the egg. Similarly, the secondary Role can manifest more strongly than the primary Role, particularly if it corresponds with your profession. Some people have the same Role in both the primary and secondary position, so will conform more closely with the Role archetype. If this is your case, you will probably recognize yourself quite easily. This section summarizes the influence of the other six Roles on Priests.

Artisan-Priests

A very creative combination, adding beauty and style to inspiration. These Priests dress with flair, though may feel guilty about having an interest in fashion. Women may look like fairy-tale princesses or enchantresses and become muses. They are likely to channel their inspiration into a creative endeavour, sometimes as artists. Their work will have a spiritual or religious flavour and may be full of complex symbolism. In daily life they will have greater mechanical aptitude than is usual for Priests. The master masons who built Europe's great cathedrals probably had this combination, as do some of the greatest composers and singers of classical and popular music. Artisan-Priests are brilliant at devising unique, colourful and fun rituals and ceremonies. They are likely to be very ungrounded and may be uncomfortable in their bodies and the material world generally, so need to exercise and do other physical activities to ground themselves.

Sage-Priests

With this combination Priests will be even more charismatic than usual, with a dazzling personality. These Priests know how to work their charm to achieve their ends and will be brilliant on the PR and promotional side. They are likely to be torn between the pulpit and the stage as career choices. A Broadway lyricist described theatre as his church and clapping and praying as looking the same. As actors or rock stars they will use their art to put across a message and their celebrity to support good causes. This is also one of the best combinations for writing and some of the greatest poets, dramatists and novelists have it. Alternatively, these Priests make successful hucksters and snake-oil salesmen. Intimacy is not their *forte* and they are uncomfortable in prolonged one-to-one interactions, but their relationships are likely to be full of drama.

Server-Priests

More gentle and low key than the average Priest, they will get on better in one-to-one relationships and be more willing to serve in mundane as well as exalted ways. They are likely to be drawn to religious and spiritual causes and to become ministers or teachers or involved in any profession where service values are prominent. They also make the best counsellors, finding it easier to work with individuals. They will be less high profile than is usual with Priests and less driven to lead, better able to function as part of a team. However, they can also display the manipulative tendencies of both Roles and become control freaks. If they stay positive, they will be greatly loved by everyone whose path they cross.

Warrior-Priests

This is a good combination for leadership positions, particularly in the military and business. However, these Priests can be very fanatical, uniting Priestly zeal with a Warrior concern for boundaries. Crusaders, Knights Templar and Japanese warrior monks typically have this combination. Objectivity will be very hard to achieve; everything will be black and white with nothing in between. You certainly don't want to be interrogated by someone with this combination. They can be effective missionaries, rising to the challenge and enjoying the adventure. They also make excellent doctors and healers, being attuned to people's bodies as well as souls. Being more practical and grounded than usual, they will be well respected in the workplace and able to set up their enterprises solidly. Their relative earthiness makes them better attuned to nature and animals than most Priests, who tend to have fears and allergies around animals. Since both Roles are extremely hardworking and can deal well with challenges and obstacles, this combination often leads to high achievement.

King-Priests

This is one of the two most cardinal combinations possible (the other being Priest-King). These Priests will have a compulsive drive to become a leader and will be phenomenally impressive in this position, whether in a business, political or religious context. Napoleon is an impressive historical example. It is likely that President Barack Obama and former prime minister Tony Blair both have this combination. It is ideal for the position of pope, although Benedict XVI does not have it. These are world-class movers and shakers, capable of having a global impact. Their word is law and few will dare to oppose them. They can be tyrannical as bosses, driving their workforce to the limit in support of the cause. Intimate relationships are difficult for them and their family is unlikely to get much of their time. However, in the positive pole they unite inspiration and action to the highest degree and are able to draw an enormous crowd of devoted followers to support their cause and achieve their goals.

Scholar-Priests

While Priests tend to see revelation as the only truth, with this combination they are more objective and will want to see evidence of the virtue and viability of a cause before adopting it. These Priests make excellent students and academics, writers, scientists, lawyers and doctors. It is also the ideal combination for a theologian, St Augustine being a famous example. Some of the greatest teachers and spiritual leaders have this combination. They are able to educate people through both knowledge and inspiration, but need to exercise awareness and self-control so as not to indoctrinate their students. They may be drawn to a monastic life where they can study as well as pray. More grounded than usual, they do well in business and politics, particularly as motivational trainers. Being both more stable and more objective than is usual with Priests, they are often better at one-to-one relationships and connect well with people intellectually as well as emotionally.

Famous Priests

St Paul, St Joan of Arc, St Francis of Assisi, Saint Bernadette of Lourdes, Martin Luther, Martin Luther King Jr, Rosa Parks, Mother Ann Lee, Chief Seattle, Sitting Bull, Black Elk, Pope John XXIII, Billy Graham, Julius Caesar, Emperor Constantine, Oliver Cromwell, Napoleon Bonaparte, Horatio Nelson, Vladimir Lenin, Adolf Hitler, Ayatollah Khomeini, Ernesto 'Che' Guevara, Grigori Rasputin, Barack Obama, Jesse Jackson, Rudy Giuliani, Princess Diana, Tony Blair, Hugo Chávez, Nicolas Sarkozy, Sigmund Freud, Carl

Jung, Dante Alighieri, John Milton, John Bunyan, William Wordsworth, Percy Bysshe Shelley, John Keats, Ralph Waldo Emerson, Allen Ginsberg, D. H. Lawrence, Leo Tolstoy, Aleksandr Solzhenitsyn, Herman Hesse, Amos Oz, George Bernard Shaw, Richard Wagner, John Lennon, Jimi Hendrix, Bob Dylan, Joan Baez, Leonard Cohen, Stevie Wonder, Bob Marley, Bono, Nick Cave, Sinead O'Connor, Miriam Makeba ('Mama Africa'), Robert Duvall, Haley Joel Osment, Friedrich Nietzsche, Ayn Rand, Robert Hunter, Anita Roddick, Germaine Greer, Timothy Leary, Scott Peck, Robert Atkins, Richard Dawkins

CHAPTER 6

The Warrior

'Courage is being scared to death – but saddling up anyway.'
JOHN WAYNE

The Warrior Personality

Warriors are the ordinal action Role, who actively seek and relish challenge, adventure and any opportunity for action. Their guiding principle is purpose and their aim is to 'get a result', which makes them extremely productive and usually successful. When the going gets tough, Warriors get going; they thrive on overcoming obstacles. Their capacity for hard work and structuring a task or environment makes them the backbone of any enterprise or organization. Tall in the saddle, they are brave, strong and true. They are the heroes and champions of humanity in war, sport, industry, exploration or rescuing a child from a burning house. Most Warriors would agree with General Ulysses S. Grant: 'Everyone has his superstitions. One of mine has always been when I started to go anywhere, or to do anything, never to turn back or to stop until the thing intended was accomplished.'

Since the word *warrior* has such strong associations with war, it is important to understand that the Role is not identical with the job function. While many soldiers are Warriors, all the Roles are represented in the military forces. However, there is an archetypal connection in that Warriors are the protectors of the tribe, guarding the population and their territory against threats, including invasion. Most Warriors would defend their family fiercely, even to the death, but in daily life they are not necessarily violent or aggressive. In fact, they handle violence better than most other Roles and avoid it where possible, understanding that the outcome of a fight is always unpredictable. The paradox of this Role is that while Warriors can be extremely pugnacious when the occasion demands or they lose control, they are generally good-natured, even gentle people. Which side you see depends on whether they see you as a friend or an enemy, and also on how you behave with them.

The goal of this system is to operate from the positive pole of your Role, which for Warriors is persuasion. Full of drive, focused and dynamic, they have a great ability to motivate people to get up and move. Extremely hardworking and productive themselves, they expect the same of others. This means that a project gets not only started but finished rather than remaining in the mind or on the drawing board. Their persuasive abilities are particularly useful in any situation where people are stuck on account of laziness, stubbornness or the fear of trying out an idea in case it fails. Warriors also make excellent salespeople, and they pride themselves on being able to sell anything to anyone.

The Warrior instinct for boundaries is central to their outlook on life. A boundary can take many forms, from a castle wall or perimeter fence to a code of behaviour for children or adults. It includes chains of command in corporate or social hierarchies – very important for Warriors. It also extends to time; if they are invited to dinner for 8 P.M. they will arrive on the dot. Boundaries need to be maintained and guarded, and only in approved circumstances can people be permitted to cross them. Rules need to be made and kept to control behaviour and maintain discipline.

At the competing Perspective, Warriors see the world starkly polarized into good and evil; they need to know if you are for or against them. A famous example is George W. Bush's challenge in 2001: 'Either you are with us, or you are with the terrorists.' If you are on the wrong side, you must be an enemy. If you are family, friend or ally, though, Warriors will be fiercely loyal, protective and supportive.

At the relationship and philosophical Perspectives, they become more flexible and tolerant in their outlook, drawn to protecting the weak and powerless, victims and underdogs, until they discover that helping them to help themselves is a more productive solution.

'My biggest challenge right now in being a Warrior is to stop defending people. In the past I have always run to their side in troubled times and tried to fix things. I have always wanted to right the wrongs. Now I try to hold them when they fall, let them go through their own lessons, and offer my input only when asked. I figure if I am meant to help they will ask me for it. I am still there for them, but would rather lead them to find

*their own answers. I used to get so angry when I would see a
wrong, and can still flare up over some causes, but am trying
now to fight with love and light.'*

HARRY, MANAGER

Warriors comprise around 18 percent of the population and
as an action Role they have a powerful impact on the world.
Families, corporations and whole nations can have a Warrior
culture. The dominant Warrior nations today are the USA
and Germany, with Spain rapidly up and coming. The
workplace, particularly corporate culture in these countries
and throughout the world, is Warrior dominated, though
the Role and personality of senior managements can act as a
counterbalancing force.

The most successful martial cultures in Western history were
ancient Rome and the Vikings, well depicted respectively
in the movies *Gladiator* and *Beowulf*. Another famously
militaristic Warrior culture was Imperial Japan, where the
armed forces of the country enthusiastically modelled
themselves on the Samurai code. The results were eventually
disastrous for Japan, as they launched themselves into World
War II. However, in the positive pole of the relationship
Perspective, Warrior cultures achieve great benefits for
themselves and the world, uniting productivity and prosperity
with democratic and peaceful goals.

The Challenge of the Negative Pole

Without action there would be no progress and development
– nothing would happen at all. Warriors are needed to
organize and persuade people and processes into action and

accomplishment. However, if they meet resistance, whether unjustified or valid, they are liable to slide into their negative pole of coercion. Persuasion becomes pressure, mounting up to an unbearable degree until Warriors become bulldozers riding roughshod over people's sensitivities. They see coercion as a justified response to a perceived threat or to others' laziness and inertia, but those others experience it as intimidation or brute force.

The Warriors' advantage is that being generally brave and practical, they are more willing than some other Roles to admit and confront the problem:

'Dealing with the negative pole ... well, first we usually openly confront it head on: attack! Sometimes it works, but as we get older, we get more tired, less resilient, and see that maybe this isn't the best plan. So we go to the opposite extreme, usually only briefly, and shut up. Keep in mind, we are Warriors, and that may only last for a few seconds or minutes. But tact finally starts to come into play, as does balancing of the emotions with the intellect and the body/beingness.'

KELLEY, MARKETING DIRECTOR

It is at the rule-bound and competing Perspectives that Warriors' coercion manifests most damagingly. Here they can become cruel, brutal and violent – unfortunately all too common a situation in many workplaces, prisons or armies, as well as some families. These Perspectives produce the playground bully, the rough sergeant major, the abusive parent or spouse, the thug. These Warriors believe that life is harsh and the world is a tough neighbourhood, so you have to fight to gain and hold your territory. Might is right. This may justify them inflicting maximum damage and injury, even killing someone. At their worst they identify with destruction and participate in it joyfully. The most extreme example is a pillaging army, laying waste the countryside and slaughtering its population without mercy. Of course other Roles can be equally violent, but there is something particularly terrifying about an out-of-control Warrior, and as an action Role they have maximum impact on others and on the environment.

At the relationship Perspective, they learn self-control and become altogether gentler. Their negative pole takes less destructive though still hurtful forms, as in the bossy manager who expects you to come into the office however ill you are and keep going till you drop – sick leave is for wimps. These Warriors can reduce people to tears, though usually unintentionally, and they will feel sorry and apologize afterwards.

Warriors typically have at least one 'battle' going on at any time, perhaps with local government, their children's school, a utility company or a difficult person. The archetypal cop movie where the detective is at loggerheads with his superiors and acts independently of the rules is a picture that is often close to the reality of many Warriors. In such cases, they are fighting for their beliefs and principles, but can find it hard to compromise and reach consensus. As John Wayne quipped, 'If everything isn't black and white, I say, "Why the hell not?"' The lesson for Warriors is that you can't always be challenging everything and the means do not always justify the ends – even when these are their highest values of justice, probity and honour.

At the philosophical Perspective, they can still exert pressure but much more subtly and softly. They understand better than any other Role that dealing with the negative pole is a major undertaking:

'Acknowledging my [negative pole] is a lifetime task. It's remarkable how pervasive it is and how deeply it permeates us. It's a constant battle. Studying it and how it operates under stress is revealing. It's like watching a disaster unfold before your very eyes. Once you are aware it's easier to stop it happening, but not always. Sometimes it's a matter of picking up the pieces afterwards and holding a post mortem to see how it all went pear-shaped.'

JAMES, IT CONSULTANT

How to Recognize a Warrior

Warriors are often easy to spot, even from behind, as they stride purposefully across the room, posture upright, clipboard in hand, issuing orders. If a Warrior is in the room, you feel their imposing presence: solid and reassuring if they are on your side; menacing and intimidating if they are against you. A Warrior in action is formidable; their considerable energy and stamina can be daunting and exhausting to others. Typically, they are always on the move, full of plans and projects, jumping into a car or onto a plane at the drop of a hat, mobile phone in hand. Warrior body language is distinctive: head and shoulders forward, eyes fixed ahead, look determined. They have the strongest, toughest bodies, are often broad shouldered and tend to be either large and rugged or stocky. The military march comes naturally to them; arms swinging, they keep pace with the drum. Sometimes they swagger as if slinging a gun from their hips, even if they are simply wearing a tool belt or a bunch of keys. Their voices are strong and deep, usually loud, and the women are sometimes mistaken for men on the telephone.

When they talk they look straight at you with a clear, direct, sometimes challenging gaze. They are the most 'in your face' Role, even more than Kings, who often conserve their power until it is needed on a grand scale. Even so, they can sometimes be mistaken for Kings, especially if they are the boss, since both are powerful leadership Roles. More intellectual Warriors can look like Scholars, as both are 'solid' Roles with a strong physique and earthy energy. Warrior women can be beautiful and become models or actresses, so you could mistake them for Artisans, but look more closely and you will notice the broad shoulders, the powerful stride, the direct gaze at the camera. Occasionally Warriors can look like Sages, particularly at a party, as both are extroverted and fun-loving, but Warriors are much blunter and less urbane. Quieter Warriors can sometimes look like Servers, as both Roles are ordinal, dutiful and hardworking.

The Warrior Role is archetypally masculine and both genders have a masculine flavour to their personality and energy. Male Warriors are the archetypal 'real men' who don't eat quiche but prefer a large steak when they come home from hunting – that is, if they have not already shot their dinner and brought it home with them. Warrior Women are usually well built with a tough physique. As children they tend to be tomboys and as adults they become Amazons, matriarchs and sometimes fishwives, happier in male than female company. It can be hard for them to adapt to the expectations of femininity, especially in a traditional society, though as ever they will rise to the challenge and find a way of making it work. However, they will certainly be happier in an environment that allows them to be strong and active and preferably pursue a career.

Warrior Style

Warriors are rarely interested in clothes for personal adornment and self-expression, though they may use them for sexual display. Mostly they would rather power dress than look fashionable, which leads them to a conservative style. Often their favourite outfit is a uniform (preferably with metal buttons), which shows the world what function, service or other activity they're about. It's important to them to dress appropriately for any occasion, particularly at work. Men like wearing suits to work, which gives them added authority. Businesswomen like to wear a sharp suit, with the broadest or most padded shoulders permissible that season, often in bold colours, particularly bright red. They are not generally interested in shopping and prefer brands that are practical, durable and good value, whether at the cheaper or more expensive end of the range.

Warriors can be quite house-proud and like to keep their homes and workspaces clean, organized and generally shipshape. They often enjoy cleaning, sometimes by turning it into a contest and competing against their own record time. Shannon Lush, an Australian 'cleaning guru', cleans to music; only a Warrior could add the flourish: 'I like squirting vinegar spray when the cannons go off during the *1812*

Overture.' Even if they are more relaxed about standards and their space looks disorganized, Warriors usually know where everything is and can lay hands on it instantly. They will expect their partner and children to maintain the same high standards and can be quite bossy about this. They enjoy socializing and entertaining, but only their closest friends and colleagues are invited into the sanctum of their home.

'I have always been very protective of my home, whether it has been one room or a nice house, and work very hard on maintenance and cleaning. I am very protective of my family and will "fight off" people I feel may not serve us well. I work hard at any job I take on and am a perfectionist. I have to complete all the tasks on my list before I allow myself to relax and enjoy the rest of the day. I can be impatient with others when they put things off and I often do their work for them rather than wait for them to do it. However, I get very aggravated at people who want me to look after them and won't take care of things themselves.'

JENNA, MANAGER

Warriors are the Role most attuned to their bodies and usually take good care of them, paying attention to nutrition and working out to develop and maintain a strong, healthy physique. Since they also have strong constitutions, they are less prone to illness than most people. On the other hand, they can easily get into fights, especially when drunk. This tendency, together with their active, adventurous lives and penchant for extreme sports, makes them vulnerable to injury, including strained muscles and backs. Being so active, if they do get ill they hate to stay in bed and are likely to cut short their convalescence. Children rarely miss a day's schooling and adults rarely take sick leave unless their doctor or employer puts a foot down very firmly. In retirement they stay active, working hard at their hobbies – not pottering in the garden but 'building raised beds, digging in plenty of manure, building greenhouses and growing a huge variety of things'. These are people who are unafraid of death and will die with their boots on:

> *'The great thing about life is that we all get to choose how high our hill is. I plan to die halfway up a massive one, rather than on the way back down a smaller one.'*
> JOHN, BUSINESSMAN

Billie Jean King: Warrior and Sporting Champion

Most Warriors love sport, as both spectators and players, and will support their team loyally through thick and thin. Being the most physically co-ordinated, strong, tough and courageous of the Roles, they excel in all sports and tests of physical endurance. The idea of a fair contest is important to them, preferably between well matched opponents, where the rules are clearly laid out, understood and adhered to and the best man or woman wins, to the loud cheers and adulation of the crowd. The gladiators of ancient Rome were archetypal Warrior heroes. Tennis is the most gladiatorial of modern sports, uniting the thrill of single combat with the challenge of perfecting the core Warrior qualities of fitness, athleticism, power, strength, stamina and toughness. No other Role can outplay a Warrior at professional tennis.

Billie Jean King is one of the greatest tennis champions of all time. In the 1960s and '70s she dominated women's tennis, winning over 40 major tournaments, including six Wimbledon singles championships and four US Open titles. Her style was extremely aggressive. She was a hard-hitting net rusher who said, 'You have to love to guts it out to win.' Warriors are the bravest Role at handling injuries and keeping going through them; King overcame several knee operations to continue playing and winning into her forties. Tennis is an excellent game for female Warriors to channel the aggression and competitiveness that it is unacceptable for women to display in most societies. Part of King's success was in transforming the energy of the Warrior's negative pole (coercion) into a constructively dynamic energy to win matches and make her mark. She was the first female athlete to win over $100,000 in any sport, for which she was personally congratulated by President Nixon.

It was not just about the money. King was a heroine of the feminist movement who battled long and hard against sexism in sport and wider society. At that time women players received much less prize money than men, and King was the most outspoken advocate for righting this wrong. As a direct result of her campaigning efforts, all the major tournaments now pay equal money to male and female players. Understanding the need for women to become unionized in order to progress, she also founded the Women's Tennis Association and set up many other foundations and enterprises for women to improve their athletic opportunities.

King was also the first prominent woman athlete to come out as gay. One of her most emotionally courageous acts was to confront her conservative and homophobic Methodist parents with her sexual orientation. At that time there was widespread prejudice towards homosexuality and she had to deal with a lot of media hostility as well as loss of earnings. Yet once again she set a milestone.

The most famous match of her career was the 'Battle of the Sexes' in 1973. Bobby Riggs was a former tennis champion, hustler and self-proclaimed 'male chauvinist pig'. He had already challenged and defeated another woman champion, Margaret Court, when he issued a challenge to Billie Jean King. She accepted. 'I thought it would set us back 50 years if I didn't win that match. It would ruin the women's tour and affect all women's self esteem.' The match was televised and watched by an audience of 50 million. King won easily in straight sets and *The New York Times* hailed her victory as another milestone for women.

Billie Jean King believes that she was born with a destiny to work for gender equality in sport and to continue until it is achieved. In 1990 she was the only female athlete on *Life* magazine's list of the '100 Most Important Americans of the 20th Century' in honour of both her sporting and campaigning achievements. Like many Warriors, she seems unable to retire and is leading as full and active a life as ever. Her persuasive and motivational talents make her much in demand as a professional speaker. Addressing university students in 2000, she urged them on: 'It's everyone's responsibility to lead, to honor, and to fight – for everyone's basic rights, for equality. Regardless of our gender, our age, our race, our religion, our appearance, sexual orientation or our abilities.'

The Warrior at Work

Warriors enjoy the workplace and are natural grafters, working extremely hard and being the backbone of any organization. They are often the first to arrive and last to leave the office, and can get quite competitive about it, going in for power breakfasts and after-work drinking sessions. Anyone lacking the stamina for this regime can be excluded from the inner circle of power. The business world has a strong Warrior flavour and Warriors generally do well in it, thrusting their way forward dynamically and getting promoted rapidly. Women Warriors adapt to or challenge male regimes and crack glass ceilings enthusiastically. While both sexes are good administrators, being practical and efficient, they will get bored with anything too routinized, needing some challenge and adventure in their working lives. Their motto is 'Let's not talk about it, let's just do it!'

Traditionally they were soldiers, and they do well at any aspect of military work, with female Warriors being unafraid to battle sexism as well as the official enemy. They are the best Role in a crisis and do well in the police and the emergency services as firefighters, ambulance drivers, security guards and bouncers. Any physical occupation suits them well, including sport, sports coaching, forestry and gardening, labouring, physiotherapy and massage. They are also attracted to occupations where their talents for maintaining boundaries and order are needed, such as school teaching, management, hospital administration and raising children.

'I have become a manager of these offices, which really amounts to becoming a "guard" making sure none of [my husband's] employees are stealing from him, and being in control of the accounts.'

JENNA, MANAGER

Warriors are the most entrepreneurial role, the most likely to succeed at running their own business, especially in practical areas like construction and transport. Freedom of action is important to them. Once they were cowboys, nowadays they are more likely to be long-distance truck drivers or airline pilots, which satisfies their need to be on the move. They also do well in retail as shopkeepers, traders and auctioneers.

Warriors are also found in the arts and media world, though mainly as managers and agents. Their talent is for ordering and organizing the creative chaos that Artisans bring into being and looking after their business interests. While most television presenters are Sages or Scholars, Warriors can bring their dynamic energy and talent for confrontation to the job, which makes exciting viewing. Joan Rivers is a good example. They enjoy being actors and stuntmen, and are in their element in all the action genres. Acting themselves in such parts gives this normally extroverted Role an opportunity to explore and understand the criminal mind and the energy of violence without resorting to it. As journalists, they like to be sent where the action is, including war zones. As authors, they are highly prolific and drawn to action genres such as action-adventure, crime and courtroom drama. Some of the best-known popular novelists are the Warriors John Grisham, Dashiell Hammett, Raymond Chandler and Frederick

Forsyth. As a literary novelist, Ernest Hemingway had an unorthodox approach to his art: 'There is no rule on how to write. Sometimes it comes easily and perfectly; sometimes it's like drilling rock and then blasting it out with charges.'

Leadership Style

Warriors can be the driving force of any organization, pushing the work and mission of the group forwards. The marketplace becomes their battleground and they do well in business, particularly as salespeople – the shock troops of capitalism. Other Roles also have selling skills, but Warriors have the energy and personality to persuade (or force) you to buy – and to close a deal. However, while excellent at strategy and tactics, they are often not as good at negotiating as they like to believe, tending to apply relentless pressure or offer inducements. This can be a handicap in sales and marketing situations where the product or service being sold is a sophisticated one. The Warrior salesperson needs to understand that they are not there simply to 'get a result' for their own side but to meet the genuine needs and expectations of the customer – in other words, to build a stable long-term relationship.

Tact, diplomacy and finesse are not typical Warrior qualities, but they are quick to learn if given proper training. They are very versatile, able to work independently but equally happy as employee or boss. They make good leaders, though prefer to be given clear instructions, aims and objectives and to report to a cardinal Role. They are the best of all the Roles as teamworkers, being able to give and take orders, collaborate well and be enterprising yet loyal. Warriors like the company of other Warriors and will spend much of their time together in like-minded groups; to push the Warrior analogy they could be called regiments. They also understand that action is very specific and other Warriors are needed in order to carry out 'missions'. Co-operation is essential.

> 'Concerning work, I can only say the obvious: apply the ethic of "know what to do and how to do it", plus an ability to work hard and a practical bent, and you get someone who really has no choice but to do a good job. I don't do things halfway, pretty much because it offends my sense of self. Hence I've succeeded at my work and have often found myself in leadership positions.'
>
> ROBERT, PROFESSOR OF ENGLISH

The downside is that if they do not feel challenged or motivated, Warriors can be among the worst performers, either becoming lazy or hatching plots and schemes. If a project gets stalled, they are likely to drop it in favour of a new one that seems to offer more scope for action. The process repeats itself until there is a backlog of unfinished schemes and works in progress. It is at this time that tough leadership comes in, and the Warrior will respect a leader who orders a halt and the completion of unfinished business. In their positive pole, Warriors are an asset to any business or enterprise and will make a major contribution to its success.

Communication Style

While the expression Roles (Sages and Artisans) are the great talkers and can keep going for hours on end, typical Warriors are strong and silent. John Wayne was famous for being taciturn, unusually among actors. His advice on acting was: 'Talk low, talk slow, and don't talk too much.' This is partly because talk wastes energy unless it has a purpose such as a fact-finding mission, and Warriors would rather direct their energy into action. Their language is plain and unadorned; they don't at all care for the long, flowery digressions so beloved of Artisans and Sages. Their communication consists mainly of issuing orders and instructions or asking questions to get their marching orders. They understand how to use talk as a weapon and in interrogation and negotiation, as well as the power of strategic silence and listening, and are well known for using military metaphors such as 'stick to your guns', 'battle on', 'indefensible claims' and 'never say die'. Since they dominate the business world, military language has taken over the workplace, sometimes to the chagrin of Sages, who dislike the clunkiness of business jargon with its focus on goals, drivers, targets and slaughtering the competition.

Warriors' style of communication can seem abrupt, abrasive and even rude to more polished or sensitive people, who can feel intimidated by it. Warriors don't intend to offend, though, and their challenging manner is sometimes a way of testing the mettle of others.

If you question a Warrior's presentation in a meeting, they will often be able to argue and bluster their way through, even if they are in the wrong. In such situations, one of their most effective strengths is their natural gravitas, which gives them a look of immovable self-assurance that is very impressive to other Roles. Their advantage in public speaking is their power of persuasion, getting straight to the point without wasting time softening up their audience.

Warriors often have a strong sense of humour, though broader and saltier than that of most other Roles. They enjoy slapstick or knockabout comedy and farce, and, being blunt and direct, they don't do irony. They enjoy pranks and practical jokes, and their teasing can become bullying if they slide into their negative pole. At this point it stops entertaining their audience, particularly their victim. When they are in a good mood, though, they are a lot of fun to be around.

They enjoy physical contact as part of the communication process – a hand on the elbow or shoulder, back-slapping among their mates. Male Warriors in particular need to be aware of the boundary between appropriate contact and harassment, particularly in the workplace. But when they are on form, other people find their warmth and lack of pretension refreshing, in contrast to the insincerity and hypocrisy of polite society.

An important point to remember when communicating with Warriors is to avoid offending their sense of honour and reputation. This is vital to them, since as action-oriented people, they need others' trust and cooperation. They can also be offended when others don't adhere to accepted codes of manners – say, not replying to invitations or not turning up at all. They are extremely sensitive and defensive around issues of respect and integrity and very unforgiving of anyone crossing this boundary, even accidentally or without harmful intent. In fact they are surprisingly thin skinned around any kind of criticism, regarding every question as a challenge. Although they understand that like everyone else they need critics, they struggle with the reality of having them. The best way forward is to say something like 'Nobody is criticizing you personally, it's just the action or words that you've taken or spoken on these occasions.' Then it is quite clear what you mean and the Warrior will happily accept that – or simply disagree, as the case may be. Above all, don't cross swords with them if you can help it, unless you are confident of winning.

Also, avoid vagueness or nuance in speech, manner or body language. Warriors don't do subtlety. They are liable to misunderstand and may take offence.

'We are direct, straightforward. Don't read between the lines with us. We'll tell you how we feel. When we are living in balance, we might even ask you if you want to know how we feel first!'
KELLEY, MARKETING DIRECTOR

In a work situation, instructions should be to the point, and ideally action-oriented. Avoid any possible ambivalence or wiggle room in interpretation. Warriors need motivating to get the best out of them, hence the typically tough-talking sales conference where remarks like 'If you don't get the contract, then don't bother coming in to work tomorrow!' are the norm. Another favourite tool is 'pep-talk boosterism' when a business motivational speaker gives the assembled ranks the realities of the current situation in no uncertain terms.

As bosses, Warriors are more interested in hearing about results than the processes needed to achieve them. The details (if required at all) can wait until either an official debriefing or, better still, after a few drinks.

The Warrior in Love

As an ordinal Role, Warriors are good at one-to-one relationships. They often think of their friends as comrades-in-arms, stick up for each other loyally and ride shotgun. There's nothing a Warrior appreciates more than a friend who leaps to their defence and wins; after that, you're a friend for life. But the game of love may defeat them. An Artisan I know was very surprised when instead of the expected invitation to dinner, her new Warrior boyfriend offered her a tank-driving lesson. Yet Warriors can also be surprisingly romantic, in a sensual way, and will appreciate the efforts of their date to dress up and create an ambience. Just don't expect them to do the same, particularly the men. A woman might spend the whole week preparing for a weekend away, but a male Warrior will just throw a pair of boots in the boot and drive off, possibly stopping to splash on some aftershave and put on a clean T-shirt.

What they enjoy is planning a seduction campaign, laying siege, the thrill of the chase. Their energy, power and animal magnetism make them highly sexy and attractive, especially to more ethereal types, and generally their persuasive skills work well for them, but they can slide into coercion, particularly after a few drinks. At the competing Perspective they are likely to boast and brag about their conquests (sometimes exaggerating them), keep scores and count notches on bedposts.

Being so athletic and action-oriented, they enjoy an active sex life, often into old age. According to José Stevens, 'They love physicality and the direct action-oriented contact of a sexual relationship. They are likely to say "Let's make love first and then talk." They want to know they can trust you physically first. They find sex grounding and nurturing and often lead amazingly sexually active lives. They tend to view sex in a matter-of-fact way and be direct, even blunt about it.' With them it's more about energy and stamina than finesse, and can get quite rough if they've had too much to drink. However, they are usually happy to learn and expand their repertoire if you clearly explain your requirements.

Warrior women can find the demands of femininity mystifying and irksome, and may rebel against the rules of the dating game. They are the women most likely to make the first move and to make the running in the relationship. It is important for them to find a mate who will appreciate a strong woman and be able to stand up to her when needed to avoid getting henpecked. They will then reward him with total loyalty and shoulder their share and more of family and domestic responsibilities.

Warrior husbands are usually good providers, taking their family responsibilities seriously but expecting complete support and loyalty in return. Their strong physical needs may cause them to stray occasionally, but their main love and loyalty will be to their wives, compartmentalizing any extramarital activity as 'flings that don't count'. However, if they find themselves the victims of infidelity, they will be shocked, hurt and enraged.

Warrior men are likely to feel at home in a more traditional marriage with clear gender divisions. Warrior women are likely to want more action in their lives than homemaking, so may prefer to reverse the gender roles.

The most compatible Role for Warriors is the King, whom they will feel honoured to serve, but unfortunately Kings are in short supply, being the rarest Role. Otherwise, Warriors' most successful partnerships are usually with Scholars. Both are 'solid' Roles, focused and grounded, with a shared earthy sense of humour and need for adventure. The inspirational Roles are tricky. Servers will look after them beautifully, but Warriors sometimes bully them, mistaking their helpfulness for weakness. There is often a strong mutual attraction with Priests, but Warriors can easily end up fighting them unless they can unite behind a cause. They enjoy the company of Sages, as both are sociable, fun-loving types, but Sages can find Warriors uncouth while Warriors can find Sage charm duplicitous. Warrior men with Artisan women comprise the classic masculine–feminine polarity and as an attraction of opposites there is plenty of room for misunderstanding, but they can enjoy collaborating on practical projects. For a detailed description of the compatibilities between Warriors and other Roles, see Chapter 9.

Parents and Children

Warriors generally make affectionate, responsible parents. They are good at instilling values, teaching good manners, setting boundaries for their children and ensuring they are kept. They tend to run the family like a military operation, which works fine in early childhood but can get frustrating for teenagers, so great battles are likely to ensue at this stage.

However, Warriors can also be quite indulgent and easily manipulated by childish charm, especially the fathers of pretty girls. Warrior women are archetypal earth mothers. They will ensure their children are well fed and clothed, do their homework and come home by a certain time – or else. They will also defend them ferociously against bullying, compensating in protection for whatever they lack in sensitivity.

'I think I instilled a sense of independence and self-sufficiency in my three children. I made sure they could hold a sensible conversation from an early age and encouraged them to express themselves clearly with confidence. I made sure they could all cook enough to survive on their own and learned useful skills like swimming, computers, driving and the art of conversation.'

JAMES, IT CONSULTANT

Warrior children are highly active from an early age, learning to walk before they talk, exploring far and wide and preferring to be outside playing games with other children than stuck inside with a book. They enjoy computer games, but not for too long at a time. What they love most is being in a gang, preferably as its leader, and heading off into all kinds of adventures, including battles with rival gangs. Girls are often tomboys, climbing trees and muddying their clothes. They prefer trousers and practical wear to pink frilly dresses. They also like gangs and may lead them.

Warrior children usually take well to school life, being at home in a structured environment with strict rules, which they will enforce enthusiastically as prefects. They can do well academically if they have a good brain and are interested, tending to prefer science and practical subjects to arts and humanities. Where they really excel is on the sports field, which makes the boys popular both among their peer group and with girls. Warrior boys flourish even in rough schools, knowing how to take care of themselves with their general air of 'Don't mess with me' and using their fists if necessary. They can be bullies, but can also stand up to other bullies and befriend and protect weaker children. Warrior girls can have a harder time, especially at schools which try to imprint a traditional concept of femininity on girls. One was told she 'wasn't being a proper female, not being quiet, being too bold, too outspoken'. But they are good at adapting and taking care of themselves, so usually end up with plenty of friends.

Teenage boys usually do well on the dating scene, being uninhibited about pursuing girls and chatting them up at parties and bars. Girls are often drawn to their masculine confidence, though more refined girls may be put off by their blunt and sometimes crude manners. Both sexes can't wait to make their way and their fortune, and often set up enterprises from their bedroom or garage before going to university. If these projects do well, they may drop out of university altogether unless made to see the importance of a degree. They become independent as soon as possible, often leaving home early, particularly if they are out of sympathy with parental values. Some stay at home if they have responsibilities like being the primary caregiver for their younger siblings or responsible for looking after a sick parent (unless there is a Server in the family to do this). If they emigrate, they usually maintain family connections and are scrupulous about sending money home if their salary is needed.

Warrior Archetypes in Myth, Fiction and Film

The archetypal Warrior in myth is the hero. Achilles was the greatest Greek hero of the Trojan War, which produced many mighty warriors. His phenomenal deeds in battle were celebrated in poems, stories and plays throughout antiquity, and more recently he was thrillingly portrayed by Brad Pitt in the movie *Troy*. Although Achilles was so strong, fit and powerful that he appeared invincible, he did have one secret weakness in his heel; hence the phrase 'Achilles heel'. This is a good metaphor for Warriors to remember that everyone has a vulnerable point somewhere; however well you defend it, death gets everyone in the end.

Like all Warriors, reputation was extremely important to Achilles. When he was dishonoured by his own king he refused to continue fighting until the wily Odysseus was sent to persuade or trick him into it. Eventually his loyalty was rekindled when his best friend Patroclus was killed by Hector, an enemy Trojan hero. This swung him to his negative pole and the gods had to restrain him from sacking the whole city of Troy in revenge. He managed to engage Hector in battle, a one-to-one contest of the kind Warriors love, and won, dragging Hector's dead body behind his chariot in a chilling act of triumph. He was never defeated in a fair fight, but finally met his end through treachery when Paris's arrow found its mark in his vulnerable heel. When he died he became a god, and his cult was widespread throughout the classical world.

The most iconic Warrior movie hero is the cowboy, well represented by Warrior actors like John Wayne and Clint

Eastwood as an emblem and carrier of core American values, a dependable, forthright protector of the weak in a world of menace. The outlaw, real or mythical, is another Warrior archetype often portrayed on film, including Robin Hood, Rob Roy, Billy the Kid, Butch Cassidy and the Sundance Kid. James Bond is the ideal competing Warrior fantasy; his current incarnation Daniel Craig brings out his action-man side to perfection. Every action movie presents positive and negative examples of the Warrior, usually in conflict with each other as hero versus villain. Hollywood movies are also full of epic superheroes and comic-based depictions of the Warrior such as Batman and Spider-man. The Terminator represents the negative Warrior functioning as an automaton, all brawn and no brain, as do Rambo, Tarzan and Conan the Barbarian. Fortunately there are plenty of more positive images to be found on film, such as the Warrior Richard Sharpe loyally fighting for his King (the Duke of Wellington) in *Sharpe's War*.

Women Warriors have fewer heroic role models, Ellen Ripley in *Alien* being a rare example. Any woman who boldly displays her Warrior nature is often likened to the Amazons, a mythical tribe of all-female warriors. They are often featured in fiction, film and video games. Wonder Woman is a superheroine based on the mythical Amazon Queen Hippolyta. Buffy the Vampire Slayer and Xena the Warrior Princess are more recent iconic examples. It is interesting that Xena began her film journey as an ally of Hercules, one of the greatest Greek heroes. She displays the positive pole of the Warrior Role in her ongoing battle to defend the weak and powerless against evil and tyranny.

How to Fulfill Your Warrior Potential

At their best, Warriors are energizing, motivational, helpful and constructive – think of a police officer effectively dealing with a saloon brawl or a good teacher sorting out an unruly class of children. However, at their worst they are gangsters or thugs, capable of causing enormous damage and injury to people and property. To fulfill their potential they need to keep their impulse to action positively directed and productive rather than futile or destructive. This section summarizes how Role and Perspective work together for growth and fulfillment.

Competing Warriors are fixated on success and winning. They are players, movers and shakers, and their ambition usually takes them as far as they aim to go. At this Perspective they are likely to go for a military career, either in the regular army or as mercenaries, which fulfills their need for adventure even better. They also thrive in business as thrusting young executives, handling the cut-throat competitiveness of corporate life better than more sensitive souls. It is important for them to be on the winning side as well as winning for themselves, and they automatically see their opponents as enemies.

In their negative pole of coercion, their natural instincts for justice and fair play can be easily overridden by their ambition. In the army they will identify with whichever side they are on without questioning the cause and enjoy the thrill of violence. In business they don't care how many people they have to trample or backstab to get to the top. The recent collapse of the global banking system is largely the result of competing Warriors' compulsive drive for short-term bonuses at the expense of long-term stability.

In their positive pole their aggression is ritualized in sport, where they provide thrilling entertainment to crowds of spectators. The archetypal image of victory is the moment of holding aloft a trophy in triumph.

Sometimes firm policies and tough tactics may be the best if not the only way of controlling firebrand Priest leaders and their followers at the rule-bound Perspective. Then Warriors' loyalty and protective instincts come to the fore and they can fight to win without inflicting more damage than strictly necessary on their enemy or opponent. The challenge at this Perspective is to get from 'winner takes all' to accepting the win-win scenario as the most productive for everyone concerned.

At the relationship Perspective, Warriors are much more self-aware and concerned about the consequences of their actions. While still pugnacious, they are more likely to become freedom fighters or campaigners in righteous causes like civil rights, feminism and the environmental movement. Tolerance is an important value and they may specialize in conflict resolution. If they join more adversarial professions like the police force or the legal system, it will be for the purpose of exposing corruption or malpractice. They are often prepared to stick their necks out for unpopular and controversial causes or to champion underdogs and victims, often at considerable risk and cost to themselves.

The action Roles have the heaviest impact on other people, so need to develop empathy and sensitivity as a counterbalance.

At the relationship Perspective, Warriors' relationships are much more nurturing and affectionate. Warriors are not naturally introspective, however, and if they become aware of their negative pole are likely to confront it head on as an internal enemy. It can be a very painful process, which may be helped by counselling or therapy. They may get impatient with slow analytical processes, preferring self-help approaches like life coaching and cognitive behavioural therapy which offer practical techniques and tools for self-development. Some forms of yoga also appeal, particularly the more strenuous varieties such as 'power yoga'.

Philosophically oriented Warriors are very relaxed, though they retain more drive and dynamism than most Roles at this Perspective and are capable of achieving a lot if they feel like it. Often their lazier side kicks in, though, after what can feel like lifetimes of hard work and drive to succeed, and gentler occupations like music, gardening, riding with their buddies and hanging out in the bar have more appeal.

Along with Kings, Warriors are the Role least drawn to the realm of abstract thought, seeing action as the best way to happiness.

'I have, I would say, a practical approach to spiritual matters as well as physical ones. I'm much more interested in what works for me than in anybody's orthodoxy, and the older I get, the truer this becomes.'
ROBERT, PROFESSOR OF ENGLISH

They prefer the more active forms of meditation such as the Buddhist-based martial arts traditions which emphasize alertness, spontaneous action, focus – natural Warrior qualities. Being the most self-disciplined Role, they are likely to stick at these and get better results than some more obviously spiritual types, who give up quickly out of boredom or laziness.

Here is an account of how it feels to be a Warrior in the positive pole at the philosophical Perspective:

'Being a Warrior means being a comfortable, grounded person who likes to get things done. A feeling of accomplishment and obtaining a result is important and I don't mind how hard I need to work to obtain that. Taking time out enjoy yourself is crucial too – we Warriors do need to relax with a few beers down the pub at the end of the day. As a Warrior I do see the world as a set of challenges and obstacles to overcome. This is not necessarily confrontational but more like a list of actions to be completed to achieve an objective. I can be focused on what I am doing to the point where I miss easier, more appropriate alternatives. My feeling is we are all in the soup together and we need to figure out the best way to sort things out. I am always willing to step up to the plate and take action and be an example to inspire others to roll their sleeves up and do something.'

JAMES, IT CONSULTANT

The formula for success, happiness and self-mastery in this system is a simple but powerful three-step process:

1. Discover your Role.

2. Integrate it with your Perspective.

3. Operate from their positive poles.

I hope by now you recognize whether you are a Warrior or whether it is your secondary Role. Identifying your Role is the first step on a lifelong journey of self-discovery. The insight needs to be confirmed and applied in daily life on an ongoing basis for best results, so requires commitment, but with practice it becomes second nature. The reward of self-transformation is well worth the effort.

Secondary Role Influences for Warriors

One of the most important factors influencing the personality variations between people who share the same Role is the secondary Role. This colours, flavours and generally modifies your personality. The combination works like an omelette: your primary Role is the egg, while your secondary Role is the added ingredient – cheese, mushroom, tomato. Sometimes the flavour is subtle, sometimes it overpowers the egg. Similarly, the secondary Role can manifest more strongly than the primary Role, particularly if it corresponds with your profession. Some people have the same Role in both the primary and secondary position, so will conform more closely with the Role archetype. If this is your case, you will probably recognize yourself quite easily. This section summarizes the influence of the other six Roles on Warriors.

Artisan-Warriors

This is a difficult combination to handle as these Roles are such opposite energies. One quality they share is touchiness, which can make for a prickly, abrasive personality, particularly at the competing Perspective. If these Warriors can learn to integrate the energies, there is rich potential in the addition of Artisan creativity to Warrior productivity. It is a good combination for music and the performing arts. Being well attuned to the human body and able to work with it more sensitively than usual, these Warriors make excellent doctors, surgeons, healers, masseurs and aromatherapists. As sporting heroes, their stylish technique will make them very enjoyable to watch and popular with the crowds. A good example is the tennis champion Andre Agassi. They dress with flair and display more refinement than usual. Women will be more feminine, and both men and women will be more sensitive and expressive in their relationships.

Sage-Warriors

This is an excellent combination for writing and public speaking. Many successful journalists and novelists have it. These Warriors make the best negotiators and salespeople, uniting Warrior persuasiveness with Sage charm and verbal skills. They are the life and soul of the party, but can also be notorious hellraisers, Dean Martin being a typical example. In relationships they are one of the most attractive combinations, being dynamic and fun-loving. It can be less fun to be married to them than go out with them, but mostly their loyalty balances their *joie de vivre*.

'I present business information clearly but always with a touch of humour if I can. Doing things in a light-hearted way with humour and a sense of fun makes it all enjoyable. I get a kick out of building a team of people to accomplish something, making plans, ticking off the milestones, having a laugh and celebrating our wins.'

JAMES, IT CONSULTANT

Server-Warriors

These Roles are very different, almost opposed energies, hard to integrate smoothly. At best these Warriors will lean more to the protective than aggressive side of their nature and be gentler than typical Warriors. They make good doctors and nurses, combining Server nurturing and comforting skills with Warrior practicality and attunement to the physical body. Both Roles are tireless workers, and any profession which requires efficiency, hard work and good interpersonal skills will suit them, such as being a family lawyer. They do well in customer services, being less belligerent than usual, and are an asset to any cause or project, doing the work of two or three normal workers. Their relationships are likely to be gentler than is usual with Warriors. This is an excellent combination for parenting and for teaching young children.

Priest-Warriors

This is an excellent combination for leadership positions, making Warriors more inspirational than usual so better able to rally the troops, workforce or family behind them. However, they can be very fanatical, conquistadors uniting priestly zeal with the Warrior strong sense of boundaries and right and wrong. You certainly don't want to be interrogated by someone with this combination. In any walk of life their sense of mission will be strong, sometimes urgent. They will be drawn to working in religious or spiritual enterprises and can be effective missionaries, rising to the challenge, enjoying the adventure and valuing the spiritual purpose. Their children may find them overly controlling and rebel against them. If they can learn to integrate these poles, they can become a great force for good in the world. The most high-profile and inspirational contemporary example is Oprah Winfrey, who has integrated the positive poles of persuasion and compassion to become the most influential woman in the media and a force for good in the world.

King-Warriors

As a double-action Role, this is a tough, formidable combination. These Warriors make powerful military and political leaders and are likely to rise to the top of any organization. Their presence is so imposing that it can scare people off, especially if accompanied by an aggressive personality and hot temper. They themselves are probably unaware of this effect and will expect people to stand up to them and demand a rise or promotion if they want one. Their bodies are strong and athletic and they can easily become sporting champions. In personal relationships they will inevitably be the dominant partner, so need to find someone who will accept this dynamic. Loyalty is extremely important to them and they will both give it and expect to receive it – or else.

Scholar-Warriors

This is a comfortable combination, since the two Roles are highly compatible. These Warriors have excellent minds and can do very well academically, though will prefer fieldwork to being stuck in a library. Career-wise, they make exceptional teachers, being well able to keep order and get excellent exam results. They also make good engineers, geologists, archaeologists and explorers, enjoying putting high-level knowledge to use in an active adventurous career. Scholar neutrality is a good safeguard against their tendency to flare up, so they will have calmer temperaments and inflict less damage on the nerves and bodies of other people than other Warriors. They also make solid, dependable partners and are likely to remain in stable long-term relationships.

Famous Warriors

Winston Churchill, Ulysses S. Grant, Grover Cleveland, General George Patton, Alexander Haig, Erwin Rommel, Nikita Khrushchev, Theodore Roosevelt, Robert Kennedy, George W. Bush, Colin Powell, Donald Rumsfeld, Condoleezza Rice, Hillary Clinton, Stephen Biko, Vladimir Putin, Prince Philip, George Gurdjieff, Henry Ford, Oliver Stone, Bette Davis, John Wayne, Clint Eastwood, Robert Mitchum, Arnold Schwarzenegger, Jane Fonda, Daniel Craig, Oprah Winfrey, Joan Rivers, George Frideric Handel, Dean Martin, Frida Kahlo, Jack London, Ernest Hemingway, John Buchan, Dashiell Hammett, Raymond Chandler, Frederick Forsyth, Norman Mailer, John Grisham, Jeffrey Archer, Hunter S. Thompson, Thomas Huxley ('Darwin's Bulldog'), Billy the

Kid, Calamity Jane, Davy Crockett, Geronimo, Jesse Owens, Babe Ruth, Jackie Robinson, Michael Jordan, Sugar Ray Robinson, Mike Tyson, Tiger Woods, John McEnroe, Boris Becker, Pat Cash, Pete Sampras, Andre Agassi, Lleyton Hewitt, Roger Federer, Rafael Nadal, Venus and Serena Williams, Bobby Charlton, Eric Cantona, Pelé, Diego Maradona

CHAPTER 7

The King

'Things do not happen. Things are made to happen.'
JOHN F. KENNEDY

The King Personality

Kings are the cardinal action Role, which makes them natural leaders. When a King is in charge of any project or organization, everyone feels motivated and confident of success. Even without a high position, they stand out from the crowd with their imposing presence, and their charisma is felt by everyone who comes into contact with them. When they rule well, the enterprise will thrive, but if they become autocratic, everyone suffers.

Many people like the idea of being a King, but few are ready to take on the responsibilities that accompany this Role. As (King) Queen Elizabeth I said: 'To be a king and wear a crown is more glorious to them that see it than it is a pleasure to them that bear it.'

'King' is such a powerful archetype that it is easy to assume that all rulers have the King Role. This is not so. There is a historical correlation between the Role and the institution of kingship, as they have evolved together. However, in the modern world there are not enough thrones to go around, and other Roles also fill them. Also, most monarchies are too circumscribed by law and tradition to allow much opportunity for leadership. For example, it is a mainstay of the British constitution that the monarch 'reigns but does not rule', which does not suit or satisfy the Role of King. It is therefore appropriate that there are currently no Kings in the British royal family, which is composed mainly of Servers, Artisans and Warriors – the most ordinal Roles.

Some of the world's greatest political and military leaders, past and present, have been Kings, a few examples being Alexander the Great, Genghis Khan, Charles de Gaulle, Mao Zedong, Indira Gandhi, John F. Kennedy, Fidel Castro and Benazir Bhutto. However, many Kings do not hold a high public position, preferring to live normal lives as regular folk.

The goal of this personality system is to operate from the positive pole of your Role. For Kings this is mastery. They are driven to excel in everything they do, great or small. They are perfectionists who will do a job over and over, driving everyone nuts, but the results will be breathtaking. They demand the same standards from others, along with loyalty, their highest virtue, but will reward those who deliver with true royal largesse.

Traditionally, honour was a top-down quality like grace, flowing from the king through the nobles to the rest of the population, and at their best Kings are heroic and honourable.

'Honour is very important to me. Not reputation, but conduct, ethics. To always do what you say you'll do, to never make a promise you can't keep. To be honest and trustworthy.'

SUSANNA

Being the most cardinal or wide-focused of all the Roles, they are also wired up to getting things done on a grand scale. Just as Sages seek their stage and Priests seek their mission, Kings seek their mandate. Jack Welch, former CEO of General Electric and one of the world's top business leaders, said: 'Control your own destiny or someone else will.' Kings are the true masters of their destiny, and sometimes of the fate of nations, putting their stamp on everything they do.

Warriors like to be given their marching orders, pointed at the task and told to get on with it. Kings call the shots and supervise the process. Whereas Warriors are good tacticians, responding to the immediate situation and seeing the best way to handle it, Kings are master strategists. They focus well, relish challenge and are ruthlessly realistic when it comes to assessing options. Part of their success comes from their ability to see the bigger picture and take a long-term view of the situation. This includes a perception of how all the parts and aspects interconnect and can be made to work together more efficiently. Kings pay close attention to detail, at least where it matters. While good at delegating, they also keep a close watch on developments and ensure everything is in place before beginning a project, whether a family reunion, a company takeover or a battle. They understand that one small thing can make the difference between success and failure, and so insist on impeccable planning.

Artisans bring in the new and Scholars conceptualize it, but Kings are the first to see the long-term potential of it. They are trendsetters who often surprise people by seeing a better way of doing something which goes against received wisdom. This may seem paradoxical, as they are innately conservative, being concerned with stability. However, since 'cardinal action' means initiating events, making things happen, exploring beyond the known horizon, they need to be above the law or a law unto themselves. They will therefore tear up the current rulebook if it no longer serves a useful purpose.

Kings are renowned for their decisiveness. They often make quick decisions based on listening to their gut instincts, which rarely let them down. The more patient ones like to gather all the evidence (often relying on Scholars for this function) and take advice, but still reach a decision as soon as possible. Once it has been taken, they usually stick with it, and it often proves to be the right one. On the other hand, they also understand the advantages of masterly inactivity in some situations. They are better able than other Roles to plan for the future, taking a long view, biding their time and letting their schemes grow and reach fruition. This makes them the best military leaders, though they can find it difficult in politics and business, where short-term gain is often preferred to long-term benefit.

Kings are the rarest Role, comprising around 2 percent of the population. Leadership on this scale has such an impact that few are needed. In our times, it can be hard for Kings to find a platform and position from where they can give their best, since democratic societies and flat management structures do not allow much scope for the exercise of power. However, leadership skills are always in demand.

Like all the Roles, Kings manifest most dramatically at the competing Perspective, from where they can become movers and shakers on the world stage. Currently business is their favourite arena for empire building and wealth creation.

Kings at the relationship and philosophical Perspectives are helping to change the face of modern business and politics to promote the greater good and are also leaders in the environmental movement. Ultimately, Kings lead in order to serve, and at this Perspective are well equipped to do so.

The Challenge of the Negative Pole

When people first encounter this personality system, they often want to be a King. The appeal is obvious, but there are drawbacks. All Roles have a negative pole and for Kings it is tyranny. Kings carry a lot of responsibility and know that they can often see the way forward more clearly than others, so they need to be in control and have their way. This can make them very willful, headstrong, impatient and intolerant of others' imperfections.

All Roles manifest their negative pole most harmfully at the competing Perspective. Here Kings are liable to be hot-tempered, overbearing and bullying until everyone quakes with fear, which does not help in getting things done in the longer term. They expect everyone to run around serving them, obeying every order and catering to every whim unquestioningly. In the workplace they fire people ruthlessly if the numbers don't add up. Any lapse of loyalty will be treated as disobedience or insubordination, which they regard as treason deserving of the most severe punishment. They will never forget a slight or injury; even if the culprit forgets, they will be unpleasantly reminded when the King finally exacts revenge. Some can hold grudges for years. A King CEO I knew used to quote an old Chinese proverb: 'If you sit by the river long enough, the bodies of your enemies will come floating by.' The ultimate punishment they impose is banishment from their presence. The sun is withdrawn and all is cold.

It is important to emphasize, in terms of this personality system, that nobody has to obey a King. Sometimes another Role will have a better view of a situation, especially in relationship issues, where the ordinal Roles are better equipped to achieve success. Anybody is entitled to stand up to a tyrannical King and tell them to get lost if they are overstepping the mark. Most people do not dare, but Kings respect strength. Warriors are the Role most likely to resist them, being bold, courageous and good at both exerting and withstanding pressure. They are more likely to succeed if they band together as a group. Sometimes tyrants need to be deposed. Alexander the Great tried to conquer the world, and almost succeeded. Finally his own army mutinied, exhausted after many years of campaigning. Alexander bowed to the inevitable and the war was over.

At the relationship and philosophical Perspectives, Kings are mellower and less aggressive. Mostly they do not intend to be despotic or frighten people and are unaware of their impact.

'All I want to do is serve, and it is so frustrating to me that my intentions and vision often seem lost to others.'

GINA, CLINICAL SOCIAL WORKER

They can still be overly directive on the basis of having a better vision of what needs to be done or what the other person's best interests are. Their drive for excellence at any level makes them hard on others and on themselves, so they need to learn to take the pressure off before everyone becomes exhausted and burns out.

'I think the negative pole comes from trying to take too much responsibility. If you feel that you are responsible for the mistakes of others, you try to control them. You end up acting like they are a malfunctioning part of you. If you take all responsibility onto yourself, you end up overwhelmed. Power and responsibility have to be delegated, both up and down. It helps to take an attitude of "helping others to do their collective thing" rather than "making others do my thing".'

SUSANNA

How to Recognize a King

Kings can be either very easy or quite hard to spot. Many have a powerful charisma which has an instant impact on everyone they meet. When they walk into a room, the air seems to fizzle and crackle around them so that they become the centre of attention. They often hold court, surrounded by their entourage or a crowd of admirers. A journalist who met Madonna (aka 'Her Madgesty') described her as being 'tiny, almost fragile, but she managed to take up all the available space: arms akimbo, legs sprawled apart like a man'. Even if Kings are not celebrities, they can walk into a restaurant and be given the best table and impeccable service while other diners try in vain to catch the waiter's eye. I experienced this once. Entering a packed-out fashionable London restaurant with a King friend, I found we were given a good table and excellent service, despite being two women on our own. Kings also have a knack of finding the best chair in the room and sitting on it as if it were a throne. I recently saw a King sitting on a throne-like rock at the top of a hill, seemingly surveying her domain from a great height.

Kings most closely resemble Warriors; both are strong leadership Roles on the action axis. However, Warriors tend to be permanently full-on and 'in your face' while Kings are more diplomatic and less 'sharp edged'. Quieter or more modest Kings may be mistaken for Scholars, especially if they are intellectuals or working in education, since both are solid Roles with an air of natural authority. In this case people need to be quite alert to notice their power, but their charisma will gradually captivate you even if it doesn't hit you between the eyes. If you ask their family and friends, it is likely they will all attest to their special magnetic quality.

'I am, most of the time, totally unaware that my presence has an impact on people. But it does show up when I speak or teach. I am told I have "a strong presence". It's totally natural to me, nothing that I think about or try to do.'

SULA, ENTREPRENEUR

Even if not classically beautiful, Kings usually look striking on account of their aura and charisma. Tall Kings look grand and imposing, while small ones have so much energy and power that you forget about their size. Whatever their size, Kings look solid, well grounded, and have a regal bearing. They usually have a strong, loud voice but don't need to raise it to get your attention. However, they 'often have a problem feeling too big or forceful, like a bull in a china shop' (Helena, USA). It is an archetypically masculine Role, and female Kings can appear masculine in looks and style, though some are quite feminine (particularly with an Artisan or Server secondary Role). Women sometimes have difficulty fully manifesting their King Role, especially in societies where they are expected to be submissive and ultra-feminine. It feels natural to them to be deferred to and to take precedence.

King Style

Fashion does not interest most Kings unless they have a Sage or Artisan secondary Role, and off duty they tend not to bother about clothes. However, they like to dress correctly and appropriately at work or on formal occasions and they have the effect of always looking right. If they turn up dressed smartly, everyone else will feel scruffy, cheap or dowdy; if casual, everyone will feel overdressed. If they are the boss, all their employees will copy their style. For both genders this is usually chic, simple and the best they can afford. Top hats and tiaras become them, as do ermine robes, designer suits and ballgowns. Naturally their favourite colours are royal blue and regal purple. Women favour subtle but expensive jewellery. Like Warriors, they are most comfortable in a uniform, which they don't have to think about and can wear with distinction, with or without an impressive array of medals.

'I find it very hard to find clothes I like! I like to look dignified, and the fashions generally look either frivolous or cheap. I'm also quite practical about my clothing. No, I don't want to buy clothes that don't keep me warm, or uncomfortable shoes, or tops labelled "Dry clean only". No, I am not getting old, I was the same at 16.'

SUSANNA

Kings have great strength and stamina, a boundless capacity for hard work. Like Warriors, they can push themselves to the maximum and beyond. Their biggest health risk is accident or injury from the extreme sports they are often drawn to in order to raise their game and find a new challenge. If ill, they are often reluctant to consult a doctor or to stay in bed. They are more likely to self-medicate with whatever is at hand and work through the illness. They have healthy appetites for all physical pleasures, which may lead to over-indulgence, weight gain and associated problems. With age, they need to learn to pace themselves or risk stress- and strain-related illness. As an action Role, they hate to retire and are likely to become even busier at this stage, in constant demand as speakers and consultants. But their self-discipline, emphasis on fitness (which they take very seriously) and strong constitutions usually enable them to live to a ripe old age, active to the end.

John F. Kennedy: A King Political Leader

Kings don't always get to the top in democracies because they are very individualistic, demanding and less willing than other Roles to compromise. However, when a King does get the top job, their impact is enormous; they take charge of their own and their country's destiny, which they can shape for decades or even centuries. Queen Elizabeth I of England was the founder of the English-speaking people's diaspora around the globe, which some leading historians see as the most significant event of the second millennium. Catherine the Great of Russia was another King who set her country's course for a long time.

John F. Kennedy is the most celebrated US president so far and an example of a King in the most cardinal leadership position available in the modern world. Shakespeare proclaimed: 'Be not afraid of greatness: some are born great, some achieve greatness, and some have greatness thrust upon them.' All these were true of JFK. He was born to greatness in that he was the son of a senior ambassador and successful businessman, Joseph Kennedy, also a King, with dynastic ambitions for his family. As a result, JFK 'had greatness thrust upon him'. His father exerted constant pressure on him, but also gave him great responsibilities, which Kings love. JFK shared his father's ambitions and demonstrated all the makings of a future President, as was noted by his elder brother and some of his fellow students at university. It is characteristic of Kings to manifest leadership skills from an early age.

His presidency gave JFK the opportunity to fulfill Shakespeare's third condition, to 'achieve greatness', and he was ready for it: 'Sure it's a big job; but I don't know anyone who can do it better than I can.' It came as a breath of fresh air to the unimaginative and hidebound political establishment of the day, and to the United States as a whole, which then (as today) felt that it was losing its sense of direction and purpose.

Kennedy ruled at the peak of US influence and added to it by his own charisma – that mysterious ability to sway others and inspire confidence that Kings possess more than any other Role. His administration was nicknamed 'Camelot' after the mythical court of King Arthur, and it promoted a similar image of youthful idealism, glamour and boundless potential. JFK commanded great loyalty and devotion from his 'knights', staff, friends, much of America and the wider world. He demonstrated a King's ability to use his charisma to 'rally the troops' and give everyone the feeling that by following him anything could be achieved.

He also understood the importance of aspirational and iconic projects, founding the successful Peace Corps and New Frontier programmes. Never settling for second best, he set out to solve all the 'problems of peace and war' and conquer all 'the uncharted areas of science and space'. For example, his visionary idea of putting men on the moon within a short time was a master stroke that did much to raise national morale.

Part of his far-sightedness was understanding the importance of the new medium of television in politics. His election victory was helped by his brilliant self-presentation in the first-ever televised political debate, far outshining Richard Nixon. He had the King's gift for oratory, particularly when it really mattered, and his inaugural address is still considered the finest ever, full of rousing sentiments and slogans, of which the most famous was: 'And so, my fellow Americans, ask not what your country can do for you, ask what you can do for your country.' Above all, his toughness and determination during the Cuban missile crisis of 1962 became a legend and this was his greatest success, showing how a King can succeed under the most intense pressure imaginable.

JFK's failures were also on a monumental, Kingly scale. The complete fiasco of the Cuban Bay of Pigs invasion can be fairly blamed on him and his typically Kingly refusal to consult properly and listen to sober advice. Worst of all was getting involved in the war in South Vietnam in support of the corrupt and rotten Diem regime in a part of the world where the USA had no significant interests. He displayed a Kingly broad strategic approach to conflict and politics but, perhaps through inexperience, lacked understanding of the complexities of foreign policy. This also showed up in his two-day negotiations with Nikita Khrushchev (a Warrior leader of the Soviet Union), which did not go at all well for JFK, who was poorly prepared. Kings are the least comfortable Role working one to one, while Warriors, as the ordinal action Role, are much more effective and can often run rings around a King or Priest. However, the encounter highlighted another Kingly skill: being more diplomatic and less sharp edged than Warriors. Kennedy was usually polished and urbane, if sometimes given to Kingly temper tantrums and a tendency to bear grudges: 'Forgive your enemies, but never forget their names.'

Kings have a long-term, wide-angle and strategic view of action. As JFK said, 'There are risks and costs to a program of action. But they are far less than the long-range risks and costs of comfortable inaction.'

While JFK had the resources of the US government at his disposal, he ran out of time and was unable to complete his mission in life. Had he lived longer, there can be little doubt that he would have learned from his mistakes and accomplished even more. Even so, he made an extraordinary impression on the whole world and his legacy will be felt for a long time to come: 'Let us resolve to be masters, not the victims, of our history, controlling our own destiny.'

The King at Work

Kings can be found in all trades and professions, but will be happiest as the one in charge, whether of a team, department, company or country. At the competing Perspective they often run for public office, holding the rank of mayor, sheriff, governor, sometimes president; in business, they'll be the manager or CEO. Working-class Kings become overseers, shop stewards or union leaders. They are more interested in power than status (though ideally both), so would rather work behind the scenes, perhaps as a mentor, than be a figurehead.

In order to achieve excellence, Kings are happy to start at the bottom, learn the ropes and master all the aspects of a business. They prefer to begin with the top company on the principle that to learn how to win and be the best, you have to work with the best. Their progress is usually speedy and may look effortless, but is supported by hard work, discipline, vision, the capacity to come up with improved strategies and processes, and perhaps luck – luck for Kings being mainly the ability to make and seize opportunities. They may come in as a secretary and become CEO within three years.

Food and drink businesses often appeal to them. Gordon Ramsay apprenticed himself to the top French chef, then opened his own restaurant and within a few years owned a chain of restaurants worldwide. The late Robert Mondavi almost single-handedly put Californian wine on the map: 'It gives me great satisfaction, because I had the notion that we could make great wines equal to the greatest wines in the world, and everybody said it was impossible.'

Kings particularly enjoy being hoteliers, which gives them a private fiefdom and access to many people. We once visited a hotel in Scotland situated on an island whose only approach was via a drawbridge. Both island and hotel, a grand baronial mansion, were ruled and run to the most exacting standards by a King, which was particularly impressive given the difficulties of finding staff in such a remote area. In the evening guests would descend to be greeted by the King at the foot of the grand staircase; he took your drinks order and engaged you in conversation for five minutes before smoothly moving on to the next guest. The hotelier was conscious of his descent from the ancient kings of Scotland buried nearby. However, his own son and heir was skulking in the cloakroom to avoid his father's dominance.

Kings like to work in large organizations and can be found heading up many global business empires. They instinctively understand the power of the media and want to control it. In the nineteenth century they were press barons, in the twentieth Hollywood moguls, in the twenty-first they are taking over new technology and the internet. Rupert Murdoch was the first big gun to exploit satellite TV, while Jeff Bezos is dominating online shopping with Amazon. Kings are not always innovators, but they are visionaries who think big and are excellent at spotting the long-term commercial potential of a new idea or invention, including long-shot winners. It may seem to others like a big risk, even a foolhardy gamble, but their self-belief is based on sound instincts and excellent judgement. As the financier James Goldsmith quipped, 'If you see a bandwagon, it's too late.'

Kings are capable of holding their nerve over a long period, sustaining losses and setbacks and finally emerging in the dominant position. They love start-ups and are willing to take big risks and extend themselves personally and financially for long-term gain. Their preference for problem fixing over routine management (which bores them) makes them not only successful entrepreneurs but also excellent consultants and troubleshooters. They enjoy the buzz and challenge of walking into a new company, quickly spotting the problems and coming up with solutions, motivating managers and workforces, setting up structures to implement the changes, then leaving others to run it and moving on to the next challenge. One entrepreneur describes the process, having set up two successful companies and transformed business practice in her industry:

'When looking back, I realized that the biggest fun was in the first few years, the raw years when I didn't really know what I was doing but just kept at it. I had to create, materialize, multi-task and figure things out. When I look back now I am amazed at my fearlessness – maybe coming from ignorance. When you are so young, you just go and do things. If you don't know how, you just figure it out, create your own system if there isn't one that you can use.

Once I had things more under control and running smoothly, I started to get bored. How many new products can you launch and get excited about? Also, I needed something to do with more and deeper meaning to the world.'

SULA, ENTREPRENEUR

Tom Peters is one of the most famous and highly rated corporate gurus. He began his career in the US navy, then worked in the Pentagon, so military strategy was an important influence on his thinking. He then moved to McKinsey & Co., one of the world's leading management consultancies. Kings rarely write books, but if they do their books are likely to have maximum impact. Peters's first (co-authored) book, *In Search of Excellence*, has been voted the greatest business book of all time and has sold over seven million copies. This and the follow-up are the only business books to have reached the #1 spot on *The New York Times* bestseller list. Its subject matter arose out of a project led by the authors on organizational effectiveness, a major interest of Kings. The book analyzes the secrets of success in business, including strategic change, empowering decision makers, personal responsibility and accountability. The methodology has been criticized for its lack of rigour (which a Scholar would have provided), but the principles and practical advice have stood the test of time. As one of the world's top business leaders, known as the *'über*-guru', Peters is much in demand as a speaker and trainer, permanently in the public eye through his syndicated newspaper column, books, articles and regular television appearances. He is truly a global business leader who has done more than anyone to shift the management debate to a broader worldwide audience.

Leadership Style

Most Kings prefer being the boss to being an employee. As employees, they work best with some general guidance and a boss who's there to help and support but not to micro-manage. They need people around them, so most would rather work in a team than alone. While not generally co-operative, they may use consultation as a reconnaissance exercise.

'It can be useful to "help" others come up with ideas the King had first, to create trust and loyalty and to persuade and modify your plans.'
HELENA

Kings are the most demanding of employers, requiring as much loyalty from an employee as from a subject, i.e., total. At the competing Perspective they are top-down managers who can be tyrannical, believing that there are only two ways of doing something: their way and the wrong way.

'Being in charge, I had to be listened to.'
STELLA, DIRECTOR

On the other hand, they will reward loyalty, capability and good service richly with high salaries, unlimited expense accounts and lots of perks. They like to delegate and, being supremely confident and aware of the importance of good support, are unafraid to appoint the strongest people to complement their own abilities. Their subordinates are required to be on the same wavelength and share their vision, but will be given a lot of independence. Most Kings prefer to be challenged by brilliant innovators than surrounded by yes-men.

At the relationship Perspective, their style of management becomes much less ruthless. While Warriors tend to throw their weight around (needing to prove themselves), Kings can be quite gentle and relaxed, but everyone will sense their inner authority and respect them as bosses. Preferring to be invited to lead rather than having to compete and push themselves forward, which offends their Kingly dignity, they may not get the promotion they deserve. If they are unhappy or unfulfilled, they will take as much time out as they need to figure out their next step. It can be an important, liberating lesson that they don't always have to be responsible for everything and can stay at home allowing their partner to be the breadwinner. They will also develop their interpersonal skills and learn to work as effectively with individuals as groups. As a result they may scale down their operations to take care of people personally. Charities, voluntary organizations and other good causes attract them, as they are places where they can serve but also run their own fiefdom. Some become counsellors and social workers, though they have to remain aware of the needs of others:

'I have to be careful not to be too directive and to maximize people's own decision-making process.'
GINA, CLINICAL SOCIAL WORKER

At the philosophical Perspective, they often lose interest in leadership, but other people are likely to recognize their worth and try very hard to get them on board. They may decide to use their expertise in business, having attained an inner integration that enables them to lead in a more compassionate, service-oriented style. One King who is now ready to move into a more public position and set up her own business says:

> '*Although I want to call the shots, I also want to be the best leader I can possibly be – leading by example, being honest, straightforward and open. I want to experiment with kinder, more empowering forms of management and create a community around my business.*'
>
> DIANE, ADMINISTRATIVE ASSISTANT

Communication Style

As with everything they do, the communication style of Kings is authoritative. Their language is direct, concise and straightforward, though less blunt, more polished and diplomatic than that of Warriors. The combination of this style, their strong voices and their tendency to sound as though they're giving orders can intimidate people. This effect is usually unintentional.

As the most cardinal Role, Kings are better at handling groups of people than individuals. Understanding the importance of talking to people in their own language to get the best results, they are often brilliant at public speaking and rallying the troops, the electorate or the workforce. They know how to get people fired up around a cause, then guide them into using this energy for action, whether this be re-engineering a company, bringing in a new political regime or banding people into mutually supporting communities for planetary survival.

Kings are not renowned for humour, which may not accord with their dignity, particularly when they are on duty. When relaxing with friends, they like to crack jokes and particularly appreciate salty humour and people who tell it like it is. They do not appreciate being the butt of someone else's joke, however, and will give the frostiest rebuff.

> '*I do have a tendency to be very serious and take things literally (when someone is making a joke, for instance). I love humour, but I personally don't joke around much and it's rarely my first response to something. Why that is, I don't know. Perhaps it's difficult to take things lightly when we're always trying to achieve mastery.*'
>
> DIANE, ADMINISTRATIVE ASSISTANT

Kings usually have a court of their closest friends or most trusted colleagues around them. If you are not one of their courtiers, you probably won't get a chance to get close to them, as they are adept at keeping people at arm's length, allowing only a select few into their charmed inner circle. However close you are, very few people get to talk to Kings as equals, though in a good mood they enjoy conversation and banter. They are much on public display yet essentially private. They usually hate small talk, finding it a waste of time, but if it is part of their job will learn to do it smoothly and graciously.

> '*People are drawn to me, yet I don't feel I am their "friend". I know that I don't "hang out". Although I might go to a gathering, it has to have a function, like celebrating someone's birthday or a meditation, and then I go to check in with the community. I am careful who I include in my community, since I feel responsible for their welfare once I make that commitment.*'
>
> DR PAULA BROMBERG, PSYCHOLOGIST

At the relationship Perspective, Kings work at their interpersonal and diplomatic skills until they have achieved mastery of them, becoming smooth operators in the workplace, gracious hosts and loyal if not intimate friends. In the process, they discover the value of mutual self-disclosure, at least with close family and friends, partly as a reality check to deal with themselves and understand how others see them. They can still be formidable, but if you have a bit of courage and self-respect and let them know when they are encroaching too far or being domineering they will be sorry to have caused offence and graciously tone it down. But never interrupt, contradict or condescend to a King, especially in public. If you are wise, you will always let them have the last word.

At the philosophical Perspective, they become brilliant at spotting potential and can team up with unlikely people from very different areas and backgrounds. They sow the seeds, then either stay and tend them or move on as appropriate. They are happy to form an alliance with you on equal terms if they respect you as a tried and trusted counsellor, but you need to prove your mettle.

The King in Love

One of the King's biggest challenges comes in the area many people take for granted – personal relationships. Part of the difficulty is that they apply their usual high standards and expectations to their relationships and few people can live up to them. Their perfectionism can scare people off, an effect that the King does not intend. Dating can be quite stressful for them, since they rarely bother to develop their flirtation skills. Dinner *à deux*, with its expectation of engaging in intimate conversation, can make them feel awkward or tongue-tied. The good news is that their charisma attracts plenty of potential partners, though they may find it difficult to make the relationship progress. Being very decisive, they tend to fall in love quite quickly and expect everything to be decided on the spot, not having the patience for a prolonged courtship. However, more emotionally sophisticated Kings are prepared to play a long game if they feel a relationship is worth pursuing. Men find it easier, since they are expected to be assertive. Women may try making the first move and be happy to make all the running, but may scare away men who can't handle such directness. On the other hand, many men will be flattered and thrilled by it, finding their Kingly power exciting. If Kings do strike a spark, their magnetism will start working for them fast.

Kings have healthy physical appetites and great stamina, and need a lot of sex. At the competing Perspective, if they don't get their needs fulfillled at home (and sometimes even if they do), they have little compunction about going elsewhere, seeing this as their right. As James Goldsmith quipped with devastating bluntness: 'When a man marries his mistress he creates a job vacancy.' If Kings do philander, they expect their family to remain loyal and steady as a rock for them, but are quick to discard an unfaithful partner, usually with no discussion.

Kings of both genders are seen as good catches. However, you need to make it clear that you are a partner and confidant, not a servant or subject. As husbands, they are good providers who usually do well at work and can make a lot of money.

As wives, they do not take easily to domesticity, becoming angry and frustrated if relegated to the kitchen and excluded from male conversation and concerns. If they can't afford childcare, they would rather be the breadwinner with a house husband.

At the relationship Perspective, Kings are much more sensitive and empathic, offering as well as expecting total loyalty. It is highly beneficial to let themselves become open and vulnerable, rather than always being strong and independent.

At the philosophical Perspective, they appreciate that each person has equality in the general scheme of things and so deserves equal respect. They also practise a more service-oriented approach to their relationships and their life in general.

> 'I have a live-in partner and I definitely am attentive to the overall welfare of this person.'
> DR PAULA BROMBERG, PSYCHOLOGIST

Two Kings together are a very challenging partnership, but if they respect each other they will collaborate rather than dominate each other. Kings have the greatest compatibility with Warriors, who will support them with total loyalty but also stand up to them if necessary. Kings and Scholars are also highly compatible as solid Roles sharing a serious outlook and interest in world events. Kings and Artisans are opposites who experience great attraction though also difficulties in understanding each other. Sages and Priests are charismatic but challenging romantic partners for Kings, being cardinal

Roles who will compete for leadership in the relationship. Priests and Kings work better professionally, sharing a broad vision but having separate spheres of responsibility. With their superb nurturing and interpersonal skills, Servers are able to soothe and comfort Kings, getting through their barrier of reserve to achieve an intimacy that few others can manage. For a detailed description of the compatibilities between Kings and other Roles, see Chapter 9.

Parents and Children

Kings expect a lot from their children and usually get it, but the overall success of their parenting project depends a lot on their Perspective. At the competing Perspective, Kings are focused on their dynastic ambitions and see their children as heirs, so push and groom them relentlessly into taking over the family business or making a good marriage. If defied, they may cut the ties and even cut the children out of their will, though they will probably regret this. Some resemble a Victorian paterfamilias or matriarch, being formal, stiff and unwilling to get involved in childcare or play with their children.

At the relationship and philosophical Perspectives, Kings still expect their children to be well behaved and respectful, but will respect them in return, be much softer with them and help them to become independent. Men are often ideal father figures, hero-worshipped by their children, while women are mother goddesses. A parenting style that combines discipline with respect, love and the ability to open doors for their children clearly has much to recommend it in an age where so many children lack boundaries and run wild.

King children often manifest their Role from an early age, ruling their family from the nursery if not the cradle. In supermarkets they sit regally in the trolley directing their parents to the food they want. Indira Gandhi, former prime minister of India, said of herself, 'My favourite occupation as a very small child was to deliver thunderous speeches to the servants, standing on a high table.'

Kings of any age hate being coerced into doing something they don't want to do or feel is wrong, which they experience as tyranny and take as an insult to their dignity. This can be a problem in bringing up King children, who expect to be listened to and obeyed, so find it hard to adjust to the lower status of childhood. Their natural bossiness can make them extremely intimidating to weak parents, and if neither disciplined nor stretched and challenged, they can become manipulative and brattish. Their younger and even their elder siblings, parents and grandparents may run errands and dance attendance on them unquestioningly, but it is better to resist being ordered about by them. They respond well to firm but fair parenting, respecting clear boundaries and discipline more than caving in to their demands. They need to be given responsibility and put in charge of something, so it's important to give them age-appropriate tasks or responsibility of their own.

'I am a King mother with a King mother and King son, i.e., three generations. I have always chafed at my mother not listening to me and seeing my "wonderful" insights, etc., and that gives me insight to my son when my son chafes with me. For a King child, the intensity of not feeling recognized and

*honoured for who one is and the accompanying indignity are
huge. And yet the King parent may not see that through their
own filter of self-importance.'*
GINA, CLINICAL SOCIAL WORKER

Some King children have a hard time at school adjusting to
the role of pupil, identifying more with the adult world.

*'I never related to children my own age very well. They
seemed incredibly shallow and petty, and to them I seemed
serious and staid.'*
HELENA

Both boys and girls will be gang leaders, and can become
playground bullies, though those at the Relationship
Perspective are likely to rule fairly and protect the weaker
pupils. They nearly always end up highly respected and
popular, surrounded by a clique of admirers like a mini-
court. On the other hand, their aura of specialness can be
problematic for them, as it can be mistaken for arrogance,
especially if they start unconsciously treating the other
children and even the teachers as their subjects. They usually
take on lots of extra duties and end up as head of school if
they don't get bored and leave early.

Girl Kings can find childhood tough, particularly in
traditional cultures.

*'Growing up in Taiwan, girls are told to be obedient and quiet,
and not ask too many questions.'*
DIANE, ADMINISTRATIVE ASSISTANT

Parents and teachers will strive to feminize a girl King's tomboy personality and strong, athletic physique, usually with zero success. While her peers are fantasizing about becoming Bond girls, she will identify with James Bond himself. It can be hard for her to make friends and she may be made to feel 'too much'. As she progresses through the school system, though, she will usually find her feet, excelling in at least one area (more likely sports than academia). She will often end up as the leader of her social set and head girl.

Dating can be tricky for a girl King, who may find the boy she likes is too awed to ask her out, but if she is fortunate she will find a bold knight thrilled to date her. I was reminiscing recently with someone about a mutual King friend. He remembered her coming into a party as a teenager wearing a long white dress with her hair piled up. Although she wasn't pretty, she looked so elegant, sophisticated and every inch a queen that she put every other girl in the shade.

Kings often shoulder responsibilities from an early age, taking life more seriously than their peers. This feels natural to them and they are surprised that others don't understand or honour this. They may become the family breadwinner in their teens or be relied on and turned to by the whole family. They do not have much time to waste in teenage angst and self-doubt, as their life task will often summon them irresistibly. It may seem preposterous to adults that teenagers take themselves so seriously, but they may feel the hand of history on their shoulder, like the young Charles de Gaulle who 'was convinced that France would have to go through gigantic trials, and that I would one day have the opportunity of rendering her some signal service'. And so it came to pass.

At university Kings often stand out, like Benazir Bhutto, who became president of the Oxford Union (one of only two women and very few non-Britons to do so) and then prime minister of Pakistan.

King Archetypes in Myth, Fiction and Film

The King is one of the most powerful archetypes. World mythology is full of heroic Kings from an era in which kingship was viewed as a sacred institution. In the Bible, the greatest monarch was King David. Chosen by God, anointed by the high priest, he charmed King Saul with his music, defeated a giant in single combat with a sling, won many battles and became King of Israel. He then founded a mighty empire and a dynasty which Christians believe is the royal lineage of Jesus. What more could be asked of a King?

In Graeco-Roman mythology, Zeus (Jupiter/Jove) was the king of the gods and ruled the pantheon from the summit of Mount Olympus. Classical gods were full of human flaws and Zeus could be a vengeful tyrant whose main weapon was a thunderbolt.

There are all too many depictions of tyrannical Kings in mythology, fiction and film, from Agamemnon of Troy to Sauron, Lord of the Rings. Shakespeare's plays, however, are peopled with positive Kings. Perhaps the most iconic is Henry V, whose speeches rallying his troops ('Once more unto the breach, dear friends...') have never been bettered. As declaimed by the great actor Laurence Olivier, they raised morale in World War II as high as at the Battle of Agincourt.

King Arthur was the 'once and future' king of Albion (mythical Britain). Mythical Kings always have to pass tests of courage, fight dragons and win battles, but are helped by magical weapons and wizards. Arthur's kingship began with a heroic act when he emerged from obscurity as a shining youth who accepted an impossible challenge and drew a sword from a stone: the mighty Excalibur. Arthur was the greatest hero of all his knights, a military ruler who united Britain against the Saxons and established an empire over much of Europe, aided by his court wizard Merlin (a Scholar, *see p.277*). He also exemplified all the Kingly-chivalric virtues of the Middle Ages: strength, honour, valiant courage, magnanimity. His Warrior knights swore total allegiance to him and found it a great honour to serve in his court. His Queen Guinevere was famous for her dazzling beauty, but her virtue was not so shining; this bit of the myth is sometimes glossed over. The Round Table symbolizes a King who is confident enough to rule through consultation as well as the sword, giving his knights a voice. Their deeds of derring-do, particularly the quest for the Holy Grail, added to the charisma of Camelot. It seems fitting that John F. Kennedy chose Camelot as the model for his own court.

There are not many mythical depictions of female Kings. Even queens and goddesses like Hera (Juno), chief goddess of the Graeco-Roman pantheon, play a subordinate role, in her case as wife to Zeus. Athena was a Greek Warrior-Scholar goddess but with some Kingly attributes. She sprang fully formed from the head of her father Zeus and remained independent, becoming his chief ally and protector. Her iconography was the main inspiration for Marianne, personification of the French Republic, who symbolizes Reason and Liberty and inspired the Statue of Liberty. The Queen of Hearts in *Alice in Wonderland* represents the negative pole well, being in Alice's words 'a bad tempered old tyrant' whose only method of dealing with difficulties is to shout 'Off with his head!'

There are two strong women in the Bible who are clearly Kings: Judith and Deborah. Judith was a heroine who became frustrated with the Israelites for not rebelling against their conquerors, so visited the enemy general Holofernes, gained his confidence and beheaded him, thus scattering the enemy and saving the country. Deborah was another successful military leader who was also a judge and known as the 'mother of Israel'.

How to Fulfill Your King Potential

Being a King is the highest calling but has some of the toughest challenges. At their best, Kings pour abundance and power on everyone, enabling prosperity, growth and fruition. They are all Sun Kings: 'The appearance of Your Majesty is as of the Sun in his strength.' But the sun can also burn pitilessly. Being the most cardinal Role, Kings have maximum impact on their environment, which gives them the power to cause much harm if they get stuck in their negative pole of tyranny. As the Roles progress in cardinality there is less scope for fulfillment. Being the most cardinal Role, it is hard for Kings to be in their element, because there are few opportunities for leadership on the grand scale. This section summarizes how Role and Perspective work together for growth and fulfillment.

Competing Kings are big hitters, high rollers, tycoons and plutocrats. Their ambition usually takes them as far as they aim to go – which for Kings is all the way. Madonna once said she wanted to be 'as big as God'. They are the greatest movers and shakers, and some achieve world domination. At this Perspective they are likely to go for a military or political career, and also flourish in the corporate world as CEOs and entrepreneurs. If they run their own business they are likely to expand it globally, taking over or eradicating all their competitors along the way. In the negative pole they relentlessly pursue growth, sometimes at the expense of stability. Their natural instincts for justice and fair play can be easily overridden and they are likely to make life very tough and miserable for all their subordinates except those who can meet their exacting demands.

However, in their positive pole of mastery Kings can achieve enormous success for themselves and their associates, rallying the troops and uniting warring factions. When the King rules well, everyone wins. There is great satisfaction and excitement to be derived from being on the winning side in a battle or election and working for the top company. Kings at their best will give you the best experience of success and victory, rewarding loyalty with enormous generosity. Their challenge is to win on behalf of others as well as themselves, since happy subjects or workers will serve their King much more faithfully and productively, increasing the chances of long-term success and stability.

At the relationship Perspective, Kings are much more benign, better able to handle an egalitarian regime and function as teamworkers as well as bosses. They understand that happiness and self-esteem are important to a successful family and workforce, though it is hard for them to learn emotional intelligence. It takes as much courage for them to explore the mysteries of the human heart and make themselves vulnerable to a fellow human being as it does for a more ordinal Role to stand on a public platform and address the crowd. But with their usual drive towards excellence they will work hard and master these skills.

More than any other Role they need to learn kindness and compassion to overcome any scorn for human weakness arising from their own strength. Like all the Roles, they can benefit greatly from counselling and psychotherapy at this Perspective. They do not like asking for help, but once they understand the benefits, tend to go for therapy in a big way. Like Warriors, they prefer action-oriented approaches like cognitive behavioural therapy and life coaching, which achieve practical results fast, rather than long-term analysis. As a result their relationships and family lives become much smoother, more fulfilling and nurturing. Many like to lead much quieter lives out of the public view in order to devote their energies more effectively to reflection and self-development. Once they have clarified their values they immediately want to spring into action for the benefit of a humanitarian cause, and often end up running charities or leading campaigns for social justice.

At the philosophical Perspective, Kings sometimes feel like retiring from the fray, but their leadership qualities make them as much in demand as ever. They are discriminating about where they direct their energies, but whatever project they choose will have an excellent chance of doing some good in the world.

'I earn my living as a psychologist and that allows me to oversee the lives of those who decide to sign on to work with me. This has been and is wonderful work for me; I see the whole picture and slowly see the person's life unfold.'
DR PAULA BROMBERG, PSYCHOLOGIST

Kings have an instinctive affinity with nature and at this Perspective may spend time alone in wilderness retreats, enabling them to be in balance and harmony with nature and within themselves. From this position they can draw on their own sources of wisdom and compassion to see the way forward. Ultimately, they lead in order to serve; once they have attained this level of mastery they can render the very highest level of service to humanity. It then becomes a privilege and pleasure for others to work with them.

While Priests tend to lead as spiritual teachers, Kings prefer to lead democratically from within the workplace, in touch with the needs of mainstream society. One King described another King working in this way:

'All his ten companies have in common that they are in one way or another making society a better place to live in. It is his way of bringing more consciousness into people's lives without being a spiritual guru and preaching. He does all this in a low-key way, working behind the scenes. He is a great example of a philosophically oriented King using his pioneering and entrepreneurial talents to do good in the world.'
SULA, ENTREPRENEUR

◆◆◆◆◆◆

The formula for success, happiness and self-mastery in this system is a simple but powerful three-step process:

1. *Discover your Role.*

2. *Integrate it with your Perspective.*

3. *Operate from their positive poles.*

I hope by now you recognize whether you are a King or whether it is your secondary Role. Identifying your Role is the first step on a lifelong journey of self-discovery. The insight needs to be confirmed and applied in daily life on an ongoing basis for best results, so requires commitment, but with practice it becomes second nature. The reward of self-transformation is well worth the effort.

Secondary Role Influences for Kings

One of the most important factors influencing the personality variations between people who share the same Role is the secondary Role. This colours, flavours and generally modifies your personality. The combination works like an omelette: your primary Role is the egg, while your secondary Role is the added ingredient – cheese, mushroom, tomato. Sometimes the flavour is subtle, sometimes it overpowers the egg. Similarly, the secondary Role can manifest more strongly than the primary Role, particularly if it corresponds with your profession. Some people have the same Role in both the primary and secondary position, so will conform more closely with the Role archetype. If this is your case, you will probably recognize yourself quite easily. This section summarizes the influence of the other six Roles on Kings.

Artisan-Kings

The totally different, almost opposite qualities of these Roles are tricky to integrate but can make a highly creative combination. The Artisan influence gives the King more style and charm than usual. These Kings will find it easier to be female – queens and divas, adding feminine wiles to their weaponry. Emotionally they can be volatile, as both Roles are quite touchy, Artisans being hypersensitive and Kings conscious of their dignity. Generally, one-to-one relationships will come more easily to them than is usual with Kings and at the philosophical Perspective they can be the most inspirational and delightful friends and colleagues. They will be highly creative and enjoy making and repairing things, bringing their usual mastery to the process. They might express their creativity by running a fashion empire or being film directors or architects designing a new city. Donald Trump appears to have this combination: 'Deals are my art form. Other people paint beautifully on canvas or write wonderful poetry. I like making deals, preferably big deals.'

Sage-Kings

This is a very cardinal combination with excellent communication skills, good for politics and public life, or any job requiring PR and public speaking. These Kings may work in the media as directors or producers, studio bosses or impresarios. A favourite creative option is to become an orchestral conductor, where their skill at seeing or in this case hearing a complex pattern can be taken to a more elevated level. They have more sense of fun than usual and can keep the company uproariously entertained all night. They will also be highly sociable, enjoying entertaining and being entertained, and having large networks of friends and contacts. If they lose their temper, they may act out their wrath in spectacular fashion. However, they are more likely to use charm and enthusiasm to gather talented people around them who will give their absolute best for them. They make highly successful and charismatic entrepreneurs, like Richard Branson, who enjoys life and work and says: 'A business has to be involving, it has to be fun, and it has to exercise your creative instincts.'

Server-Kings

Ultimately, Kings lead in order to serve, and this is the best combination to facilitate the process. Kingly leadership qualities integrated with Server interpersonal skills make this one of the most appropriate and effective combinations for leadership in a democratic society. These Kings understand that it's often easier to lead by offering than by requesting something and will be more aware than usual of people's emotional and practical welfare. As a result, they find it easier to work one to one. One Server-King I interviewed has a successful career as a clinical social worker in healthcare. These Kings particularly favour charities and other good causes. They will be softer and gentler than the average King and may be hard to recognize initially, to themselves as well as others. Their relationships will be smoother and easier than is usual with Kings. They may experience some frustration at the competing Perspective if their Server influence holds them back from pursuing their projects as relentlessly as they would like, but the problems will probably be outweighed by the benefits.

Priest-Kings

This is one of the two most powerfully charismatic combinations possible (the other being King-Priest). These Kings will be dynamically inspirational, able to draw an enormous crowd of followers and supporters, and will have a compulsive drive to become leaders. These are world-class movers and shakers capable of having a global impact. Their word is law and few will dare oppose them. However, they are much more driven by the idea of a higher good or spiritual ideal than usual, so can establish a new ideology or religion, dealing easily with any resistance. Some cult leaders have this combination. The institution of sacred kingship embodies this idea, as with the Egyptian Pharaohs, Chinese and Japanese Emperors and the Biblical Kings. These Kings can be formidable bosses, driving their workforce to the limit in support of the cause, but will also inspire people to give their best. Family life and intimate relationships are difficult for them and their family is unlikely to get much of their time, but the whole family can be swept up and exalted in service of a great cause.

Warrior-Kings

As a double action Role, this is a tough, formidable combination. These Kings make excellent leaders and are likely to rise to the top of any organization. Their presence is so imposing that it can scare people off, especially if accompanied by an aggressive personality and hot temper. The Kings themselves are probably unaware of this effect and will expect people to stand up to them and demand a rise or promotion if they want one. They relish one-to-one conflict more than most; quick to start a fight, they will usually win it. Their bodies will be strong and athletic and they may become sporting champions or sports coaches. In relationships they will inevitably be the dominant partner, so need to find someone who will accept this dynamic. Loyalty is extremely important to them and they will both give it and expect to receive it – or else.

Scholar-Kings

This is a strong, solid and effective combination, integrating knowledge and action. As John F Kennedy said, 'Leadership and learning are indispensable to each other.' These Kings make excellent lawmakers, judges and head teachers. Academics with this combination are likely to be heads of departments, successful even as women among men, or to become government scientists or economists like John Kenneth Galbraith.

'I absorb information easily and almost compulsively. Unlike a Scholar, though, I'm mostly interested in information with

a practical application, which here is in understanding the world and people around me. I do more thinking than reading, extrapolating and interpolating the information until theories become tools. For me, mastering knowledge is like becoming deft with a tool or familiar with a map. It's not an end in itself, it's something you use.'

HELENA

These Kings may find marriage and parenting difficult, as both Roles can be distant and are not renowned for their interpersonal skills, but will benefit from having a warm, loving partner who can provide the emotional foundations for the family.

Famous Kings

Alexander the Great, Charlemagne, Attila the Hun, Genghis Khan, Lorenzo de' Medici, Catherine the Great, Boudicca (aka Boadicea), William the Conqueror, Richard I (the Lionheart), Queen Elizabeth I, Arthur Wellesley (1st Duke of Wellington), Otto von Bismarck, Simón Bolívar, Charles de Gaulle, Douglas MacArthur, Togo Heihachiro, Isoroku Yamamoto, Mao Zedong, Indira Gandhi, John F. Kennedy, Fidel Castro, François Mitterrand, Golda Meir, Benazir Bhutto, Saddam Hussein, Raisa Gorbachev, Madeleine Albright, Sarah Palin, Arianna Huffington, Aristotle Onassis, J. Paul Getty, John Muir, John Kenneth Galbraith, Hugh Hefner, Helena Rubenstein, Jack Welch, James Goldsmith, William Randolph Hearst, Rupert Murdoch, Ted Turner, Lee Iacocca, Jeff Bezos, Donald Trump, Richard Branson, Tom Peters, Louis B. Mayer, Sam Goldwyn, John Huston, Orson

Welles, Katharine Hepburn, Sean Connery, Patrick Stewart, Jack Kerouac, Jessye Norman, Thomas Beecham, Colin Davis, Herbert von Karajan, Madonna, Deepak Chopra, Robert Mondavi, Gordon Ramsay

CHAPTER 8

The Scholar

'Doing what little one can to increase the general stock of knowledge is as respectable an object of life as one can in any likelihood pursue.'

CHARLES DARWIN

The Scholar Personality

Scholars are the integration Role, who stand alone on their axis as seekers after truth. In the process they gather, interpret and store knowledge, which they are well equipped to do, being thoughtful, curious and objective. They can be found on the cutting edge of science, technology and any branch of learning, possessing an astonishing capacity to get their heads around the toughest intellectual problems and come up with solutions. A recent example is the discovery and recording of the light that shone from the first stars in the universe. All Scholars love to share and communicate their ideas, whether as writers, teachers or trainers. The 18th-century Scholar Dr Samuel Johnson exemplified the Role, being a poet and wit as well as compiler of the first dictionary: 'To talk in public, to think in solitude, to read and to hear, to inquire and to answer inquiries, is the business of the Scholar.'

The term *Scholar* is strongly associated with the professional function of scholarship, but the Role is not identical with it. Scholars have developed and mainly run the education system, science and the learned professions, but other Roles have also made valuable contributions. The archetype of the Scholar at ease with solitary intellectual labour still holds true, though nowadays with a computer in the place of the quill and parchment of the medieval monastery. Yet eventually Scholars' curiosity and adventurous spirit do lead them out of their studies, since they like to experience a wide diversity in their lives. As a result, they are likely to follow several different careers and have a number of hobbies and interests.

Scholars value knowledge, which is the positive pole of their Role. Any true Scholar will disobey the command not to eat the fruit of the tree of knowledge; it is their favourite food. The world is their school or lab, full of opportunities to study and experiment.

'I see the world as one big classroom and my life as that of the perpetual student, which leaves little room for boredom but sometimes not enough time to fit everything in.'
ANN, ADMINISTRATIVE ASSISTANT

At the rule-bound and competing Perspectives, Scholars get their knowledge second hand – from school, books, the media – and make a career out of teaching it. At the relationship and philosophical Perspectives they understand you don't own knowledge until you've experienced and validated it for yourself. They may therefore reject formal education and instead go to the jungle to study tribal culture; sing or compose to understand music; live in a cave to experience higher states of consciousness.

The scholarly function of integration is a highly complex, demanding and long-drawn-out process, requiring specialist skills, a calm, stable temperament and great stamina. Most people do not have the interest or patience for such work, but Scholars positively enjoy it. Some dedicate their life to compiling a dictionary or studying one species of insect. Many are amateur historians and archaeologists, rooting around in libraries and archives, trudging the fields with metal detectors, unearthing local traditions, running special-interest societies or websites. Most will want to dig into the history and culture of a place before going on holiday there. I know one who astonished her family by doing a doctorate in ancient Middle Eastern languages the moment her children left home and now spends her leisure time as an unpaid museum researcher deciphering fragments of stone tablets from long-vanished temples. Scholars also enjoy genealogy, and may spend years compiling their own family tree. This is a particularly satisfying activity that brings together their historical interests with their natural talent for detective work.

Whether they do their research in libraries or online, Scholars in the positive pole will subject it to rigorous testing. They have better attention spans than average, rarely suffering from attention disorders. This enables them to go into books, articles and online browsing in more depth, an important ability which much of the population is losing due to the more entertaining aspects of the internet and other media. They are the Role most at home in the information age and the knowledge economy, being the brain behind computers and the internet. As well as their own research, they perform an important service for other Roles by organizing the anarchic vastness of the web into user-friendly sites and browsers and moderating forums and chat rooms (though other Roles also do this). Only when they are satisfied that they have gathered enough solid evidence to claim as proof will Scholars make the results available to others.

The inner quality that most helps Scholars search for truth is their neutrality. They are the only neutral Role, neither cardinal nor ordinal but balanced between, at the resting point of the pendulum. Neutrality enables them to be very objective and practical, seeing all sides of a situation, which makes them excellent diplomats, moderators, facilitators and gatekeepers. On the other hand, they can easily swing into ordinality or cardinality as the situation requires.

'I enjoy both going off around the world on adventures and also staying home and baking cakes.'
NICOLA, WRITER

Ordinal Scholars are typically geeks and nerds, but cardinal Scholars become adventurous pioneers, heroic explorers and mountaineers, such as Marco Polo, Christopher Columbus, Edmund Hillary and Scott of the Antarctic. They can also become powerful leaders, harnessing their knowledge to promote a radical new idea or lead a cause. The former

British prime minister Margaret Thatcher is a Scholar who began her career as an ordinal industrial chemist but rose to become one of the most famous and controversial political leaders of the late 20th century, helped by what her daughter called her 'blotting-paper brain' and memory 'like a website'. Interestingly, the current German chancellor, Angela Merkel, is also a former chemist and a Scholar. Here is a typical Scholar self-analysis:

'I have a very neutral attitude and am a great mediator, seeing all sides of a given situation. I have often been puzzled by my ability to remain neutral in situations that are otherwise very dramatic and explosive to others. By neutral I mean having the ability to see all sides of a situation, being able to empathize with conflicting motivations and interests, being able to take a meta-perspective. I think that others value this quality.'

YVONNE, ORGANIZING CONSULTANT

Scholars comprise around 15 percent of the population. They prefer to live where knowledge is valued, ideally as members of the intelligentsia, so are happiest in liberal, scientifically oriented Western cultures rather than religious and/or superstitious cultures. Specifically, they love university towns like Oxford and Harvard. The collegiate system of universities and monasteries enables them to pursue their researches uninterrupted but well supported. Well-stocked libraries connect them to the past while new technology plugs them into the future. At the relationship and philosophical Perspectives, they are more inclined to leave their academic sanctuaries and become rootless cosmopolitans, globetrotting to wherever the cutting edge is located.

The Challenge of the Negative Pole

Scholarship at its best requires enormous skill, intelligence, patience and stamina, which not all Scholars can manage. They can easily give up, get lost or take short cuts. When this happens, they slide to their negative pole of theory. They jump to conclusions without properly researching and testing their ideas. They believe they know something because they've Googled it. This leads them to feed people false information as well as become vulnerable to blind belief, which it is their job to safeguard people against. It is the plague of the internet, where you have to wade through mountains of rubbish, including the wildest conspiracy theories and most demented gobbledegook set down as if they were gospel. The other side of the 'Hitler Diaries' hoax *(see page 22)* was that the world-renowned historian Lord Dacre authenticated the scoop, which was subsequently exposed as a crude forgery. Known ever after as 'Lord Dacre of the Diaries', he never fully recovered his reputation.

As with all the Roles, the negative pole manifests most damagingly at the competing Perspective, making Scholars opinionated, pedantic, ponderous, narrow- or closed-minded and over-analytical, unable to see the forest for the trees. As teachers they become didactic, relying on outdated notes and droning on interminably till their students fall asleep. They can get so bogged down in cataloguing and list-making that they forget to look up and enjoy the sunset. All spontaneity gets lost in the process. They may collect hundreds of recipes but carry on cooking the same old dishes because they haven't finished classifying the recipes. If they get lost they would rather blame their partner's map-reading skills than admit that the map could be wrong. A woman whose house stood on the ever-shifting border between Russia and Poland was told that her house was once more in Poland. She replied, 'Thank goodness! I couldn't stand another Russian winter.'

The negative pole becomes more subtle at the relationship and philosophical Perspectives. Scholars are more detached and less engaged with other people and life in general than the other Roles, often preferring to stand on the sidelines rather than jump in and participate fully. This more vicarious approach to life is a valid choice, but can make them overly withdrawn and reclusive.

'I like the neutrality of being a Scholar and feel it makes me a more balanced person, as I tend to see both sides of a thing. The pitfall is that at times I may have more difficulty committing to a cause, an idea or a simple life decision.'
ANN, ADMINISTRATIVE ASSISTANT

The Scholar's challenge is to stop sitting on the fence of their neutrality and move from evaluation to action.

'I can get stuck in gathering information and never feel that I know enough to take action.'
SARAH, SCHOOL PSYCHOLOGIST

The antidotes to theory are direct experience and experiment. The goal is to convert the crude matter of hypothesis into the pure gold of true knowledge. This is the true meaning of the Philosopher's Stone, and the Scholar's gift to other Roles.

> *'Knowing my Role helps me to appreciate what I'm good at rather than comparing myself unfavourably to others or envying them their natural talents and proclivities. It helps me to see my strengths and weaknesses more clearly and without the taint of judgement. It helps me to know that while some features are immutable, others are things to be aware of so that I don't act unconsciously from the negative poles but move as much as possible towards the positive poles. Ultimately, I think this has helped my spiritual evolution in a big way.'*
>
> SARAH, SCHOOL PSYCHOLOGIST

How to Recognize a Scholar

Scholars can be hard to detect when you first meet one. They can be as beautiful or handsome as any Role, but they are not usually striking in appearance. Their neutrality, coupled with a reserved manner, can make them appear bland and aloof, though talking about their favourite subject makes them much more animated. Scholars have an intellectual or bookish appearance even outside academia. They often have a high forehead (hence the epithets 'highbrow', 'egghead' and 'pointy-head') and a thoughtful, slightly quizzical expression softened by kind eyes. Ordinal Scholars can conform to the stereotype of the bespectacled geek, though cardinal Scholars who lead more active lives can come across quite forcefully.

Traditionally, scholarship has been seen as a quintessentially masculine activity, and both sexes tend to have a solid and dependable feel, though often tempered with gentleness. Men can look quite androgynous, though they do have a penchant for beards, particularly in academia. The determination and seriousness required for the pursuit of knowledge can give female Scholars a slightly masculine appearance, as seen in portraits of women academics and professionals. These are not girly girls; once out of their teens they rarely giggle and never gush. However, they can also be feminine and attractive in their own way, especially at the relationship and philosophical Perspectives, where they become less earnest and lighten up.

Scholars' capacity for absorbing impressions, including conditioning from their family or profession, means they can easily take on the colouring of other Roles. They are most likely to be mistaken for Warriors, particularly if they are more dynamic and action-oriented than usual, since both are solid, earthy Roles. Their air of authority can also make them seem like a quiet King. More ordinal, family-minded, emotionally expressive Scholars can seem like Servers. They can sometimes be intense and passionate, and if they are also spiritually inclined they may look like a Priest. Artistic, expressive, style-conscious Scholars may sometimes be mistaken for Artisans. Occasionally a Scholar with a Sage secondary Role who is more fun-loving than usual with a well-honed wit may look like a Sage.

Often if you have difficulty figuring out someone's Role because nothing leaps out at you, they turn out to be a Scholar. If you suspect someone of being a Scholar, Shepherd

Hoodwin recommends the litmus test question: 'Are you a packrat?' Scholars always have something they are collecting, accumulating, storing – stamps, postcards, recipes, CDs or, of course, books. Books are one of the biggest giveaways. A Scholar's home will be overflowing with books, not just on shelves but on every available surface, piled on the floor and stacked high on their bedside tables. Nowadays, however, many Scholars are reducing their book collections, preferring to get their information from the internet. In their leisure time they may also be 'birders', trainspotters or fossil collectors.

Scholar Style

Naturally, Scholars tend to dress neutrally. Unlike Sages, they don't want to draw attention to themselves and would rather blend in with the crowd. Grey, brown, green and black are favourite colours, and they prefer solid block colours to patterns. Comfort, ease and convenience are paramount for them, so they can look dowdy. Sometimes, though, just as an exception to prove the rule, they can allow themselves an ostentatious flourish as a mark of distinction, such as the bright bow tie of the professor or an eccentric hat like Sherlock Holmes's deerstalker.

> *'I like to have fun with fashion periodically and shake things up a bit even if I am not up on what is fashionable at the moment.'*
> ANN, ADMINISTRATIVE ASSISTANT

Occasionally women Scholars might play with the idea of putting a rebellious pink streak in their hair, but will probably end up with discreet low-lights. Until the 1960s pipes were very much part of a male Scholar's image, and the Harris-tweed clad academic or writer (or prime minister Harold Wilson) puffing away on his pipe was firmly set in the popular imagination.

Like Warriors and Kings, Scholars like to dress appropriately for the occasion, often feeling most comfortable in the simple black gown worn down the ages by academics, lawyers, clergymen and doctors. An academic, once asked why he was dressed in a mortar-board hat and buckled shoes, replied, 'My dear fellow, why ever not? This is what gentlemen Scholars always wore in the eighteenth century.' Tradition rules. QED. End of discussion.

Being a 'solid' Role, Scholars can be as hardy as mountain goats and survive in conditions that would thwart even Warriors. This is essential for the more extreme forms of information gathering, which might entail spending months in mountains and jungles. Only a Scholar would risk their life by letting a rare mosquito bite their arm in order to study the reaction.

Action-oriented Scholars enjoy exercise and sport. Most understand the need to balance intellectual with physical activity, discovering that their brains function more efficiently after a brisk walk, swim or session in the gym. But if they become obsessed with a study or research project, they can neglect their bodies. Long hours at the computer or poring over books affect their posture, so they end up with the habitual Scholarly stoop, stiff neck and weakened muscles.

The downside of their ability to absorb and store information is a tendency to hold and store emotions in their bodies instead of letting them go, causing aches and pains. When Scholars fall ill, they like to find out everything about their condition, comparing treatments and experimenting with different remedies. Their tough constitutions usually guarantee them a long and healthy life, though, and their insatiable curiosity provides them with new interests in their retirement.

Charles Darwin: A Scholar's Heroic Quest for Knowledge

Scholars' commitment to truth is absolute, whether they seek it in the external world or the inner realm of ideas. They are rarely content with received opinion, being wired up to push back the boundaries of knowledge. This often leads them into clashes with academic, state and religious authorities, but they are prepared to defend unpopular and controversial views against orthodoxy at the cost of their reputations and jobs. Under oppressive regimes they may be branded as 'heretics' and persecuted. While other Roles are more likely to bend and back down in response to threats, Scholars are literally prepared to risk their lives to defend truth. Socrates, the founder-father of Western philosophy, was put to death by the Athenian authorities as a social and moral critic who challenged the dominant authority that 'might is right', saying, 'Where the wind of the argument leads, there we must follow without fear.' Two of the greatest Renaissance scientists, Copernicus and Galileo, fell afoul of the Inquisition, and the philosopher Giordano Bruno was burnt at the stake as a heretic. They then became venerated as martyrs to science.

Charles Darwin, the most famous naturalist and geologist of the 19th century, was widely vilified in his lifetime, though not martyred. The Victorian age produced many geniuses, but he had the greatest impact on his own time and ours. His discovery of the principle of natural selection, also known as the theory of evolution, transformed the worldview of millions of people. Until this point, despite 300 years of scientific endeavour, Christianity had still been the dominant ideology, offering a crude 'creationist' theory of the origins of life. The palaeontologist Stephen Jay Gould wrote, 'We are fortunate (in the biological sciences) to have as our founder someone who was wholly admirable.'

Darwin was a quiet, solitary child, who loved exploring the countryside around his home. Like many Scholars, he was an obsessive collector, especially from nature. He was sent to a school where the main emphasis was on Latin and Greek, which he found tedious and pointless, getting low grades, to the disappointment of his father, who thought he lacked intelligence. This is typical of Scholars at the relationship and philosophical Perspectives; they have a strong sense of what knowledge is important to them and disdain what society thinks is a proper education. Obeying his father's wishes, Darwin studied medicine, but was shocked by the butchery of its methods, so switched to theology. Yet he had little interest in the subject and devoted most of his energy to collecting beetles on his long walks.

His passion for the natural sciences was rekindled when he met botanists and geologists who profoundly influenced his thinking and probably sowed the seeds of evolution in his mind – guiding him at last to his true calling. Among those teachers was a freed black slave who taught him taxidermy. This made him understand – unusually for the times – that there was little difference between races, and he became an abolitionist. For the rest of his life, he had an abiding hatred of slavery and cruelty in all forms. This is important, since the theory of evolution has sometimes been twisted to justify racism. He said: 'If the misery of our poor be caused not by the laws of nature, but by our institutions, great is our sin; but how this bears on slavery, I cannot see; as well might the use of the thumbscrew be defended in one land, by showing that men in another land suffered from some dreadful disease.'

Scholars will sacrifice much and travel to the ends of the Earth for knowledge. Soon after graduating, Darwin was offered an unpaid job as a naturalist for a round-the-world survey lasting several years on HMS *Beagle*. He jumped at the opportunity: 'If a person asked my advice before undertaking a long voyage, my answer would depend upon his possessing a decided taste for some branch of knowledge, which could by this means be advanced.'

On the voyage he contracted a serious, painfully debilitating illness which was to last for years. Despite this, during and after the epic journey, he persevered with his beloved collecting and sorting on a grand scale. Like many Scholars, he was a natural recluse, so found it easy to switch between ordinal and cardinal modes, retreating back to his study after his big adventure. Correctly anticipating the wrath of the scientific and religious establishment, he delayed as long as possible publishing his great work *On the Origin of Species*, quipping: 'It is like confessing to a murder.' Fortunately the exhaustive detail of his research and the thoroughness of his experiments ensured that despite the many objections to his theories, the sheer weight of evidence would eventually overcome all opposition apart from the most bone-headed fundamentalists.

On the Origin of Species was a bestseller, despite or because of the negative publicity. This book and his other publications propelled Darwin onto the big stage and made him the leading public intellectual of the age. However, he preferred to live a quiet life as a gentleman Scholar and family man, avoiding the excitement of public debate and controversy. He was aided at several stages by Warriors, particularly his 'Bulldog', Thomas Huxley, who protected him from the attacks of conservative religious figures.

Darwin was not thrilled that having successfully challenged one fundamentalist ideology, his own free-spirited enquiry became dogmatized. 'I was a young man with uninformed ideas. I threw out queries, suggestions, wondering all the time over everything; and to my astonishment the ideas took like wildfire. People made a religion of them.' The irony is that if Scholars' radical ideas do get accepted, Priests are likely to make a new religion out of them. Today's heresy is tomorrow's dogma. Nevertheless, Darwin deserves his position in the pantheon as one of the foremost architects of the modern scientific worldview.

The Scholar at Work

In tribal societies, Scholars would have been shamans or medicine men; in the medieval world, scribes or chroniclers.

Nowadays the white-coated scientist is the iconic Scholar. Academia is their natural home, but any kind of teaching, training and research appeals to them. Their favourite job would be running a think tank. Being good at absorbing knowledge and passing exams, they dominate the traditional professions, particularly medicine and the law. Other occupations using a broad knowledge base such as publishing and the media will also appeal. Scholars are useful if not essential in most professions and as the neutral role can fit in well almost anywhere. Their main requirement is mental stimulation, though they can enjoy basic technical work if it includes a problem-solving element, such as plumbing and electrics, car mechanics or running the office IT system. Most will feel deeply frustrated if confined to mind-numbing routine tasks, even at professional level. Many a Scholar who has found themselves in a desirable post, perhaps family medicine or tax law, eventually wants to escape and wishes that they had done something else in life. The thought of yet another patient or client with a routine problem coming to consult them is enough to make them want to reach for a drink.

On the other hand, Scholars' definition of 'dull' work differs from that of other Roles. They are the world's great record-keepers and can be happy as historians, librarians, curators, registrars, accountants, even bookkeepers. No other Role would be able to sustain the intellectual labour of lexicography: compiling words into dictionaries, encyclopaedias, thesauruses. Nowadays Scholars flourish in creating such resources online, wikipedia being one of the great contemporary Scholarly achievements. When TV documentaries make their obligatory descent into a vast basement stacked to the ceiling with books and boxes, this treasure of ancient manuscripts, pottery fragments or old bones is guarded and maintained for posterity by Scholar archivists. To other Roles it would seem a dungeon, but to Scholars it is a sacred calling. Paradoxically, they are oriented to the future as much as the past, and excel as futurologists, climatologists, financial analysts and trendspotters. Since we live in exciting but uncertain times, good forecasting skills are much in demand.

Scholars enjoy using their linguistic skills creatively as professional writers. Dr Johnson described his dictionary-making as 'harmless drudgery' and dreamed of becoming a poet, which eventually he did. Scholars make the best critics and reviewers, having more ability than other Roles to get beyond personal taste and current fashion to objective criteria. They make good journalists, especially on the investigative and comment side, taking great pains to check their facts and sources. As authors, they dominate the non-fiction genres and even their novels are well researched, acutely observed and historically accurate. Many of the greatest novelists were Scholars, including Jane Austen, Charlotte Brontë, Thomas Hardy, Henry James, Iris Murdoch, J.R.R. Tolkien, Margaret Atwood and the recent Nobel Prize winner Doris Lessing.

Scholars team up well at work with most Roles, particularly Warriors. Scholars understand that their knowledge is of limited value without action, while Warriors know that action without underpinning knowledge can be harmful. These two Roles run most schools, as well as collaborating in the army, the police, business and politics. They enjoy combining action and knowledge out in the field as archaeologists, geologists, anthropologists and explorers. Being in nature is healing to Scholars' busy minds and of course an interesting field of study. Many ornithologists, botanists, gardeners, guides and trackers are Scholars. They are good with animals, who find their calm neutrality non-threatening, and make excellent vets, zookeepers and animal trainers. Being curious, discreet, methodical and able to blend in well, they also make good detectives and secret agents. Sir Francis Walsingham, Queen Elizabeth I's spymaster, was a Scholar.

Leadership Style

In the modern workplace, the Scholar is a key figure. Their neutrality and knowledge base make them indispensable all-around players in the team. Few teams will stay functioning for long unless there is at least one Scholar playing a significant part as a mediator bridging the gaps between the various Roles. They are often chosen to be the team leaders in situations where rivalry is intense, including politics. Other politicians can often reach consensus on a Scholar as the default if not the first choice for the post of president or prime minister (for example, George Washington, Woodrow Wilson, Richard Nixon, Clement Atlee, Margaret Thatcher). The leadership position is not something that Scholars themselves normally seek – they are seldom particularly ambitious, except at the competing Perspective, and rely on others to put them forward and look after their interests. Once in a responsible supervisory or managerial job, however, they can often come out of their determined detachment and blossom into a formidable champion for their organization.

Perhaps the hardest thing for Scholars is to assert themselves, speak out when needed and fight their corner against the plots and schemes of colleagues. They believe intelligence and capability are enough, not appreciating the need for social and political skills to advance their career. The easy camaraderie of office life that most people take for granted can be quite painful for them. They get upset and angry if overlooked for promotion in favour of a less bright but more charming colleague. They don't see the point of exchanging gossip by the water cooler, lunching with colleagues or schmoozing bosses, and so are excluded from the grapevine. As a result they may miss out on rumours of promotional opportunities. All too often, they may know the answer to a problem or the best way out of a tight spot, but remain quiet, perhaps preferring to mull over the pros and cons of the situation. Worse still, they may not forcefully demand the resources they need to do their job properly or run their department.

The way out of this detachment is either mentoring by an older hand (ideally a Warrior), or management training, such as assertiveness courses. Alternatively, and this is the aim of this book, a person can become aware that they are a Scholar, be alert to the impartiality of their role and consciously counteract it when the time comes for decision and action.

Communication Style

Scholars' aim in communication is to present their truth as accurately and objectively as possible. They understand better than any other Role the fallacy of the absolute statement and generally will not express a strong opinion until they can support it in a court of law. Their language is peppered with provisos – 'on the other hand', 'it could be argued' – along with a whole spectrum of conviction from the cautious ('maybe') through greater confidence ('probably') to near-certainty ('usually'), which is as close to the absolute as most Scholars get. When a Scholar in the positive pole asserts an opinion with total confidence, they are worth listening to seriously, as their claims will be backed up by extensive research, much thought and balancing of conflicting evidence, while other Roles would be content with a straw poll or even a hunch. However, in the negative pole Scholars can be opinionated and sometimes charmless, interrupting stories to correct facts and rejecting compliments as exaggerations.

While Scholars do not crave the spotlight as much as the cardinal Roles, they do want to share their knowledge. At the competing Perspective they have a tendency to lecture their audience as if they were in a classroom, so can become bores, but at the relationship Perspective they become more sensitive to their listeners and can present information interestingly. At their best, with a subject they know and love, they can hold an audience enthralled as charismatically as Sages. With practice and experience, they are mostly good at public speaking, though they don't improvise well and prefer to use notes. At other people's talks they usually take notes as part of their recording function. They like to have a platform for their ideas, preferably a newspaper column, but a blog will do. Most public intellectuals are Scholars, though Sages and Priests compete for this position. While Sages like to get together at a party and Warriors like to work together on a project, the Scholar's favourite venue is the conference, where they can exchange ideas without getting bogged down in small talk, which bores them.

> '*Sometimes I feel lonely. I yearn for community with others of a scholarly bent though not necessarily confined to the strictures of academia. I have been able to synch up with other musicians, but the lack of depth in most of our discussions has often left me wanting more.*'
>
> JOSEPH, ENGINEER

Like Sages, Scholars love words and are equally adept at using them, but more in service of truth than entertainment. They are the natural arbiters and custodians of language and culture. Sages coin new words, while Scholars note, collect, define and compile them into dictionaries. Sages are interested in developing language creatively and wittily, while Scholars are more concerned with rigorous meaning. Dr Johnson expressed his goal with his dictionary as 'I have laboured to refine our language to grammatical purity, and to clear it from colloquial barbarisms, licentious idioms, and irregular combinations.' One of Scholars' best communication skills is the ability to simplify information to the level of their listeners or readers without patronizing them. This ability makes them excellent TV presenters who can turn abstract ideas into riveting viewing.

Scholars often have a good sense of humour, though not everyone gets it. Their strength is in puns and wordplay, which makes them good at solving and compiling crosswords. They do irony better than any other Role and can be very funny with a dry, world-weary wit delivered in a deadpan way. But because they keep a straight face and don't signal that a joke is on its way, if anything underplaying it, their audience may miss it. They therefore need to learn to deliver their humour with more expression and panache to get laughs.

Scholars are the least sociable Role. Many would rather stay at home with a good book than go to a party and some avoid social gatherings altogether apart from small get-togethers of friends. When they first meet people, they tend to blend into the background in order to study without being observed. This is a useful ability for novelists and spies, both of which activities appeal to Scholars. As a result, other people may not notice them, especially in a group of talkative Sages and Artisans, charismatic Priests and domineering Warriors. In comparison to these noisier Roles, Scholars can appear quiet, unassuming and emotionally withheld. In fact, they experience emotion as deeply and intensely as anyone, but its expression is more reserved, especially in public.

The best way to communicate with a Scholar is to ask them questions about what they're working on or reading, or for their views on the issues of the day. Scholars can answer an impressive range of questions off the top of their head or track down the answer on the internet in a few minutes, which makes them a useful resource for people. Woolly-mindedness is their worst bugbear, so be cautious about sounding off to them on topics you know nothing about, as your ignorance will be quickly and pitilessly exposed. Since they prefer to connect mind to mind initially and are uncomfortable with self-disclosure, they may get embarrassed or clam up if you launch straight in with personal questions.

At the relationship Perspective, they develop their emotional and social skills in balance with their intellects, becoming much warmer and friendlier. One characteristic they share with Priests is that people will often confide in them, though more in search of their expertise and non-judgemental objectivity than the compassion and empathy that Priests offer. People do not so much pour out their hearts and souls to Scholars as ask for advice with problems they are wrestling with in order to get a balanced overview of the issues.

At the philosophical Perspective, Scholars blossom, resembling Shakespeare's verse portrait:

> *'He was a scholar, and a ripe and good one.*
> *Exceedingly wise, fair-spoken and persuading;*
> *Lofty and sour to them that loved him not;*
> *But to those men that sought him sweet as summer.'*

The Scholar in Love

'When a Scholar goes to seek a bride, he should take an ignoramus along as an expert,' advises the Talmud. While this sounds brutal, there is a certain truth in it. In their negative pole of theory, Scholars are inclined to overlook the finer points of interpersonal relationships and are not always the best judges of a prospective partner; in fact they can be quite naïve. As a result, they can be knocked for six by a sexual attraction that catches them unawares, feeling lost if they can't deal with a situation rationally. Many Scholars end up with unsuitable partners for this reason, hence the Talmudic advice to take along someone who is less learned but more worldly wise.

At the relationship or philosophical Perspective, Scholars are much better balanced and will find their love lives much easier to handle, though they will still have a tendency to intellectualize the process:

> *'We take an academic approach, studying, dissecting, evaluating, until that swell of emotion overtakes the mental process and the feelings can finally allow us to be swept off our feet. Then, after the initial grand passion, we settle back down to studying, dissecting, evaluating the how, why and progress of the relationship.'*
>
> ANN, ADMINISTRATIVE ASSISTANT

Their neutrality can work well for them romantically. People accustomed to wearing their heart on their sleeve can be intrigued and captivated by Scholars' cool intellect and reserved mystique. They become curious and challenged to get behind the smooth façade – melt the ice maiden, kindle the fire of the inscrutable man. They may succeed, at least temporarily. Scholars can be passionate, though rarely as dramatically as an Artisan or Sage, and would rather not be teased and pressured into expressing undue emotion. They have strong physical as well as intellectual needs and an earthy sensuality that rebalances their intellectualism. Although they can be a bit wooden or inhibited, they are keen to learn, and with a sympathetic partner can become skilled and sensitive lovers.

Scholars' still waters run deep, in contrast to the shallow sparkle of some other Roles. However, their neutrality is for real, so their partner may feel frustrated and misled when they discover this, believing that there's nothing there. This result is more likely if the Scholar is stuck in the negative pole. At the relationship and philosophical Perspectives, they learn emotional intelligence and can express and communicate their inner states and feelings directly. As a result their partner is more likely to appreciate the advantages of having a more objective and stable partner who can handle and balance out their own emotional excesses and rise above momentary flare-ups. Because of their low-key manner, Scholars are not always instantly recognized as a good catch unless they are doing very well professionally, but they are a good prospect for a long-term relationship. They make steadier partners and more reliable breadwinners than some of the more glamorous but flightier Roles, as well as providing intellectual companionship.

Their most compatible partner is often another Scholar. This can make one of the best and most loving marriages. Otherwise, their best partner is often a Warrior, who will respect the Scholar's knowledge while revitalizing them with their boundless energy. Scholars feel exalted by Kings, who can harness their ideas to a bigger cause. Servers can be good for them, nurturing and supporting them while drawing them out emotionally. Charismatic Priests are likely to attract them but clash with them over values and beliefs. They are highly attracted by the style and vivacity of Artisans, and though their differences can prove tricky, they share an independent spirit as well as a fascination with new gadgetry. They are often dazzled by Sages, and this relationship can work well if both are intellectually oriented. For a detailed description of the compatibilities between Scholars and other Roles, see Chapter 9.

Parents and Children

Scholars are primarily interested in children as young minds to be educated, and sometimes prefer being teachers to parents. At the competing Perspective, the old Latin saying *Aut libri aut liberi* (Either books or children) often applies, with books the preferred choice. Scholars find children distracting and can be quite cold and remote, often retreating to their studies. At the relationship Perspective, they become much more interested in the process of child development and accepting of children as they are. Being good mediators, they are concerned with fairness and will avoid favouritism better than most people. They enjoy the educational side of parenting and are good at answering their children's questions with infinite patience and helping them with their homework. They are likely to give them improving outings and treats such as visits to museums and art galleries, but more active Scholars will also play with them and take them to sporting events. At the philosophical Perspective, they become much warmer and more fun, and can make delightful parents.

Scholar children often learn to talk early, in fully formed sentences. They love books and will want to be read to by their parents, but as soon as they learn to read (usually very fast) will prefer to read to themselves, racing through every book in the school library.

'Sometimes my mother says she's sorry she got me interested in books, because it became impossible to keep me away from them.'
VIIVI, RESEARCH ASSISTANT

Nowadays they also take to computers at an early age and it can be hard to tear them away from the screen to get them playing outside. They also enjoy jigsaws and word-based games like Scrabble. They are often quiet, serious and studious, and will ask lots of questions about everything. It is important to allow and encourage this tendency, which comes from a genuine curiosity and desire to learn, not to annoy. If the parents don't have the time and ability to answer their questions, they need to direct them to sources of knowledge, otherwise they will get extremely frustrated.

Scholar girls are often tomboys. If they are not reading or on the computer, they would rather climb trees than play with dolls.

'Growing up, I was brainy and learning came easily to me. I had no idea that was not the case for everyone. I loved to read. As a child I loved to play outside and engaged in neighbourhood pick-up games of softball and kick the can. However, as a girl growing up in the 1950s and '60s, athletic endeavors were not encouraged. The combination of my predisposition toward the life of the mind and an absence of external encouragement resulted in a lack of development of physical skills. This would have been so helpful as a child. Sadly that energy instead fueled the endless activity of an overactive mind, yielding a tendency to think more than do.'

REBECCA, CLINICAL PSYCHOLOGIST

Scholar children usually flourish at an academic school with good teaching, becoming star students and passing exams easily. They sometimes become bookworms, which can make them unpopular and even bullied. It is important to encourage them to be more outgoing and active, make friends, enjoy sports and creative activities. It is not uncommon for Scholar children to confuse their teachers by doing brilliantly at subjects they're interested in and are well taught, and spectacularly badly at subjects that bore them or are badly taught. A Scholar I interviewed, who grew up in China, explained how a very advanced culture had become used as an instrument of oppression:

'As a Scholar I fit well in Chinese culture. However, the social structures support more the negative pole of theory. For example, we had to do heavy studies of Chinese history (5,000 years of data) and memorize all Confucius's words and Lao Tze's Tao Te Ching, *but their daily lives told a different story. China is still an imperial empire. The head of government would use Confucius's words as rules and threats to control people. Basically people live in repressed fear under debatable theories.'*

YUNG, DANCER

As teenagers, Scholars at the competing Perspective often get into top universities and do brilliantly, ignoring all distractions as they climb the academic ladder. The teenage dating scene can be quite difficult for them, though, particularly for girls in families where intelligence is not valued for women.

'I was told that men don't like brainy girls, so I should develop a more bubbly personality or I wouldn't get any dates. I learned to put on a fluffy, feather-brained act, but got really confused. I couldn't really accept myself for many years until I finally found a fellow-Scholar who loved my mind.'

JULIE, EDITOR

At the relationship and philosophical Perspectives, they go to university if it suits them, but are more likely to reject this obvious route to knowledge as boringly predictable, preferring to go off on their travels and adventures and get their knowledge in more unorthodox ways, as Darwin did.

'For most of my life, I had no "life goal". In high school, most people would say, "Oh, I'm going to be a doctor," or whatever. I never had a desire to "be" any particular thing when I grew up. I just wanted to know lots of stuff; I really enjoyed learning. But I always felt bad because I had no desire to grow up and be a this or a that. Finding out that I'm a Scholar and Scholars often just like to learn things made me "okay".'

JOHN, TELECOMMUNICATIONS

Scholar Archetypes in Myth, Fiction and Film

Athena was the Greek goddess of wisdom and philosophy and patron deity of Athens, the most scholarly culture of the ancient world. As a wise counsellor, she helped many of the Greek heroes on their quests. A good mediator, she ended a family feud to provide the *Odyssey* with its happy ending. Her beauty was serene, but serious and aloof. Nowadays she is often depicted in university libraries accompanied by an owl and a serpent, symbols of learning.

The Greek myth of Pandora's Box offers a variation on the Garden of Eden myth. Pandora was the world's first woman and was given a box by the gods but forbidden to open it. Of course curiosity got the better of her; she opened the box and all the evils of the world flew out. Every Scholar is a potential Pandora, until they learn better judgement.

The mad scientist is a Scholar parody popular in fiction and film. Dr Frankenstein is the most famous example, invented by the Scholar author Mary Shelley. Other iconic movie examples are Dr Strangelove, and the James Bond villain Dr No.

The ideal Scholar archetype is the 'wise old man', shaman or magus. The most famous mythical example is the wizard Merlin, King Arthur's most trusted counsellor. People were afraid of Merlin's magical powers but respected his wisdom. His downfall came from falling in love with a beautiful enchantress who coaxed the secrets of his powers from him and used them to imprison him. Male Scholars often have a naïve susceptibility to female beauty, so this is a plausible fate.

Prospero, the philosopher duke of Shakespeare's play *The Tempest*, was based on the real-life Scholar Dr John Dee, Queen Elizabeth I's court astrologer, who was seen as a Merlin figure. Prospero prefers studying to ruling ('My library was dukedom large enough'), so loses his throne to traitors, but gains self-mastery on the island where he is shipwrecked. When he learns to use his magical powers wisely and compassionately he becomes a true Magus, declaring, 'I'll break my staff ... and drown my book,' which he no longer needs. More recent fictional/film examples of the Merlin archetype are the wizard Gandalf in *The Lord of the Rings* and the wizard headmaster Dumbledore in the Harry Potter novels.

Portrayals of Scholars in movies are often disappointing and implausible, since the majority of film actors are Artisans. Some fluffy librarians spring to mind, who forget their books the moment they take off their glasses. *A Beautiful Mind* was a biopic of the mathematician John Nash, whose mind was not revealed beyond the cliché of equations scrawled on blackboards. Scholars are better portrayed in science fiction films, such as the series *Star Trek*, where they run the spaceships along with Warriors and Kings and are given their own planets, such as Vulcan or Trill. Mr Spock, Data (a robot), Jadzia Dax and the hologram Arnold Rimmer in the *Red Dwarf* sitcom are all clearly identifiable as Scholars.

Sherlock Holmes, the archetypal Scholar detective, has been frequently depicted on screen. His creator, the Scholar novelist Arthur Conan Doyle, said: 'Detection is, or ought to be, an exact science, and should be treated in the same cold and unemotional manner.'

Scholars can be romantic heroes, but are usually more reserved than other Roles. Most typical are Mr Darcy and Mr Knightley, creations of the Scholar novelist Jane Austen, though their scholarliness is sometimes sexed up when they are acted by Artisans and directed by Sages.

Jane Eyre is the creation of another Scholar novelist, Charlotte Brontë. Unusually plain for a romantic heroine, she is redeemed by her intelligence, honesty and steadfast soul, which finally win her a Byronic hero husband.

How to Fulfill Your Scholar Potential

Scholars carry a major responsibility, since the integration of knowledge underpins the work of all the other Roles. At their best, they are pundits who advance the sum of knowledge and the cause of understanding. Whether poring over old manuscripts in a library, expanding computer databanks, concocting remedies in a lab or discovering new species deep in the rainforest, they leave the world richer as a result. At their worst, they are pedants who entangle themselves and others in the false consciousness and confusion of woolly, wild or untested theories. This section summarizes how Role and Perspective work together for growth and fulfillment.

At the competing Perspective, Scholars are intent on making their way in the world and coming out on top. Their goal is to become award-winning scientists and professors at top universities with lots of letters after their name. An academic degree is their equivalent to the Warrior's sporting trophy. They often succeed, but in the negative pole may become arrogant know-alls. They are also liable to exploit their assistants and colleagues, using their work for their own glory, sometimes without due acknowledgement. At this perspective they can easily become obsessed with a branch of knowledge, getting bogged down in over-specialization. Some are walking encyclopaedias, full of undigested facts and data that are useful for winning quizzes and passing exams but do not lead to any deeper understanding. Their relationship skills are minimal and they can often end up either alone or in an unsuitable relationship. However, in their positive pole they can add immensely to the sum of knowledge, sometimes making huge breakthroughs and important discoveries that change our understanding of the world and advance civilization. The great universities are staffed by competing Scholars who provide an environment for other people at this Perspective to gain the glittering degrees that will take them on to worldly success. Their lesson is to get beyond the selfish pursuit of knowledge to advance their own career and to produce useful knowledge that will benefit humanity.

At the relationship Perspective, Scholars start to enquire into the deeper meaning and purpose of all branches of learning. They also realize that Descartes's famous dictum 'I think, therefore I am' is not the whole truth, even for Scholars. They therefore begin the arduous journey from IQ to EQ, developing their emotional intelligence to achieve a balanced personality. They are liable to feel helplessly at sea in the storminess of personal relationships, so often seek help from professional counsellors and therapists. With their usual curiosity, they are likely to explore the full panoply of therapies and self-help approaches on offer before settling on whatever works best for them.

As with all Roles, they may need to retreat from active participation in society at some stage, but since they value the solitary life more than most people will find this process less arduous and more interesting. They are likely to reject organized religion in favour of alternative spiritualities, possibly joining a religious movement that promises personal growth and enlightenment. Their fascination with the human mind may lead them into careers as psychologists or psychiatrists, or social scientists studying human behaviour at a collective level. They can become fine writers, composing subtle yet powerful poetry out of the pain of life. Service is important to them, and they want their work and knowledge to benefit people, particularly those who need it most, so often do a lot of *pro bono* or voluntary work. They are more likely to teach at a rough school than a top university.

At the philosophical Perspective, their intellectual development expands from micro-specialism to the bigger picture, understanding how it all hangs together. They begin to plug into a deeper truth and become a messenger for it rather than claiming ownership of knowledge, and are thus able to receive and communicate true enlightenment. The continuing search for underlying principles to the endless stream of information in the world leads them to the most advanced and rarefied branches of science, philosophy and metaphysics. Most of the extraordinary ideas coming out of modern physics, like parallel universes or intelligent life-forms retrospectively creating the laws of nature, come from philosophical Scholars, generally to the dismay of more conventional colleagues. They accept that life is a mystery to be lived, not a problem to be solved. Many cultivate spiritual practices like Zen Buddhism, which help their busy, noisy minds quieten into 'no-mind'. They tune in to nature as a spiritual resource and may become shamans. Some become mystics, getting enormous contentment from leading a contemplative existence and teaching anyone interested in sharing their wisdom. One 'everyday mystic' described his practice as:

'Be still, pray, meditate, study, contemplate, attain a balanced perspective, put yourself in others' shoes.'
JOSEPH, ENGINEER

◆◆◆◆◆◆

The formula for success, happiness and self-mastery in this system is a simple but powerful three-step process:

1.   *Discover your Role.*

2.   *Integrate it with your Perspective.*

3.   *Operate from their positive poles.*

I hope by now you recognize whether you are a Scholar or whether it is your secondary Role. Identifying your Role is the first step on a lifelong journey of self-discovery. The insight needs to be confirmed and applied in daily life on an ongoing basis for best results, so requires commitment, but with practice it becomes second nature. The reward of self-transformation is well worth the effort.

Secondary Role Influences for Scholars

One of the most important factors influencing the personality variations between people who share the same Role is the secondary Role. This colours, flavours and generally modifies your personality. The combination works like an omelette: your primary Role is the egg, while your secondary Role is the added ingredient – cheese, mushroom, tomato. Sometimes the flavour is subtle, sometimes it overpowers the egg. Similarly, the secondary Role can manifest more strongly than the primary Role, particularly if it corresponds with your profession. Some people have the same Role in both the primary and secondary position, so will conform more closely with the Role archetype. If this is your case, you will probably recognize yourself quite easily. This section summarizes the influence of the other six Roles on Scholars.

Artisan-Scholars

This is a tricky combination of very different energies, but great for creativity and original thought. These Scholars like to study something, then do something creative with it. It can be hard for them to decide upon a direction, to choose between arts and sciences, creative or intellectual activity:

'I'm a research assistant who'd rather be an illustrator.'
VIIVI

The ideal is to integrate the different interests or energies, for example illustrating natural history books. Many inventors have this combination, being well equipped to create, research and test their prototypes. It is also good for any work involving machines, innovations, fixing things and solving technical problems. These Scholars do particularly well in the worlds of IT and multimedia as engineers and software designers. Their sensitivity can make for painful relationships, but they will be more stylish and better dressed than usual.

'I am making "me" a case of study, yet I would like to splash some colour, shape it in some form and find it a little more amusing.'
YUNG, DANCER

Sage-Scholars

A superb combination for writing which gives these Scholars the ability to express and communicate ideas accessibly and entertainingly for a mainstream audience. Their style will be more accessible, polished and witty than that of the average Scholar or academic and will be likely to contain jokes, puns and other wordplay. Their fiction will be sharply observed, wickedly though discreetly satirical, witty and polished. It is probable that Jane Austen had this combination. These Scholars also make good journalists, able to wade through and distil the raw data fast, so their articles will be well researched and authoritative. As radio DJs they combine a vast knowledge of music with communication skills without needing a live audience. They make some of the best teachers, workshop leaders and public speakers, combining the teaching and communication skills of both Roles and with more charisma than usual. They are more sociable, sophisticated and urbane than the average Scholar, which makes them popular as friends and colleagues and desirable as romantic partners. They usually have good relationships with their partners and children.

Server-Scholars

This combination makes for a softer, friendlier personality, with better emotional intelligence than is usual with Scholars. These Scholars enjoy work that combines knowledge with service, so make ideal librarians, patient and helpful in handling enquiries as well as good with the books. They are also excellent teachers, kind and patient with slow learners as well as star students. As pharmacists, they combine knowledge with helpful advice and a friendly, comforting manner. Their empathy and interpersonal skills make them good healers and they usually prefer evidence-based approaches like herbalism and homoeopathy. Their relationships are likely to be warmer, more comfortable and nurturing than usual with Scholars.

> *'Since my early 20s I have been studying aspects of human development and relationships – psychology, spiritual teachings, organizational development, and more. I've trained and practised as a psychotherapist, professional organizer, and coach. ...I've spent a great deal of time seeking to better understand ADHD (the Scholar seeking information, knowledge and understanding with endless curiosity) to help myself better understand my clients and the many organizing challenges they face in daily life. Everything I learn helps me identify and work with their unique ways of being and functioning.'*
>
> YVONNE, ORGANIZING ASSISTANT

Priest-Scholars

It is important for these Scholars to study a subject they find inspiring rather than knowledge for knowledge's sake. As they are likely to be drawn to the study of religion, philosophy or metaphysics, this is the ideal combination for a theologian or sociologist of religion. They will establish an intellectual framework for the visions of Priests, or critique these visions if they see them as woolly and misguided. Once they accept a cause, they can be easily drawn out of their neutrality into the inspirational zone and will work well with Priests and Servers. They make good teachers, public speakers and workshop leaders, able to motivate people to learn enthusiastically. They may be drawn to a monastic life where they can study as well as pray. In relationships they will have more charisma than usual and be able to inspire and be inspired by their partner and children.

Warrior-Scholars

This is a comfortable combination, since the two Roles are highly compatible. These Scholars will be interested in knowledge that is useful and practical, such as teaching business administration or leading workshops on corporate team building. They are more enterprising and better able to set up a business and hold their own in the rough and tumble of the business world than more introverted Scholars. Warrior drive and relish for challenge helps them flourish as consultants. They make exceptional teachers, coping better than most Scholars in rough schools where they need to keep order as well as teach. Enjoying nature and the outdoor life, they make excellent geologists, archaeologists and explorers, putting high-level knowledge to use in an active, adventurous career. Their toughness, athleticism and teaching skills make them good sports coaches. They can also flourish in the military and police forces, particularly as detectives and intelligence offers, well able to hold their own in these Warrior-dominated environments. Their relationships are more assertive than usual:

> 'My Warrior influence sometimes makes me defensive and a bit bellicose in close relationships, but also protective and motherly.'
> EVELIN, TRANSLATOR

Generally they are loyal and lovable friends and partners, warm-hearted, intellectually stimulating and more active and dynamic than usual.

King-Scholars

They will have tremendous gravitas, even grandeur, and good leadership skills. Their ideas will be received with great respect and they often achieve a high position or platform from which to hold forth. As academics, they are likely to be heads of departments or major research institutions, often in a practical or scientific field. They are more likely than usual to take to politics and public life, combining Scholarly mediation skills and ease in assimilating information with Kingly authority and leadership skills. It is likely that former British prime minister Margaret Thatcher (the 'Iron Lady') had this combination. They also make excellent judges. One I interviewed worked as a consultant specializing in organization design, change management, leadership and team development and conflict resolution. These Scholars may find marriage and parenting difficult, as both Roles can be distant and are not renowned for their interpersonal skills, but will benefit from having a warm, loving partner who can provide the emotional foundation for the family.

Famous Scholars

Socrates, Plato, Aristotle, René Descartes, Immanuel Kant, Ludwig Wittgenstein, Bertrand Russell, Noam Chomsky, Galileo Galilei, Nicolaus Copernicus, Isaac Newton, Alexander Fleming, Michael Faraday, Marie Curie, Louis Pasteur, Charles Darwin, Karl Marx, Marco Polo, Christopher Columbus, Robert Scott ('of the Antarctic'), Edmund Hillary, Alfred Kinsey, Margaret Mead, Hannah Arendt, John Maynard Keynes, Alan Turing, Tim Berners-

Lee, Stephen Jay Gould, James Lovelock, Niall Ferguson, Johann Sebastian Bach, Ludwig van Beethoven, Arthur Miller, T. S. Eliot, Samuel Johnson, Jane Austen, Charlotte Brontë, George Eliot, Thomas Hardy, Arthur Conan Doyle, Henry James, J. R. R. Tolkien, George Orwell, Aldous Huxley, Iris Murdoch, Thomas Keneally, Peter Carey, Martin Amis, Ian McEwan, Margaret Atwood, Dan Brown, Philip Pullman, Marcel Proust, Anthony Hopkins, Vanessa Redgrave, Francis Walsingham, George Washington, Woodrow Wilson, Richard Nixon, Al Gore, Clement Atlee, Harold Wilson, Margaret Thatcher, Gordon Brown, Angela Merkel, Osho Rajneesh, Pope Benedict XVI

CHAPTER 9

The Roles in Relationship

Your Role is one of the most important influences on your relationships as well as on your personality. Whatever your Role, you can get on with any and all of the other Roles in love, friendship and work. However, some combinations are innately more or less compatible, all things being equal. On the other hand, even the trickiest and most challenging combinations have some similarities and the potential for a happy long-term relationship.

This chapter summarizes all the different possible combinations, with an emphasis on romance and marriage or long-term relationships, but some guidance on friendship and the workplace. These dynamics hold equally true in same-sex relationships.

Please take these brief descriptions as an approximate guide to help you recognize yourself and your partner and the dynamic of your relationship, rather than a prescription of who should or shouldn't be together. The aim is to provide insights to deal with any problems and misunderstandings arising out of Role clashes, and also to recognize and develop the positive potential of the Roles.

Perspective is an equally important influence; a relationship with someone of a less compatible Role but the same

Perspective has a much improved chance of success. 'Mirror-image' relationships can also work particularly well, i.e., if your primary Role is the same as your partner's secondary Role and vice versa.

Artisans

Artisans get on well with each other, sparking each other to new heights – as long as they are not rivals. They understand each other's need for space and can usually appreciate each other's mode of creativity. In daily life a man needs to appreciate his wife's dress sense and cooking skills, ideally down to the subtle detail, and notice any little changes of home décor. A woman needs to admire her husband's skills and talents and compliment him appropriately. As marriage partners they need to work hard to make sure the practical aspects work and the bills are paid, since they tend to be other-worldly.

Artisans are highly communicative, so will never run dry in conversation with each other, sometimes continuing deep into the night. They will never be the long-married couples sitting silently in a restaurant for the entire meal. Their relationships will be passionate and volatile, full of emotional drama – invented if there is nothing real going on. One moment they will be twin souls, the next slamming doors. It may appear to outsiders that they are on the brink of divorce, but they are probably just clearing the air.

Artisans and Sages

Artisans and Sages are often mutually attracted and are a highly compatible combination in work and love. They balance each other, tune in to each other, tolerate any mood swings well and enjoy each other's style and sophistication.

Typically, a Sage film director will marry his Artisan leading lady, a Svengali his protégée. Traditionally, it works better with the Sage as the male partner, being more cardinal, but can be fine the other way round if the male Artisan doesn't mind being eclipsed or upstaged now and again. These are the glamour couples, particularly at the competing Perspective. They will be seen in all the right places, will host the best parties in the neighbourhood. The Sage will appear to be the dominant partner, especially at parties and in public, but will often defer to the Artisan's expertise in one-to-one relationship. Both enjoy the merry-go-round of emotional dramas, preferring stimulating contrasts to bland harmony. In arguments the Sage will score all the verbal points while the Artisan will win through adept emotional manipulation, including suddenly changing tactics or ground rules.

It is likely to be a fun marriage, fulfillling on many levels. Commitment is an important value for both and should carry them through any sticky patches, especially if both remain in their positive poles.

Artisans and Servers

These make good friends and partners, both being skilled at one-to-one relationships. Servers often have a natural, unadorned loveliness and sweetness of character, which Artisans appreciate in contrast to their own artfulness. These two will enjoy dating, as both are quite charming and the Server is a ready admirer of the Artisan's style and talent.

Servers look after their partners well, which Artisans need and appreciate, since they like a clean, well-ordered home but left to their own devices are prone to making it chaotic. Typically, the Artisan will cook and the Server will wash up. The Server will happily do the basic childcare, which the Artisan would prefer to be excused in favour of telling bedtime stories, buying new clothes for the children and making them toys.

This marriage will probably contain less drama than many Artisan relationships, as Servers tend to be accommodating or to find discreet ways of getting their way without a scene. They prefer being married to cardinal Roles who can lead them to a higher good, but if they believe in the Artisan's creativity will happily support their work. They need appreciation, though, so it is important for Artisans not to take them for granted and to express praise for their support.

Artisans and Priests

This is one of the most magical combinations. These are the two 'highest frequency' Roles with easy access to the realms of vision and imagination. They each have a different kind of charisma and glamour, and when they meet and kindle, the flames rise sky-high. Priests often have strong sexual needs to balance their high aspirations and are highly susceptible to the charms of a beautiful woman or man, while Artisans are always seeking inspiration for their creativity and a Priest provides a never-ending source.

This relationship is one of the most romantic in its early stages and can easily lead to marriage. It can get problematic later, however, as Priests like to control people and need to ensure that everyone, including their partner, is on message. Artisans will be full of admiration for their Priest, and may support their mission, but are mutable in their beliefs and outlook. They don't respond well to pressure or preaching and hate being boxed in, so these two can fall out quite acrimoniously.

Both are intense Roles, which can lead to explosion or burnout, though also to the most catalytic emotional experiences. The best recipe for success is for the Priest to include the Artisan in their mission, putting their creativity to work for the cause and giving them a free rein within their area.

Artisans and Warriors

An Artisan woman and Warrior man are the classic romantic opposites, experiencing maximum attraction and misunderstanding. He is captivated by her feminine cuteness, she is wowed by his macho toughness.

> 'I admired him as a wonderful art creation (he is really very beautiful), and he looked on me as an exotic butterfly.'
> LIUDMILA, BIOCHEMIST

Once married, the difficulties manifest. Artisans are fluid and play with boundaries, while Warriors construct and defend them, seeing the world in black and white. However, they can enjoy collaborating on projects. Both appreciate good construction and functionality and enjoy using their hands to create a garden, restore a classic car or renovate a house. Warriors enjoy tearing down walls while Artisans reconstruct the space.

The Warrior needs to show enthusiasm for the Artisan's creations, however humble. A mortified Artisan once told me how she and her builder had constructed an ingenious wine rack out of pipes. When her Warrior husband came home his blunt comment was: 'Not bad for DIY.'

In relationships between male Artisans and female Warriors each needs to enjoy the fact that the wife wears the trousers and organizes the practicalities and finance, while the husband provides the colour and style and is probably better dressed than his wife.

A more traditional style of relationship may work better:

'There is nothing like being married to an Artisan to prevent becoming an old stick-in-the-mud. There is a kind of symbiosis involved in this relationship of opposite roles. I'm the person who finds the things my wife loses, but that's only one aspect of my role as Mr Infrastructure in our marriage. I do the grounded, necessary stuff that makes the household run, and fundamentally I like doing that. It suits me.'
ROBERT, PROFESSOR OF ENGLISH

Artisans and Kings

These two also experience great attraction of opposites. Artisans are drawn to the solid majesty and magnetic power of Kings, who give them a sense of the bigger picture, a grander vision of life's possibilities. They also enjoy the glamour, sumptuous lifestyle and opportunities for public display that often accompany life with a King. In return they give Kings the gift of intimacy, put them in touch with the finer points of style and create a beautiful home – a palace, if they can afford it – all of which Kings appreciate.

The emotional side can be challenging. Kings in a rage are formidable and Artisans are not well equipped to handle aggression (though they may find the raw power quite exciting), so the King will need to learn to rein in their temper while the Artisan will need to find ways of standing up to them.

As with Warriors, this combination tends to work better when the Artisan is female, but it can also work well in reverse. One of my friends, a female King, used to live with an Artisan artist. She earned enough money from her job to buy the flashy cars they both enjoyed, while he painted avant-garde pictures which were much admired even if nobody bought them. They both enjoyed the glamorous lifestyle of the London art world.

Artisans and Scholars

This is one of the trickiest combinations.

'I think that Scholars can get along well with just about anyone except Artisans (I think their unpredictability is too bizarre for a typical Scholar).'
JOHN, TELECOMMUNICATIONS

Both can be intrigued and often attracted by their differences – the low-key Scholar dazzled by the Artisan's style and vivacity, the high-flown Artisan intrigued by the Scholar's intellect and gravitas – but familiarity can lead to disillusion, with Artisans becoming irritated and frustrated by Scholars' reluctance to engage with their emotional dramas, while Scholars become fed up with Artisans' intensity and demands for attention. One Scholar said of his Artisan wife: 'I love her like fury, but it's like being trapped in a brown paper bag with a bluebottle.' A typical result is that the Scholar husband shuts himself in his study with his computer for hours on end while the Artisan wife resorts to long complaining phone calls to her friends.

On the other hand, their differences can be constructive. The Scholar can become more creative, expressive and sensitive as a result of the relationship, while the Artisan can learn to stand back from their creations and evaluate them more objectively. They share a fascination with experiments and a love of the latest gadgets, and both enjoy being alone, so can respect each other's need for space.

'I have been married to a Scholar for 18 years. When I met him, it was instant comfort, like putting on well-worn jeans or slipping your foot into your favorite slippers. So easy to be with him! He didn't invade my space.'
MEREDITH, ATTORNEY/MEDIATOR

Sages

Two Sages can have the most fun in the world with each other as friends and colleagues, though will find it harder to live together. Each will compete furiously for the limelight and delight in upstaging the other and their relationship can become a screwball comedy.

'There is usually not much room for more than one Sage. When more than one is present, it will be a very entertaining time, though it can be heated and can go negative, as there is a load of ego in a Sage!'
MICHAEL, BUSINESS MANAGER

It works fine as long as they can treat their rivalry lightly, as a game, and not undermine each other too much in public.

Their public appearances will be unpredictable. One time they may appear the world's most devoted couple, the next it's *Who's Afraid of Virginia Woolf*? Which scenario is real? They themselves may not be able to answer, or decide if the play is a tragedy or comedy with a happy ending. They can actually enjoy the theatricality of their rows, though if one is unfaithful, the other is likely to retaliate in kind. Stability is more likely if each gives the other plenty of space to play and perform to other audiences.

At home they like to keep open house for friends, relatives, even strangers. Their biggest challenge is to learn to listen to each other; their recipe for success is to share the limelight.

Sages and Servers

These often end up as partners, sometimes to the surprise of the Sage's friends who have witnessed a series of relationships with more glamorous people. But the Sage is displaying wisdom in this choice, which suits their needs well: Servers are the Role best equipped to give the care, nurturing and support that will enable the Sage to shine and enjoy themselves while doing the minimum of household chores.

Servers themselves will enjoy looking after a cardinal Role who has an impact on the world, and on a higher level they have high emotional intelligence, so can help Sages become more emotionally balanced.

On a lower level, the Sage may exploit the Server dreadfully, taking for granted an endless supply of freshly ironed shirts and round-the-clock nursing when they are sick. The darkest possibility is that the Sage may be understimulated and start having affairs, and the Server is more likely than some other Roles to put up with this abuse long-sufferingly. Nevertheless, Servers will leave if pushed too far, which is usually a result neither partner wants. So it's important for the Sage to show appreciation for the Server and give them some fun and a share of their worldly success to keep them happy and revitalize their flow of inspiration.

Sages and Priests

These often work well together if the Sage takes the Priest's mission seriously and the Priest values the Sage's talent for presentation and wowing the audience. They are often attracted to each other as romantic partners, since both are highly charismatic. However, differences of values soon emerge: Sages find Priests too serious, while Priests find Sages too goofy. This can be resolved by learning to appreciate their different but complementary communication skills. Both are bright and quick-witted, and Priests admire Sages' poise and polish, while Sages admire Priests' conviction.

Both are leadership Roles, so are likely to start competing for dominance in the family – and less playfully than two Sages. Their relationship will work better if they give each other a lot of space and have their own separate projects or work (unless their work is very well arranged to give each the platform they need).

For their best chance at happiness, Sages need to allow Priests some of the limelight, while Priests need to use their inspiration and counselling skills to help Sages become and remain their best self. Each can enhance the other's success – the Sage showing the Priest the importance of laughter in getting people to accept their message, the Priest revealing how wit and humour can be directed into a good cause.

Sages and Warriors

This is quite a challenging combination, as they have very different energies and values. Sages can find Warriors uncouth, while Warriors can find Sage charm duplicitous. Warriors and Kings share a belief in loyalty as their core value, while Sages talk about commitment but find it hard to give, which can become problematic in long-term relationships with both Roles. It can work well if there is a higher than usual overlap, for example if the Sage is more physically oriented and the Warrior more intellectual than usual.

'I have been married to a Warrior and it took some effort to learn to speak his language since he saw everything as either

black or white. His integrity was unequalled, though, and once I learned his language, communication became not only much easier but also deeper, since I understood him so much better.'

LYDIA

Both Roles share a sense of fun and enjoy practical jokes and teasing. They do need to be careful with their disagreements, however, since Sages use their anger for effect while Warriors really mean it, which can cause serious misunderstanding. Sages will do anything to avoid serious confrontations, preferring a charm offensive. If forced into a difficult encounter, they prefer to use their considerable tact and diplomacy or deflect aggression with a joke. If challenged or opposed, they tend to back down readily.

Both Roles are prone to over-indulgence in the pleasures of the table and they may need to help each other watch their diet and alcohol intake, as well as rein in their sexual appetites – with other people at least. Together they are likely to have an enjoyable sex life, with the Sage bringing finesse, the Warrior physical pleasure.

Sages enjoy making plans, but walking their talk is sometimes a step too far. A King or Warrior partner will help them get moving and realize their projects instead of just hanging out in the pub or expending their wit on yet another dinner party.

Sages and Kings

Sages and Kings make a very high-profile relationship and are likely to become a glamour couple on their own social circuit if not a bigger stage. Both are leadership Roles and the King is likely to win the battle for dominance, leaving the Sage annoyed and frustrated.

Kings enjoy Sage style and glamour but may not appreciate their more light-hearted side, while Sages can find Kings heavy and overbearing. For the marriage to work, the King will need a better sense of humour than usual and the Sage will need to be restrained about using wit as a weapon against their partner (since Kings are very touchy, which can lead to a rapid escalation of conflict).

Nevertheless, these two can have a lot of fun together. Both tend to look beyond work and home life for fulfillment and will be active socially and in other spheres. It is a good combination for outwardly focused projects. A King might set up a theatre for his wife while she assembles a glittering guest list for a fund-raising dinner. A Sage married to a King might agree with Woody Allen that 'In my house I'm the boss, my wife is just the decision maker.'

Sages and Scholars

These two Roles have a lot in common. They will keep each other interested, if not entertained, better than any other pairing. Sages can help Scholars to lighten up, laugh at themselves, bring more wit and flair to their arguments and see the importance of entertaining as well as convincing their audience.

'I love being able to make a Scholar non-neutral! Hehehe.'
MICHAEL, BUSINESS MANAGER

301

In return, Scholars help Sages ground their flights of fancy in reality, research and fact checking to give their arguments more depth and substance.

> *'I do well with a strong, mentally capable partner.'*
> MICHAEL, BUSINESS MANAGER

This combination works particularly well if both are writers, teachers or professional communicators. However, these two can get quite competitive, and Scholars may resent being outshone and upstaged by a more flamboyant partner, while Sages will not appreciate being corrected on facts while in the full flow of an anecdote. It can work well if the Sage can show generosity in sometimes allowing the Scholar into the limelight and the Scholar can graciously accept playing second fiddle most of the time and find their own independent area in which to shine.

These two can make good sexual partners, as both find mental stimulation an important component of attraction. The emotional side of the relationship is harder, once the first flush of romance has passed, since both Roles tend to shy away from what they see as the messiness and minefield of feelings. They will find this aspect much easier if both are at the relationship or philosophical Perspective. Here is an account of a Sage and Scholar marriage that worked brilliantly:

> *'My husband was a Sage academic, so we were very compatible. He was a man of duty, so worked hard at his research – again, something that fitted my temperament. Yet*

he could kick back, too, and we liked to sit with a glass of wine and talk about our day or how TV rotted the mind (to use his phrase) or how we could live once resources became more expensive. We were also sociable and he enjoyed getting people together who ordinarily didn't see much of each other, largely so that they would get to talking with each other and comparing ideas. That, of course, suited me very well, too. He was funny and liked to play little games with our cat or our daughter, something the cat didn't much like but the daughter did. And he could also be helpful by charming me out of a bad mood with a joke or something that made me laugh. I also appreciated the fact that he was an excellent teacher and so could answer many questions that I had, never making me feel as if I should know the answer already. Instead, he always made me feel as if I was really smart to ask such a question.'

NICOLA, WRITER

Servers

Servers get on well with each other, particularly as friends and colleagues, understanding each other's needs and values and working together brilliantly in a team. As lovers, they can't do enough for each other and will compete to see who can be the more devoted. A marriage between them is likely to be stable and enduring, and they will provide a nurturing environment for each other and their children. They can get a bit frustrated in that they prefer serving a more cardinal Role who will provide a wider vision and higher cause. At worst a relationship between two Servers will be a bit dull and over-practical and at best they will keep each other inspired and provide a loving home for their children.

Servers and Priests

This is a highly compatible combination. Both are inspiration Roles and each understands the other's need for an ideal or cause to serve. They will be dedicated to each other and to the Priest's cause or mission.

Servers are in fact happier than any other Role to play second fiddle to a Priest's mission, looking after them beautifully, tirelessly and uncomplainingly, supporting them in every way and not expecting much in return. They also know how to top up their Priest's inspiration when they are flagging and can soothe, comfort and nourish them till they perk up again. They are happy to keep the home fires burning, including childcare, while the Priest is off on their mission. This goes for Server husbands too.

However, in the longer term Priests can take Servers for granted and not make them feel special, so a Server can end up feeling hurt, neglected and resentful. If pushed too far they may even walk out, especially if an ultimatum is ignored, which will leave the Priest feeling astonished as well as aggrieved. To keep the relationship working, Priests need to show appreciation of their good fortune in attracting such a devoted mate and Servers need to make their needs clear to their busy partner in order to get those needs met.

Servers and Warriors

These two make one of the trickier combinations, since Warriors are the Role least interested in either giving or receiving inspiration. However, they do appreciate being looked after and having someone to do the jobs they don't want to do so they can get on with their own projects. Unfortunately, they are liable to mistake the Server's pliability for weakness, which can bring out their bossy and bullying side. They will tend to order the Server around and get impatient if everything isn't just so. The Server can get quite depressed as a result, feeling their service isn't helping the common good in any way.

This partnership can work if each understands, honours and appreciates the other's virtues, but this takes self-awareness, which neither Role is known for. Their best chance is if each can take on some of the other's best qualities and work together on a shared project. Also, both are hardworking and family-minded, so the family unit will be strong and stable.

Servers and Kings

Servers and Kings can make good if generally unequal partners. Servers of either sex feel honoured and privileged to look after a King and be part of a greater enterprise. They won't mind being behind the scenes, though may not gain as much control as they would like. Nevertheless, they are quite resourceful at finding ways of doing so.

With their superb nurturing skills, Servers are able to soothe and comfort Kings and get through their barrier of reserve to achieve a physical and emotional intimacy that few others can manage. Kings do, however, need to be sensitive about remembering a Server husband or wife's existence and being grateful for their support rather than treating them as a servant. For their part, Servers will need to raise their game if they are not to be left keeping the home fires burning while the King is out in the world. They may not mind, but unless they remind their King of their value the situation may deteriorate.

Servers and Scholars

This can be a good combination as long as the Server sees the Scholar as serving the common good in some important way. A Server wife will be happy to book her husband's trip to a conference and pack his suitcase, but will expect to be taken along occasionally, especially if she suspects she needs to keep an eye on him. It can also work well in reverse, with the male Server feeling proud of his intelligent wife and supporting and encouraging her endeavours to write a book or combine studying with working and motherhood. He will also be willing to work extra hard at his job and domestic duties and be a stay-at-home father if his wife has a successful job and needs to work late or go away a lot.

The Scholar, being neutral and particularly understanding of the other Roles, will generally treat the Server with care and respect, which is important to them and something they don't always get from other Roles. However, scholarly reserve can be quite difficult for Servers, particularly if the Scholar spends too much time locked in their study. For the relationship to work, Servers need to be sensitive to Scholars' need for private study time and Scholars need to make efforts to come out of their shell and participate in family life. To achieve a truly equal and companionable relationship it helps tremendously if the Server is intelligent and educated, as in order to feel fulfillled in a relationship Scholars need a partner who enjoys discussing ideas.

Priests

Priests often get along with each other extremely well. Since they are a small minority among the Roles and frequently misunderstood, when they find each other they may feel they have found a soulmate. However, they often find it easier to be together as friends, or better still co-workers in a shared cause, rather than lovers or marriage partners. Each Priest has an inbuilt need to be the leader and will probably find it hard to give way to their partner, however much they love them. If they can understand this dynamic and have separate spheres of action and/or be flexible about giving way and taking turns to be dominant, then their partnership can be one of the deepest and strongest. However, they do need to ensure they both give enough time and attention to their children rather than getting too carried away by their mission and neglecting family life.

Priests and Warriors

These two Roles are often highly attracted to each other, because their energy is so opposite. Warriors are solid yet dynamic, with an earthy sexuality and direct approach that Priests find refreshing, grounding, even healing, while Warriors themselves can be captivated by Priests' charisma and intensity.

As sexual partners, it can be an exciting relationship. As a marriage, it is more challenging, since both Roles are great fighters and their differences are liable to bring them into constant conflict unless they can unite behind a cause. If they can do so, they can become comrades-in-arms and make an excellent team. Warriors often have a cynical streak, however, and distrust what they perceive as Priests' flakiness, while Priests get frustrated with Warriors' refusal to rise and fly with their vision. As a couple they are likely to have different ideas about boundaries, especially when it comes to childcare. This is therefore an inherently difficult combination, but both Roles are very hardworking, so can achieve a lot together if they have enough commitment.

Priests and Kings

This is one of the hardest Role combinations for marriage or any other relationship, since both are adept politicians with a need for leadership and may have little understanding or sympathy for the other's point of view. Priests tend to bend with the breeze, while Kings are single-mindedly consistent. Kings are perfectionists wanting every detail in place, while Priests only care about their vision and are impatient with preparation.

In the workplace it can work well if they have separate spheres of responsibility. In a relationship they may experience a lot of initial attraction, since both are highly charismatic in different ways, but the differences can quickly become problematic. They will have to work hard to make a marriage succeed. It will help if they can have different spheres of influence and a strong shared purpose. Neither is keen on domestic work and childcare and both will resent it if they feel they are doing more than their share, so it helps if they can afford to pay others to do this or persuade them to volunteer. Their children will probably feel they don't get enough parental love and attention, or it may come in an intensive burst of love and treats, then the parents are off again.

Priests and Scholars

This can be a good combination if both are intellectually oriented and share a worldview and values. Scholars often understand and therefore get on better with Priests than any other Role apart from Servers, which Priests appreciate, since they often suffer from being misunderstood. Scholars themselves enjoy being swept off their feet and caught up in the flow of the Priest's high energy. If the Priest returns the attraction it can make for a steamy love affair, but the stability of a long and successful marriage is harder to achieve. Priests can find Scholars too analytical and critical, while Scholars find them flaky, and they are liable to fall out over ideas and beliefs. Priests tend to agree with Ecclesiastes: 'He that increases knowledge increases sorrow,' which Scholars find bizarre, countering with 'Know the truth, and the truth shall set you free.' Both will need to work hard at communication, as the Scholar may feel they are engaged in a 'stimulating discussion' while the Priest resents being 'analysed' and 'criticized'.

For a stable and happy marriage, both partners have to accept that the Priest's mission is the binding force and the personal relationship is secondary. At the same time, Priests need to understand that a marriage needs nurturing and commitment and they should not treat their partner as a maid or footsoldier in their cause. As long as they have a shared vision, however, they can enjoy a stimulating and mutually beneficial partnership, the Priest appreciating the Scholar's solidity and intellectual support, the Scholar feeling exalted by the Priest's inspiration.

Warriors

Warriors generally get on extremely well with each other as friends, colleagues and lovers once they have established the pecking order and know where they fit in the hierarchy. Otherwise there will be a power struggle between them. They understand each other's ways, however, and are not offended by bluntness and directness as some other Roles can be. Their relationship will be quite boisterous and they tend to spar a lot, which looks like conflict from the outside but is generally playful. However, if they do fall out they can fight savagely – verbally, physically and in the law courts.

> 'With other Warriors, it's war!'
> KELLEY, MARKETING DIRECTOR

Their understanding of boundaries applies to marriage, too, so while they are an item they are the most loyal of friends but once they fall out they become enemies. However, being generally good at conflict resolution, they often manage to resolve any difficulties before getting to that stage.

Warriors and Kings

This is a highly compatible pairing on the action axis, excellent for stable long-term relationships. Warriors are the only Role unafraid to stand up to a King, so can prevent them becoming too tyrannical. It is easier if the King is male, since he will be the dominant partner, at least in public, but it can work fine vice versa if the Warrior recognizes his wife's Kingliness and feels privileged to serve and protect her.

Warriors feel honoured to be married to a King and will literally lay down their life if required. Kings can relax easily with a Warrior, who understands them better than other Roles do and is not afraid of them. The pair can lose their tempers with each other and get into ferocious conflict, but can also actively enjoy power-struggle arguments. Eventually they are likely to resolve their differences, especially if they can stay in their positive polarities.

Warriors and Scholars

Warriors and Scholars are one of the most frequent pairings, being 'solid' Roles with high physical compatibility. They both enjoy adventure and exploration and share an earthy sense of humour. Warriors respect Scholars' knowledge, and can help them harness their information more productively. Scholars are revitalized by Warriors' boundless energy and activity, which help them get out of their heads and away from their computers.

However, the Warrior always wants to 'do it now' and can find the Scholar too slow, getting impatient with their need to research thoroughly and mull things over before deciding anything. They will call them a stick-in-the-mud, while the Scholar will resent being pressured. Warriors also love to pick a fight, while Scholars tend to avoid conflict at all costs. Warriors want to take sides, while Scholars want to examine all sides. Both need to learn to air their differences constructively rather than destructively and aim for win-win solutions.

If all goes well, however, their qualities are so complementary that they can make for one of the strongest and most enduring partnerships – as friends or colleagues as well as spouses. Their family life will be particularly well organized, the Scholar taking care of the paperwork and the Warrior organizing domestic life.

Kings

Two Kings together make a very challenging partnership, as both are so dominant that they may not find a way to live together as equals, but it can also be very stable and successful. The Kings will be on the same wavelength – a rare and precious experience for both. If they also have a shared vision and values, they can make a superb team and provide their children with the best possible start in life. However, since each is used to being dominant, if there is an argument or fight they will both find it hard to give way. It works better if both partners are at the relationship or philosophical Perspectives, which will give them a good chance of achieving an equal relationship based on mutual respect and understanding, which is much harder for Kings with other Roles.

Kings and Scholars

These make good business associates and can also be good friends, sharing a serious outlook and interest in world events.

> *'I notice that I enjoy Scholar types – their involvement
> in study and learning and their neutrality offer me good
> companionship.'*
> DR PAULA BROMBERG, PSYCHOLOGIST

Kings respect knowledge and will listen if they judge the Scholar to be an expert. Scholars feel exalted by Kingly energy, which gives their ideas and projects form and direction, a practical outlet. In olden times, to be known as 'the King's Scholar' was a great honour and privilege. However, Scholars' primary allegiance is to truth, which can create painful conflicts if they disagree with their King.

The pair can make good marriage partners, but since neither is great at small talk and flirting, the interpersonal skills that get a relationship started, they may need to be formally introduced or thrown together and experience strong sexual attraction to begin going out.

Scholars make good, loyal and supportive partners if they believe in their King, are consulted and listened to occasionally and are allowed a sphere of their own. Scholars can be stubborn and Kings self-willed, however, so each will have to learn to be flexible and conciliatory to avoid endless arguments. Kings expect to have the last word, which Scholars can only accept if they agree with it.

Scholars

Scholars get on very well with each other and this can make one of the best and most loving marriages, as long as they are on the same wavelength and share their main values.

They will understand and respect each other's neutrality and independence and never tire of discussing each other's ideas and the issues of the day, sharing their insights and discoveries. It's important that one but preferably both partners has the opportunity to keep learning and discovering (just try to stop a Scholar!), to refuel their conversations. If so, they will never get bored with each other's company.

The main risk is that since Scholars generally tend to avoid emotion, the relationship can become a bit dry, so both partners need to make an effort to acknowledge and explore their own and each other's emotional states, to keep the juices flowing. Then they have a good chance of developing an immensely strong, supportive and enjoyable marriage that will deepen into lasting love.

CHAPTER 10

Taking It Further

I hope that by now you have discovered your Role, or at least narrowed it down to a couple of possibilities. If you're still unsure, don't worry. While some people recognize their Role easily, others take longer, needing time to reflect and observe themselves in action and in their relationships. Sooner or later your true Role will become clear to you. It is also worth consulting family or friends, who sometimes have a clearer picture of us than we do of ourselves.

In addition to the Role and Perspective, there are five other sets of traits or aspects which add to the complexity and uniqueness of your personality. The summary chart on page 317 shows the complete personality profile in diagram form. It was created by Dr José Stevens at Pivotal Resources and is used by most teachers of this personality system. (This is a slightly adapted version, with permission.) You can see that the Role is one of several layers that make up the personality, albeit the most fundamental layer, core or essence. If you feel interested and inspired enough to explore the system in greater depth, some of the books and websites in the Resources section following this chapter give detailed descriptions of these traits. The consultancies listed offer consultations and training to help you find your Role and other traits and put it all together in context.

Here is a brief summary of the main traits:

Goal

This is the broad aim of your life and like the Role takes different forms according to whether it is on the expression, inspiration, action or integration axes. Your goal is an aspiration or life task that motivates you throughout your life. Everything that happens to you can be used to fulfill your goal, but as with all the elements of this system you have to stay in the positive pole in order to achieve it. For example, growth is the cardinal inspirational goal. If you have a goal of growth you will be more intense and driven in pursuit of your aims, preferring challenges over easy options, new experiences over the tried and trusted. Personal development will be very important to you. Your personality will therefore have a certain Priest-like flavour.

Mode

This is the driving force or vehicle which powers your whole personality, being the method by which your goal is achieved. The best metaphor is a car engine. Passion, power and aggression are cardinal modes like powerful engines; they can travel fast but are expensive to run and high maintenance. The ordinal modes (caution, reserve and perseverance) are like smaller family car engines, slower with less power, but more economical and reliable. Observation is the neutral mode corresponding with the Scholar Role. Someone with observation mode will be highly observant and acutely aware of their surroundings, objective and a bit detached, good at research and gathering information – in other words, a bit like a Scholar.

Personality Chart

	Expression		Inspiration		Action		Integration
	Ordinal	Cardinal	Ordinal	Cardinal	Ordinal	Cardinal	Neutral
ROLE	+ Creativity ARTISAN − Self-deception	+ Communication SAGE − Verbosity	+ Service SERVER − Bondage	+ Compassion PRIEST − Zeal	+ Persuasion WARRIOR − Coercion	+ Mastery KING − Tyranny	+ Knowledge SCHOLAR − Theory
GOAL	+ Sophistication DISCRIMINATION − Rejection	+ Unconditional love ACCEPTANCE − Ingratiation	+ Simplicity RE-EVALUATION − Withdrawal	+ Evolution GROWTH − Confusion	+ Devotion SUBMISSION − Exploited	+ Leadership DOMINANCE − Dictatorship	+ Free-flowing RELAXATION − Inertia
MODE	+ Deliberation CAUTION − Phobia	+ Authority POWER − Oppression	+ Restraint RESERVE − Inhibition	+ Self-realization PASSION − Identification	+ Persistence PERSEVERANCE − Inflexible	+ Dynamism AGGRESSION − Belligerence	+ Clarity OBSERVATION − Surveillance
ATTITUDE	+ Investigation SCEPTIC − Suspicion	+ Coalescence IDEALIST − Naivety	+ Tranquility STOIC − Resignation	+ Verification SPIRITUALIST − Dogma	+ Contradiction CYNIC − Denigration	+ Objective REALIST − Subjective	+ Practical PRAGMATIST − Opportunist
OBSTACLE	+ Sacrifice SELF-DESTRUCTION − Suicidal	+ Appetite GREED − Insatiability	+ Humility SELF-DEPRECATION − Abasement	+ Pride ARROGANCE − Vanity	+ Selflessness MARTYRDOM − Victimization	+ Daring IMPATIENCE − Intolerance	+ Determination STUBBORNESS − Obstinacy
CENTRE	+ Insight INTELLECTUAL − Reasoning	+ Truth HIGHER INTELLECTUAL − Communication	+ Perception EMOTIONAL − Sentimentality	+ Love HIGHER EMOTIONAL − Intuition	+ Productive MOVING − Frenetic	+ Integration HIGHER MOVING − Desire	+ Aware INSTINCTIVE − Automatic
PERSPEC-TIVES	+ Survive SURVIVAL ORIENTED − Ruthless	+ Structure RULE BOUND − Inflexible	+ Competent COMPETING − Selfish		+ Insightful RELATIONSHIP ORIENTED − Confused		+ Wise PHILOSOPHICAL − Detached

Attitude

Your attitude in this personality system refers to your general outlook on life. It is the lens through which you perceive the world and everything that happens to you, good or bad, including your relationships. The attitude is one of the easiest traits to recognize and verify in yourself and other people. Everyone knows what an idealist, realist, cynic or stoic looks like and most people can easily say which of these seven attitude fits their personality. For example, realism is the 'King' attitude and makes you more capable than usual of looking at the bigger picture, even if you are an ordinal Role. Faced with choices, you can see all sides of the situation, weigh up the pros and cons objectively and take action accordingly.

Obstacle

In some versions of this philosophy it is called the Chief Feature, in others the Dragon. By whatever name it goes, it is dysfunctional and is the cause of most people's self-inflicted suffering. The seven obstacles bear some comparison with the Seven Deadly Sins of Christianity, but in this system they are seen psychologically as fear patterns rather than morally as sins. The aim is to identify your obstacle so you can overcome it, achieve your goal and live happily. It is often easier to spot other people's obstacle than your own – from the frustration and annoyance you feel in its presence. There are for example the moaning martyrs, the impatient drivers hooting and speeding, the stubborn CEO who refuses to see that things are changing faster than he would like. José Stevens has written an excellent book on the obstacles called *Transforming Your Dragons*, which is listed in the Resources.

Centring

This is also known as 'reaction style'. Centring is your preferred way of operating in life; it governs how you react to and deal with information and impressions from the world and your life experiences. Mostly only the ordinal centres are used – intellectual, emotional and moving. The intellectual centre is most prominent in Western culture, but there are advantages to each of the centres. For example, emotional centring is on the inspiration axis and makes you sensitive and empathic, responding from the heart and feeling things intensely, like a Server or Priest. The moving centre makes you physically very well co-ordinated, athletic and energetic. You are more likely to work out in the gym regularly and go out dancing on Saturday nights, and if you are a woman you will find it much easier to walk in high heels. The moving centre correlates with the action axis and is useful in enabling you to put your ideas into action rather than just talking about them.

◆◆◆◆◆◆

As with the Roles, none of these traits is better or worse, higher or lower. All have their positive and negative pole and can help you in different ways to achieve success and happiness. Since they correspond with the Roles and most people have a combination of traits on different axes, everyone's personality has some flavour and characteristics of the other Roles. This gives you variety and flexibility, and makes it much easier to understand and relate to people with different Roles – and to be understood and accepted by them in turn. One way in which this system is being used successfully is in teamwork training, bringing a depth and clarity of understanding that contributes greatly to the collaboration and harmony of a team.

The broader aim is to discover all your traits and put them all together into one whole: the pattern or map that makes up your total personality. Understanding the system as a whole will give you a complete picture and even deeper understanding of who you are. However far you want to go with this process, I wish you an interesting and enjoyable journey.

Resources

Life Roles Training

Life Roles Training is a consultancy service co-founded by Elizabeth Puttick and Robin Puttick based on the Personality Types system. Our aim is to give you a map of your Personality Type that you can use as a powerful tool for personal and professional development. Our methods include detailed questionnaires and analysis, personal interviews and coaching. We offer both individual consultations and corporate training. We also present an international programme of talks, seminars and workshops.

www.7personalitytypes.com

Pivotal Resources

Pivotal Resources is an international management consulting and education company co-founded by José Stevens, PhD, with Lena Stevens, which includes Power Path Seminars™. We are committed to offering dramatic improvement in your effectiveness as a business or corporate leader, trainer, professional therapist or as an individual striving for excellence and success in our fast-paced world. Our core approach is Personnessence™, a personality typology we have developed which uses the Seven Roles in the context of a broader philosophy. José Stevens is the author of ten books and numerous articles including:

Transforming Your Dragons: How to Turn Fear Patterns into Personal Power (Bear & Co., 1994)

The Michael Handbook, co-authored with Simon Warwick-Smith (Warwick Associates, 1994)

The Power Path: The Shaman's Way to Success in Business (New World Library, 2002)

http://thepowerpath.com

The Institute for Management Excellence

The Institute for Management Excellence offers practical tools for business and corporate clients, including communication skills, project management and a range of management and training services. We combine creativity with proven approaches to solve complex business challenges. Our motto is: 'It's Time ... for new ways of thinking and new ways of doing business.'

The website is also an important online resource for information on the Personality Types and the general Michael Teaching, including books, websites, teachers and consultants, online groups and news. It includes the Personality Game, a fun way to learn the different aspects of the system backed up by lots of explanatory articles. The emphasis is on the practical self-development and professionally oriented aspects of the system.

www.itstime.com

Runora LLC Organizational Development & Market Resource

In the USA market we offer automated online services to businesses, organizations and institutions in the areas of market research, organizational development, hiring, retention and benchmarking. We take the guesswork out of understanding your customers and your employee DNA by offering a sophisticated psychometric and behavioral assessment tool. The benefits are alleviation of stress, time saved through online convenience and efficiency, affordability and highly accurate results.

For the USA and international markets we offer speaking engagements, workshops and seminars in various topics including UnderstandingYourPersonality®, a leadership program for organizations providing practical tools for success and excellence in the workplace.

www.runora.com, www.understandingyourpersonality.com

Keys to Balance®

Keys to Balance® is a versatile program based on the Personality Types system, which offers inspirational insights into great leadership, dynamic team work and effective communication. Itstrengthensproblemsolving,collaboration and stress management. Keys to Balance® offers a practical toolbox and many eye-opening ways to discover and accept the differences in people and make the best of any people situation. We offer trainings and coaching for executives, managers, teams and individuals. Keys to Balance® trainings are offered in English, Finnish and Swedish.

www.dolphino.net

Shepherd Hoodwin

Shepherd Hoodwin is an intuitive, workshop leader, channel, author and teacher who offers a range of services including healing, therapy and counselling. He specializes in the Michael Teaching and lives in Laguna Niguel, California. Email Shepherd at sgh@summerjoy.com if you would like to receive his Perspectives newsletter or be on his Forwards list. His blog is http://newagevillage.com/perspectives. His books (all published by Summerjoy Press) include:

The Journey of Your Soul, Loving from your Soul and *Enlightenment for Nitwits.*

http://summerjoy.com

The Michael Teaching

There are many books, articles, websites and online forums on the Michael Teaching, mainly taking a metaphysical or philosophical approach to the system. The best and most comprehensive resource is www.michaelteachings.com. The website carries detailed and very well organized information on all aspects of this personality system, including an extensive archive of articles and a very clear, useful FAQ section. It also hosts the largest and most active discussion list on the Michael Teaching.

www.michaelteachings.com

Acknowledgements

Many people have kindly helped me with this book. I'd like to thank everyone at Hay House UK for their support and enthusiasm, particularly my publisher, Michelle Pilley, for her inspiration and encouragement. Many thanks to Lizzie Hutchins for her excellent editing – perceptive, tactful and hawk-eyed.

Warmest thanks and gratitude to José Stevens, who taught me most of what I know about this personality system, including its deeper dimensions and its practical adaptation for self-development. Very special thanks to Philip Wittmeyer, my sternest and best critic and an expert on the Michael Teaching, who read and commented on the entire manuscript and came up with many helpful insights and suggestions. Teachers, trainers and consultants who use this system in their work have been immensely kind, helpful and generous with their time. Barbara Taylor answered many questions, read and commented on material and shared her invaluable database. Runa Bouius and Carita Nyberg were very insightful on the application of this system to professional development and corporate training; they also read material and provided some inspirational case histories. Dave Gregg is the creator and moderator of the main website and the largest discussion group on the Michael Teaching, invaluable resources which helped me test and develop ideas. Shepherd Hoodwin's books are highly enlightening and entertaining, and I thank him also for commenting on material and for a most enjoyable correspondence.

Many students and practitioners of this system helped me by allowing me to interview them, writing about their experiences of what it's like to have their Role and field-testing my questionnaire. They come from all over the world, including North and South America, Britain and Europe, Australia, Russia and China; as a result the book has true cross-cultural relevance. Their responses have validated and enlivened the content of this book, though some appear anonymously by request. I'd like to very warmly and gratefully thank Clementine Mitchell, Tarin Davies, Tina Fisher, Elisa McDonell, Hugh Nicklin, Yvonne Trostli, Barbara Hartman, Tuija Kamppi, Diane Ho, Meredith Johnson, Ed Hamerstrom, Glenn Stewart, Yung Lerner, Kelley Koehler, Donimo Shriver, Liudmila Vlasenko and her parents Antonina Fyodorovna and Pyotr Petrovich Vlasenko, Claire McKay, Dr Paula Bromberg, Donna Jarrett, Ann Howell, Jean McKinney, Jill Petersen, Michael Huttinger, Luna Belsona, Mary Lewis, Lowry Pei, Caterina Arends, Deborah Gavel, Sylvia Mcleod, Rebecca Mueller, Elizabeth Forster, Patricia Wisdom, Vivian Hitchman, John Little, Joseph Carotenuto, Navid Fatemi, Cheryl Varner, John Thrasher, Matt Pallamary, Michael Bartlett, Wendy Innis, Evelin Poll, Joe Maher, Michael Bartlett, Rossinna Ippolito and Lydia Ott. It was important to test the questionnaire and material on people unfamiliar with the system, and I'd like to thank the following people for their participation and feedback: Harriet Vered, Roy

Vered, Anupam Barlow, Ann-Marie Gallagher, Iain Edgar, Eileen Campbell, Erica Brealey, Suzanne Evans, Sarah Sutton, Sam Ellis, Mary Finnigan, Chris Gilchrist, Rebecca Abbott, Martine Batchelor, ShivaDas, Charlie Johnson and Malcolm Burgess.

Finally, and above all, I'd like to thank my beloved husband Robin. Words cannot express what I owe him, but his input and emotional, moral and creative support at every stage of our shared ongoing journey have helped make this book what it is. It is only fitting that it is dedicated to him with much love.

We hope you enjoyed this Hay House book. If you'd like to
receive our online catalog featuring additional information
on Hay House books and products, please contact:

Hay House, Inc.
P.O. Box 5100
Carlsbad, CA 92018-5100

(760) 431-7695 or **(800) 654-5126**
(760) 431-6948 (fax) or **(800) 650-5115 (fax)**
www.hayhouse.com® • **www.hayfoundation.org**

◆◆◆◆◆◆

Published and distributed in Australia by:
Hay House Australia Pty. Ltd., 18/36 Ralph St., Alexandria NSW 2015 • *Phone:*
612-9669-4299 • *Fax:* 612-9669-4144 • www.hayhouse.com.au

Published and distributed in the United Kingdom by:
Hay House UK, Ltd., 292B Kensal Rd., London W10 5BE •
Phone: 44-20-8962-1230 • *Fax:* 44-20-8962-1239 • www.hayhouse.co.uk

Published and distributed in the Republic of South Africa by:
Hay House SA (Pty), Ltd., P.O. Box 990, Witkoppen 2068 •
Phone/Fax: 27-11-467-8904 • info@hayhouse.co.za • www.hayhouse.co.za

Published in India by: Hay House Publishers India, Muskaan Complex,
Plot No. 3, B-2, Vasant Kunj, New Delhi 110 070 • *Phone:* 91-11-4176-1620 •
Fax: 91-11-4176-1630 • www.hayhouse.co.in

Distributed in Canada by: Raincoast, 9050 Shaughnessy St.,
Vancouver, B.C. V6P 6E5 • *Phone:* (604) 323-7100 • *Fax:* (604) 323-2600 •
www.raincoast.com

◆◆◆◆◆◆

<u>**Take Your Soul on a Vacation**</u>

Visit **www.HealYourLife.com®** to regroup,
recharge, and reconnect with your own magnifence.
Featuring blogs, mind-body-spirit news, and
life-changing wisdom from Louise Hay and friends.

Visit **www.HealYourLife.com** today!